Religion and Nation

STUDIES IN FORCED MIGRATION
General Editors: Stephen Castles and Dawn Chatty

Religion and Nation

IRANIAN LOCAL AND
TRANSNATIONAL NETWORKS IN BRITAIN

Kathryn Spellman

Berghahn Books
New York • Oxford

First published in 2004 by

Berghahn Books

www.BerghahnBooks.com

©2004, 2006 Kathryn Spellman
First paperback edition published in 2006
Reprinted in 2006

Library of Congress Cataloging-in-Publication Data

Spellman, Kathryn.
   Religion and nation: Iranian local and transnational networks in Britain /
   Kathryn Spellman. p. cm. – (Studies in forced migration; v. 15)
   Includes bibliographical references and index.
   ISBN 1-57181-576-7 (alk. paper)--ISBN 1-57181-577-5 (pbk. : alk. paper)
   1. Iranians–Great Britain–Social conditions. 2. Iranians–Great Britain–Religious
   life and customs. 3. Muslims–Great Britain–Social conditions.
   4. Iran–Emigration and immigration. 5. Immigrants–Great Britain.
   I. Title. II. Series.

DA125.I68S64 2004
305.891'55041–dc22

                                                                    2003063912

British Library Cataloguing in Publication Data

A catalogue record for this book is available from the British Library

Printed in Canada on acid-free paper

ISBN 1-57181-576-7 (hardback)
ISBN 1-57181-577-5 (paperback)

Contents

Preface

When visiting Iran in the summer of 1999 I came across a woman in the public restrooms in Isfahan's bazaar whom I shall always remember. After a wonderful day of wandering around Isfahan, my hair started to fall loose from the obligatory headscarf. I walked into the restroom, feeling hot and tired, and started to pin it back into place. I noticed a woman, who was wearing the proper *hejâb*, a black chador and black stockings, staring at me. I began to feel uncomfortable as she continued to look at me, up and down, in a seemingly disapproving manner. Many questions came to mind. Was it my style of dress – the colourful headscarf and thin overcoat – she didn't like? Was I showing too much hair? Was she one of those 'hardliners' one reads about in newspapers (but I had failed to come across throughout my visit)? Did she have problems with Western women? I said 'Excuse me' in Persian, *bebakhshid*, several times as I finished tying my scarf. When I started to walk out she stopped me and with a mischievous look on her face, she slowly took off her chador. Her hair was purple (not from henna), *really* purple, and styled in a punk-like fashion. She giggled and said, '*doost dârî*'? [Do you like it]. As we laughed together it became clear that she was making a point of showing me that much was happening in Iranian society.

In many ways my experience in Isfahan symbolises the time I have spent with Iranians over the years. By means of many questions and exchanges it has been a pleasure breaking through many of the existing stereotypes and misconceptions held between Iranian and Western cultures and societies. This book is a small attempt at understanding some of the rich and complex layers of Iranian history and culture and how they continue to be lived on and through networks of Iranians who live in Britain.

Acknowledgements

The following chapters reflect the help of all the Iranians who have given me their time during the course of this project. Foremost is the incredible hospitality and generosity of the many Iranians living in London who have shared their knowledge and experiences with me. I am extremely grateful for their support.

I am indebted to a number of people for their assistance with this book. My deep appreciation goes to my Persian teacher, Parvaneh. Her help has been invaluable throughout this study. My sincere thanks to: Anoush Baghdiantz, Ian Dougal, Joanna de Groot, Jason Edwards, Ilian Haralanov, Anna Enayat, Deniz Kandiyoti, Homa Katouzian, Kate Morris, Mehdi Moslem, Xavier Munōz, Kamal Parsi-pour, Armando Salvatore, Alex Seago, Idoia Turro, Caroline Wintersgill and Matthijs Van den Bos for reading parts of the text and making helpful remarks at different phases of this project. I want to thank my friends who participated in the 'Public Spheres and Muslim Identities' Summer Institute, who gave me very constructive comments and engaged with me in lengthy discussions. Of course, the shortcomings in this work are my responsibility alone.

I would especially like to thank Sami Zubaida, who has been a constant source of knowledge and encouragement over the years. It has been a great honour and pleasure being his student.

I owe a special thanks to Karin Hesse-Lehmann and Albrecht Lehmann for their whole-hearted support, enthusiasm and insightful comments.

Nima Zahed has been an important part of this work. His love, patience and encouragement have guided me through every stage of this project.

This book is dedicated to my parents, Martin and Patricia Spellman, and my brothers and sisters in gratitude for their love and support.

Introduction

Religious Identity
in the Process of Migration

An estimated one million people left Iran during the course of the 1979 Iranian revolution and the establishment of the Islamic Republic.[1] For the past twenty-five years the waves of Iranians who emigrated to Britain, who are politically, religiously, socio-economically and ethnically heterogeneous, have found themselves in the ongoing process of settlement. The aim of this book is to explore facets of this process by examining the ways in which religious traditions and practices have been maintained, negotiated and rejected by Iranians from Muslim backgrounds in relation to the political, economic and social situation in Iran and Britain, and have served as identity-building vehicles during the course of migration. This investigation moves the spotlight away from the more visible and politicised Islamic movements to the everyday lives of Iranian Muslims living in London. It begins by introducing the wider field of studies that focus on religion during the process of migration. We shall see how the bulk of Britain's academic, political and popular discourses on minority religions have been developed in response to the settlement experiences of immigrants from its former colonies in the post-war period. The following also provides an overview to majority–minority relations that Iranians encountered upon their arrival in Britain.

Many research projects have shown that religiosity is often heightened by changes that occur in the process of migration.[2] The social significance of religion for migrants has often been categorised under the headings 'cultural defence' and 'cultural transition'. As Bruce points out,

> when there is a people with a common religion dominated by an external force (of either a different religion or none at all), then religious institutions acquire an additional purpose as defenders of the culture and identity of the people. The role of religion in cultural transition involves religion acquiring an enhanced importance because of the assistance it can give in helping people to cope with the shift from one world to another.[3]

The implications of cultural identity have been central in questions relating to the contemporary migrations of people to Britain and the way they come to terms both with one another and with the dominant culture. The literature contains many, and sometimes conflicting, approaches which basically can be divided between the primordialist and instrumentalist perspectives. The primordialist view holds that identity flows from shared cultural-religious essences or symbolic values; the instrumentalist perspective maintains that individuals or groups assert particular identities because they provide a means to maximise their interests.[4] The primacy of cultural–religious divisions has been criticised by writers who argue that differential notions of culture fix collectivities, thereby mystifying them. As Eickelman and Piscatori observe:

> The fundamental difficulty with both the primordial and instrumentalist perspectives is that they predicate the formulation of identity upon a reality that appears abstract and somewhat independent of those persons or groups who perceive and participate in it. The specific difficulty with the instrumentalist approach is that it imputes to actors an ordering and clarity of goals, but these goals are necessarily dependent upon ever-shifting cultural and social contests and are often ambiguous as a consequence.[5]

Critiques of such approaches have rightly pointed out the dangers of compartmentalising identities in the pursuit of a political project.

The following section discusses the various ways in which primordialist and instrumentalist perspectives have both been used in academic, political and popular discourses in analysing the significance of religion during the process of migration. We shall see how until the middle of the 1980s sociological studies of migration, race, ethnicity and religion gave little attention to the dynamics of religious traditions and practices in relation to processes of migration in Britain. This started to change in the 1980s and 1990s when religious identity became a feature of majority–minority relations and in turn played a more central role in both primordial and instrumental perspectives.

Sociologists of religion, particularly before the middle of the 1980s, were not engaged in studies that concentrated on the religions of ethnic groups. Roy Wallis and Steve Bruce observed that the sociologists of religion let this expansive area of study be 'high-jacked' by race and ethnicity and the sociology of race.[6] The ethnic school often formulated ethnicity as a shared culture and treated ethnic groups mainly as static communities facing problems of integration, assimilation and transmitting the shared culture to the second and third generations. By wrongly assuming that 'ethnicity' is always the primary identity marker of a group, this type of approach often treated religion as a passive and fixed concept, usually one of many other concepts such as language, dress, and food, used to define the 'ethnic group' or the concept 'ethnicity'. This perspective often presupposed that social and cultural institutions were primordial, and therefore able to reveal the essential characteristics of an ethnic group.[7] The main problems with the primordialist project are that it treats groups as insular and internally homogeneous with fixed cultural and symbolic values, and secondly it fails to think through the implications of ethnic groups constructing, maintaining and transforming their ethnic boundaries. This critique, which stems from Fredrik Barth's conceptualisation of ethnicity, draws attention to the constitution of markers of differentiation rather than its cultural characteristics.[8] As Brah points out, 'if ethnicity, following Barth, is not about communicating an already existing "difference" the political project, then, is crucially about identifying how narratives of "commonality" and "difference" are constituted and contested, and how these are marked by the conjuncture of specific socio-economic and political circumstances'.[9] This approach seeks to explain how the dynamic and changing significance of cultural difference and sameness are related to a range of signifiers, such as religious traditions and practices, and how and why they are drawn upon in varying combinations under specific situations.

Despite the efforts of Barth, the ethnic school continued to be criticised during the 1980s for not paying enough attention to the changing economic and political processes whereby markers of differentiation are constituted.[10] Sociologists who were mainly concerned with race and racism denounced the studies coming from the ethnicity school, for implicitly or explicitly reifying the 'white family' as the ideal norm and, as such, pathologising any differences in black community life. The criticisms of the assimilation model were also in response to the growing racial tensions directed towards non-white groups in the 1970s; minority groups increasing demands for rights and privileges; and the emergence of cultural racism practised by the New Right. It is important to point out that at this time migrants, who were mainly workers and their offspring from South Asia and the Afro-Caribbean, were principally defined in terms of their country of origin. Although this continues to be the case, religion has featured more dominantly in the vocabulary of identities.

Changes in the Academic Study of Migrant Religions in Britain

There has been a growing trend in many countries and groupings facing chronic political and economic problems to base their politics on markers of identity, such as religion and ethnicity, in order to reorganise and mobilise mass popular support. As a result it has often been assumed that Western-led modernisation – in both its capitalist and socialist forms – is inherently different from and, therefore, incompatible with the fabric of other cultures who require their own unique social, economic and political systems. The critiques of the Western nation-state model have challenged Western theories which forecasted parallel outcomes in the process of modern social development. Such critiques have generated many contradictory reactions. There has been a growing trend, for instance, for Western commentators (for a variety of reasons and motivations) to assert that cultural–religious identities and differences have a determining role in the way social life is experienced. This has been especially true in recent years as the 'Islamic revival', which has often been misperceived as a homogeneous movement, has increasingly been portrayed as a determining force in the way in which social life is constituted.

The growing presence of Muslims living in Europe has also led to a increasing number of discussions and debates concerning the public recognition of minority religions and their leaders, in light of the liberal and secular organising principles of European states. Starting with the New Right, the following section examines how religion, and in particular Islam, has received much greater attention. The Salman Rushdie affair in 1988–89 was particularly central in crystallising a number of apparent tensions, and in questioning the compatibility of Islamic values and Western principles. Debates on Muslim presence in British society have also become more centred in political, popular and academic discourses since the atrocities of the terrorist attacks in New York and Washington D.C. on 11 September 2001.

During the 1960s and 1970s, due to many factors such as the questions and debates concerning the changing dynamics of ethnic and religious identity in contemporary Britain, the economic recession, and the future of British national identity in light of the European Union, migrant groups (who were expected either to assimilate or return to their home countries) were increasingly seen as a 'problem'. The series of Immigration Acts and Race Relation Acts that developed during this period were largely in response to social and political tensions surrounding the settlement of South Asian and Caribbean ex-colonial workers. The 1962, 1965, 1971 and 1981 Immigration Acts effectively stopped immigration and placed colonial migrant workers on similar legal footing with guest workers. The 1981 Immigration Act was particularly significant for the reason that it redefined British nationality in terms of *jus sanguinis*, which meant that a person having been born on British territory no longer determined citizenship. To be British a person must be born to parents of whom one is a British citizen.[11] It is worth noting that the debates and development of legislation concerning the inflow and management of migrants were carried out by both left- and right-wing politicians.[12]

The New Right

A number of right-wing ideas and policies, based on 'common sense' political arguments that build a relationship between an 'intuitive' concept of culture and those of religion and nation, were incorporated into mainstream political debate and practice. Commentators such as Margaret Thatcher, Enoch Powell and writers of the *Salisbury Review* articulated their concerns about the unnatural process of immigration for both the immigrants and the host county, and how it would ruin the British, traditional way of life.[13] They deployed forms of rhetoric which set out to defend and preserve Britain's culture, traditions and history from too many foreigners.[14] Barker writes: 'The alleged invasion by foreign culture implies a particular theory of nation and of race. For the New Right, the nation is constituted by the homogeneity of culture, and the problem of race lies in the fact of cultural difference. Alien cultures (not inferior, merely different) necessarily undermine social cohesion; this necessity derives from human nature. Such cultures must therefore be eliminated either by assimilation or by removal.'[15]

Portions of the press have also played an important role in implementing and publicising these codes of references to 'difference' and alien cultures. As Nancy Murray states: 'Powell's racial interpretation of the nation,[16] with its imagined unity and Burkean reverence for tradition, as well as his supposition that it is "natural" to want to be with one's "own kind" and protect home territory from the incursions of strangers, have found a home in the range of national papers'.[17]

Since the late 1980s religion has taken on a new mode of signification within the discourse of the New Right, in asserting that religious beliefs and practices, particularly Islamic belief and practices, are inherently different from Christian and secular practices, therefore making it unlikely that the increasing numbers of Muslims immigrating to Britain will successfully assimilate to British culture.[18] In what follows I shall focus on the New Right's 'common sense' political language and the ways it has politely been used in the past twenty years to essentialise Muslims in Britain as a threat to the British way of life. Critiques of the New Right's portrayal of Muslims in Britain, which can be loosely categorised in two main bodies of thought, namely the liberalism of multiculturalism and the anti-racism of the Left, will also be introduced.

Muslims in Britain

The 'Muslim community in Britain' is a blanket term that has increasingly been used in politically driven campaigns to promote, on the one hand, fear and hostility towards Muslims who are a supposed threat to the essential values of Western civilisation and, on the other hand, to promote solidarity amongst Muslims in order to defend themselves from religious discrimination and gain public recognition of communal and religious exigencies. This includes, for example, the acknowledgment of faith-based schools, the recognition of religious holidays, the allowance for observance of prayers and dietary requirements. Before sifting through the various conceptions and misconceptions that have been projected on and by Muslim people, let us briefly consider what lies behind the 'Muslim' label.

As a result of the Census (Amendment) Act 2000 the 2001 census results included data on religious subgroups. It was the first time since 1851 that a question on religion was asked on a British census. According to the British Office of National Statistics, Islam is the second largest faith, after Christianity, with nearly 3 percent, or 1.6 million of the population in the United Kingdom, describing their religion as Muslim. 3.1 percent of the population stated their religion as Muslim in England.[19] According to Peach's estimates, 'the probable Muslim population in Britain in 1951 was about 23,000. By 1961, there were about 82,000 Muslims in Britain, by 1971 about 369,000, by 1981 about 553,000 and by 1991 about 1 million'.[20] The *Muslim News* analyses the statistics by breaking them down by the country of origin: 'Of the total Muslim pop, 1.2 million are of South Asian origin. Of these, 675,000 are Pakistani, 257,000 are Bangladeshi and 160,000 of Indian origin. There are 150,000 Turks, 350,000 Arab & African. The rest are other ethnic backgrounds. 10,000 are either white converts or of Afro-Caribbean origin.'[21]

The first Muslims to settle in Britain were a small number of Yemeni Arabs, Somalis and Indian seaman, who worked mainly in Liverpool, London, Cardiff and Tyneside during the nineteenth century.[22] The first recorded mosque in Britain dates back to 1860 in Cardiff; and the first purpose-built mosques were constructed in Woking in 1889 and Liverpool in 1891.[23] The need for labourers after the Second World War led to the biggest influx of Muslim immigrants (and eventually their families) coming from mostly rural backgrounds in the Indian subcontinent. During the 1960s and 1970s a number of South Asian Muslims, from mostly urban and professional backgrounds, arrived in Britain after being expelled from East Africa. The remaining immigrants and refugees from Muslim backgrounds, as listed above, mainly arrived from 1970 onwards. By 1985 there were 338 mosques registered in Britain and an estimated 1,000 by 1997.[24]

The migration patterns and birth rates of these various groupings of people have distinctive experiences that must be analysed in their historical specificity. The circumstances for leaving a country (recruited for labour, political strife, conflict and war); the places and experiences they encountered before reaching Britain; the changing legal, social-economic and political frameworks and barriers they face in Britain; and the transformations of the 'home' country are all conditions which need to be explored. It is also imperative to analyse the positioning and the changing dynamics of the groupings in terms of class, religion, gender, education and generation in relation to the other members of the group, other minority groupings and the dominant culture. Most of the research on Muslims in Britain has focused on those originating from Pakistan, India and Bangladesh. It cannot be assumed, due to demographic differences and the profound diversity of Muslims in Britain, that the results of these studies represent other ethnic and national groups such as Iranians and Iraqis.

In many discourses, however, religion has become the overriding marker of identity, which is problematic not only because of the historical specificity of different minority groups' situations, but also the profound variations in their religious identification and practice. As Vertovec and Peach point out:

> Both images of Islam and Muslim people do gross injustice to the broad historical and geographical plasticity and creativity of Islamic writings, social forms, institutions and practices as found in numerous 'schools' of Islamic law, mystical brotherhoods, devotional and popular traditions, minority Muslim traditions (such as *Ismaili*, as well as *Ahmadiyyas* and *alevis* who are often not accepted by the 'mainstream' Muslim population), and regional variations of teachings and practices (even in countries of limited size). Such images also mask contemporary variations in the manifestations of Islamic belief and practice throughout the world which reflect the nature of any local rural-continuum, class and status structures and levels of education, both religious and secular.[25]

A number of national and international events in the late twentieth century, including the Iranian revolution, the Salman Rushdie affair, the Gulf war, and issues surrounding halal meat, dress and other Muslim requirements have led to many questions on the accommodation of Islam in British society. Many more queries on Islam's place in the West have been raised after the 11 September 2001 terrorist attacks in New York and Washington D.C.

Discussions surrounding Islam in the West have been problematised by essentialist images of Muslim leaders and practices which often underemphasise the range of discourses and practices of those from Muslim backgrounds. Portions of the media have been influenced by comments made by conservative political figures such as Winston Churchill MP, Ray Honeyford, Jean-Marie Le Pen and Franz Shönhuber, who conflated religion with culture, and considered it to be natural or authentic, and therefore 'different' from British culture.[26] Samuel Huntington's (1993) much discussed representation of Islam as a civilisational enemy to Europe (which is mirrored by anti-Western rhetoric of many Muslim militants) has become part of the 'common sense' language and cultural stereotyping reinforced and reproduced by commentators of the New Right and segments of the media.[27]

Poole's study on media representations of British Muslims demonstrates how stories are differentially shaped in an assortment of newspapers in relation to political circumstances and motivations. She writes:

> The absence of normal stories in which Muslims appear, and the narrow diversity of roles that result from the selection of stories seen as specifically dealing with 'Muslim affairs', results in a consistently narrow framework of representation. This firmly established itself in the 1990s, but stemmed from events in the late 1980s (the Rushdie and Honeyford affairs) that defined 'what it meant to be Muslim' and that attempted to construct a closure around these definitions.[28]

Poole's study made the important point that the media should not always be criticised for misrepresentation and demonstrated how British newspapers do not only project negative images of Muslims in Britain. She argued that there is a need, however, for better descriptions in news stories which represent the rich variety of Muslim life, including that of the non-practising Muslims.

The rise of Islam as a prominent marker on the world stage and culturalist notions of Islam have encouraged Muslim organisations and political commentators to join together to form British Islamic institutions in order to cater to religious and social needs and respond to the rise of 'Islamophobia'.[29] The enormous controversy over the Salman Rushdie affair revealed many of the tensions and transformations which developed during this period. On the one hand it can be argued that the anti-blasphemy campaign and Khomeini's death sentence against Salman Rushdie damaged Muslim space in the public sphere and led to further anti-Islamic sentiment. On the other hand, the episode was central in developing a culture of action and legal struggle for rights among some British Muslims. Vertovec writes:

It is possible to interpret the rise of Islamophobia in Britain alongside advances in Muslim recognition through a kind of linked or circular operation. In one process, as a result of the increased vilification of Islam in the media and discrimination against Muslims in everyday spheres (both fuelled by assumed connections between British Muslims and international Islamic extremists), a variety of countermeasures – including changes to legislation, various institutional guidelines, and public policy adjustments – have been advocated by Muslims groups, Muslim media, and public bodies composed of Muslims and concerned others such as interfaith groups and antiracists.[30]

Such tensions and countermeasures will continue to materialise as a result of the 11 September 2001 terrorist attacks.

Multiculturalism and a New Politics of Representation

In response to the increasing levels of prejudice towards Muslims (and others) in Britain, multiculturalist and anti-racist discourses have become focused on questions surrounding cultural–religious difference. Should, for example, marginalised groups be handled within the normal parameters of the political system or should special institutional arrangements be engineered to make up for exclusion and discrimination? Discussions regarding the analysis of cultural difference have developed alongside debates revolving around critiques of oriental and colonial studies – the most notable being Edward Said's, who argued that the Orientalist paradigm in the social sciences constructs the Orient as stagnant, irrational and backward, and in contrast accounts the Occident as changeful, rational and progressive.[31] In short, Said's critique, through a Foucauldian perspective on discourse and power, argues that Orientalism is a discourse of domination constructed by Europeans who define and control the Orient (and the Third World in general) and thereby silence and suppress the voices of oppressed groups. Said's critique triggered a crisis in some social scientific disciplines by raising questions about difference, representation, interpretation and the analysis of power in the construction of the 'Other'. The ethnic school came under attack for displaying ethnocentric tendencies in the representation of ethnic groups resulting in the propagation of their marginal positions. Whereas the emergence of post-Oriental scholarship has usefully challenged the authority of 'expert' accounts and has instigated a more context-dependent, sensitive, approach to studying society, there has been a tendency of privileging 'cultural difference' as the primary indicator of an ethnic minority group.

Post-Oriental scholarship has, for example, lent credibility to the multiculturalist problematic: that of preserving difference and recognising and facilitating cultural diversity.[32] Such differentialists demand that religious communities, with their own unique traditions and rules, be publicly recognised in the public sphere. The emergence of the politics of religion and community amongst Muslims in Britain has involved organisation, articulation and the construction of frameworks created by multiculturalist and community leaders, who selectively draw upon criteria in order to engineer an identity of a commonly shared religion and community.[33] This is tricky, however, because in order to establish special group rights to balance out historically produced conditions of discrimination, there is a tendency to prioritise and fix certain identity markers, which do not take into account the variety and/or (re)emergence of other telling identity markers and how they shift across time and place. For example, in the pursuit of safeguarding Islamic practices in Britain, multiculturalist and Muslim community leaders have sought self-consciously to define Islam as an ethnic group in order to generate a greater response from English courts. Jorgen Nielson observes: 'The pressure imposed on Muslim organisations by European official, legal, political and bureaucratic expectation, is such that Islam has to become an ethnic identity.'[34] Conflating religion and ethnicity in this way, however, makes it difficult to account for the diverse ethnic composition of Muslims in Britain and the various ways in which religious beliefs and practices are shaped and negotiated in and between different groupings. According to Yuval-Davis: 'The liberal construction of group voice can inadvertently collude with authoritarian fundamentalist leaders who claim to represent the true "essence" of their collectivity's culture and religion.'[35]

The liberal communitarians (and the New Right) have been criticised from the Left for ignoring questions of power relations and failing to recognise the dynamic character of culture, ethnic and racialised identities. It is often observed that liberals concentrate more on keeping the migrants living in their insulated communities, specified as 'traditional', instead of campaigning against exclusion and for political rights.[36] As Werbner points out, 'cultural difference has become the basis for an exaggeration of difference and, with it, the incommensurability of cultures. Racist differentialism and liberal or social communitarianism – ideologies of the Right and Left – abandon universalist notions of responsibility, of the individual as a life project, in order to revalorise closed cultures, roots and traditions'.[37]

Alternative Models of Cultural Pluralism

An alternative model of cultural pluralism was developed in the late 1980s by writers such as Homi Bhabha, Paul Gilroy and Stuart Hall. Instead of focusing on the processes of assimilation and acculturation of ethnic groups within nation-state borders, there have been a number of new concepts, such as 'diasporic', 'hybrid' and 'creolised' used to discuss the movements of population and settlement across and between national boundaries. Çaglar writes that, 'these concepts draw attention to the processes that generate an interpenetration of diverse "logics", producing new forms of boundary crossing that allegedly destabilise or subvert the hierarchies imposed on differences. Contrary to the dualistic logic of resistance-assimilation that characterised modernisation theory, here no single mode has a necessary overall priority'.[38] Striving to develop non-essentialist approaches in studying other cultures, these writers aim to express the complexity of practices and cultural formations of plural identities by moving towards explorations of 'new ethnicity' and the culture of difference as emerging hybrid identities. This approach is invoked as a challenge to essentialism because it suggests a new vision of justice which gives primacy to difference, local knowledge and heterogeneity.

Stuart Hall has sought to detach 'ethnicity' from essentialist discourses of 'race', 'culture' and 'nation', and constructs a more positive conception of ethnicity. What he had in mind was a new politics of expressive cultures of Britain's black settlers, projected through film, popular music, dance and other cultural forms.[39] Gilroy, also by turning the focus away from bounded and holistic approaches to ethnic minorities, builds on Hall's 'celebration of difference' in constructing a liminal third space, located on the boundary between insiders and outsiders. Those who are marginalised can make use of this vantage space to create counter-narratives that evoke and impact on the constructed boundaries and limitations of the adoptive nation.[40] These writers also rightly emphasise the constantly changing and contested nature of British culture and identity. According to Hall,

> identity is like a bus! Not because it takes you to a fixed destination, but because you can only get somewhere–anywhere–by climbing aboard. The whole of you can never be represented by the ticket you carry, but you still have to buy a ticket to get from here to there. In the same way, you have to take a position in order to say anything, even though meaning refuses to be finally fixed and that position is an often contradictory holding operation rather than a position of truth.[41]

Hall's approach, which is grounded in Gramsci's theory of hegemony, sets out to create alliances among the margin against conservative forces by engaging in the following three-step strategy: 'First, through an opposition to the given order; second, via recovery of broken histories and the invention of appropriate narrative forms; third, through the definition of a position and a language from which speech will continue'.[42] For example, Islam strategically constructed as a political force fused with 'the British' or 'black people' is thought to create a new ethnicity or hybrid identity which may link people with a diasporic culture stretching across national boundaries, and in turn challenge ethnocentric definitions of English cultural purity.

Writers such as Hall, Gilroy and Bhabha have introduced thought-provoking material which has encouraged rethinking of essentialists' arguments. They have rightly set out to de-couple ethnicity from 'culture', 'nature' and 'nation', and have shifted the focus of analysis away from the processes of assimilation and acculturation within the homogenised boundaries of a nation-state, to a more inclusive and nuanced investigation of the diasporic experience. Employing the concept of hybridity, the politics of identity and the celebration of cultural–religious difference can be misrepresentative, however, should the project stem from bounded notions of pre-existing, holistic cultures. Çaglar, for instance, makes the apt point that creolisation and hybridisation could lead to bounded cultural forms, and in turn adopt the very reifications they were seeking to overcome.[43]

There is a danger in the politics of identity of assuming that fusing identities, such as 'British Muslims', will necessarily destabilise existing hierarchies.

This could also inadvertently prevent other alliances from forming which could improve the conditions of marginalised groups. As Eade writes, 'clearly many "British Muslims" share similar economic and social problems and uniting solely around the banner of Islam can prevent them from co-operation with non-Muslims in specific struggles over such issues as gender, employment, housing, racial violence, immigration controls and the future of young black British citizens.'[44] Another problem with this type of approach is that it seems to focus mostly on the movements of intellectuals, artists and political activists, and assumes that everyone else in the margins is able to (and wants to) celebrate the fusion of old and new identities.

A more nuanced definition of cultural hybridity provides a way to stay clear of some of these trappings. Drawing from a distinction, made by Bakhtin, between 'organic' and 'intentional' hybridisation of languages, Pnina Werbner points out that 'cultures may be grasped as porous, constantly changing and borrowing, while nevertheless being able to retain at any particular historical moment the capacity to shock through deliberate conflations and subversions of sanctified orderings'.[45] Whereas 'organic' hybridity conceptualises the inevitable, and often unconscious, processes of cultural exchange and transformations, 'intended' cultural hybridisation is more reflexive and potentially used to resist and transgress normative orders and power hierarchies. Werbner's analysis also throws light on the fine line between the liberating possibilities in employing transgressive hybridity forms and the limits and dangers, which could overstep the boundaries of acceptability, backfire and in turn create barriers between and across cultures. She discusses these intricate processes through an examination of the debates that arose after the publication of the *Satanic Verses*.[46]

As the following chapters demonstrate, the efficacy of concepts such as 'hybridity', 'new ethnicities' and the 'diasporic space' depends on how they are measured and guided by empirical research. Through specific case studies this study hopes to highlight the intersecting processes which foreground the conditions that shape cultural production and the inevitability of hybridised Iranian identities in London. It hopes to build on perspectives that question the categories and essential differences between East and West; traditional and modern; popular forms of religiosity and textual; Muslim and British; assimilation and resistance.[47]

Theories asserting such putative levels of difference, however, continue to be drawn upon to explain the prominence of 'Islam' in politics. Ernest Gellner's cyclical theory of 'Muslim society', for example, argues that Islam provides an alternative route to modernity and therefore is an exception amongst the world's civilisations because it is immune to secularisation. According to Gellner, Islam has long been split into a high tradition of urban scholars which is scriptural and characterised by order, texts and sobriety, and a low tradition which is rural, informal, and more concerned with emotion, ritual and magic. He considered such distinctions as unchanging historical categories which periodically rupture into conflict when reformers 'revived the alleged pristine zeal of the high culture, and united tribesmen in the interests of purification and of their own enrichment and political advancement'.[48] The rise of the modern state in the Muslim world, Gellner argues, is characterised by the low tradition of the tribes being replaced with a purified, high Islam.[49] This book will argue that positing such dichotomies as fixed and coherent sociological entities is misleading and ignores the range of Muslim beliefs and the way they are interpreted and practised according to current conditions.[50]

The Organisation of the Book

I became particularly interested in religious practices in the early stages of this project as I listened repeatedly to Iranians from Muslim backgrounds criticise the brands of Islam propounded by the Islamic Republic and other Islamist groupings around the world (particularly in Britain). I was told time and time again that 'real' Shia Islam cannot be judged by politicised notions of Islam, nor the negative stereotypes and media images that portray Muslims as 'radical fundamentalists' and 'terrorists'. I believe that focusing on Iranians who wished to practise a religion actively, in light of the negative sentiments towards the many and different interpretations of Islam, to be an important area of research.

Many of the approaches discussed earlier have not been informed by detailed empirical studies of how religions are practised and constructed by individuals in local situations. This book moves away from the more visible religious/political projects and explores the everyday lives of Iranians living in London. Although a religion may share common symbols and a vocabulary of religious and cultural terms, it cannot be assumed that the symbols and terms are constant and, therefore, uniformly shape social experience. Instead of assuming that religious dogma, texts and symbols determine the way religions are experienced by individuals, it is my intention to build on studies that recognise varying expressions and relations of practice and representation of religions both across time and place, as well as across and between groupings.[51] As Asad writes, 'different kinds of practice and discourse are intrinsic to the field in which religious representation (like any representation) acquire their identity and their truthfulness. From this it does not follow that the meanings of religious practices and utterances are to be sought in social phenomena, but only that their possibility and their authoritative status are to be explained as products of historically distinctive disciplines and forces'.[52]

By focusing on a range of Iranian religious practices that are manifested through the Iranian women's Shia Muslim religious gatherings, Iranian Sufi orders and Iranian Christian organisations (which consist of Iranian Muslim converts) the chapters ahead will illustrate that 'Islam' cannot be discussed as fixed and rigidly bounded. An examination of the transformation of social and religious meanings found in the range of Iranian religious practices and traditions in London, whether they are considered to be heterodox or orthodox, traditional or modern, Muslim or Christian, for women or for men, and so on, depends upon an understanding of the way in which they are defined and sanctioned by both the various religious and political establishments and the variegated allegiances of the practitioners. I will show how religious spaces can be vehicles and barriers to political, social and economic expression, and potentially, stepping-stones to wider public spheres.

In order to explore the very continuity, discontinuity and modifications of Iranian religious forms and beliefs in London, this study involves an inquiry carried out on two interconnected levels. Following Zubaida's approach, I examine the links between the religious networks under investigation and political discourses in Iran during the last century. This will illustrate the transformation of the religious practices in relation to socio-political processes and demonstrate that religious practices and beliefs shift, change and disappear at various historical conjunctures.[53] The primary focus, based on material gathered from a fieldwork study carried out from 1996 to 2000, is centred on the construction of Iranian religious networks in London, in light of the events surrounding the Iranian revolution and post-revolutionary Iran and the political and social processes in Britain. In line with writers such as Eade and Brah, this study will 'convey fully the diverse complexity of the constructional process in which individuals engage as they confront the tensions between different definitions of belonging and between social and individual identities'.[54] This type of research requires an examination of the interplay of religious practice and political, economic and cultural forces across and between national boundaries, which in turn marks the relationship between religious practice and gender, class, age and ethnicity.

Transnational Dimensions

The social significance of the increased importance of religious traditions and practices has often been associated with coping strategies in dealing with the newness of settlement and/or a way of asserting ethnic pride, which is usually in response to social exclusion. They are often considered in terms of perspectives such as instrumentality, which is when 'religion represents a set of resources for the fulfilment of particular objectives to do with health, wealth and happiness'[55] and solidarity, when communal boundaries are drawn and provide a local social base for belonging and differentiation. They can not, however, be fully understood solely in the boundedness of the local London context. The following chapters will demonstrate that religious groupings are identity-building vehicles that involve negotiations with several systems of representation. Religious networks are linked to religious 'communities', both real and 'imaginary', stretching across national boundaries. As Michael Humphrey[56] argues, 'local identities forged in the city are interconnected to a variety of supra-local discourses on cultural identity and social membership. These can have fairly limited dimensions such as family or village community within a global context as well as broader "imagined communities" such as diaspora, national and transnational identities and histories'.

A number of the Iranian local networks that I will discuss in the upcoming chapters are created and informed within a broader context of social dialogue, articulated by my informants who travel between London, destinations in America (usually Los Angeles) and Tehran, and participate in pilgrimages to Mecca and other holy shrines. Local experience also becomes intertwined with the preservation of an invented or reinvented religious past. These traditions are often constructed anew in order to characterise a return to a legitimate, great, pure and authentic Iranian past, with hopes of masking the negative stereotypes and images associated with 'Muslims' and 'Iranians' found in the London context. According to Hobsbawn, 'we should expect it [the invention of tradition] to occur more frequently when a rapid transformation of society weakens or destroys older social patterns or produces new ones to which they were not applicable'.[57]

The particular circumstances that Iranians come across in British society and the ongoing relations with networks that stretch across the wider Iranian diaspora must be analysed in light of the changing political backdrop in Iran. This book argues that the revolution, the period around the end of the Iran–Iraq war and Khomeini's death, and Mohammed Khatami's presidency in 1997 are particularly important historical conjunctures for understanding the choices and practices of Iranians in London and elsewhere.

Chapter 1 provides an overview of the Iranian Diaspora and its political and cultural dynamics. It highlights the events surrounding the Iranian revolution and post-revolutionary Iran, and the resulting waves of emigration.

Chapter 2 introduces a mapping of the range of Iranian networks in London. To my knowledge this study is the first sociological investigation of Iranians living in London. It was necessary, therefore, to gather demographic information, detect settlement patterns and to note impressions and experiences for further studies to build on.

The focus narrows in Chapters 3, 4 and 5 to the analytic objective of this study, which is to show the importance of religious traditions for some Iranians during the process of migration, and how religious practices are reworked and shaped in relation to the political and socio-economic processes in both Britain and Iran. Chapter 3 concentrates on popular Shia Muslim women's gatherings called *sofreh*. I look at the performance of the *sofreh* gathering in the past and currently in Iran and assess its changing meanings and roles. The continuities and reinterpretations of this tradition in London are then examined.

Chapter 4 is about two Iranian Sufi orders that have developed in London since the revolution, namely, the Nimatullahi and the Maktab Tariqat Oveyssi Shahmaghsoudi. This investigation demonstrates the maintenance and reformulation of Iranian Sufi orders in London and how they serve as a social and religious base of belonging and differentiation for Iranians seeking the 'authentic' and 'purest' form of Islam. Presenting the discourses and practices of both Sufi orders will demonstrate that 'Sufism' does not signify or denote a set of unchanging characteristics.

Chapter 5 deals at length with Iranians from Muslim backgrounds that have rejected Islam and have converted to Born-Again Christianity and attend the Iranian Christian Fellowship located in Chiswick. Despite Christian missionary work in Iran since the nineteenth century, this is the first time a number of Iranians (living both inside and outside Iran) have become Christians. I will place this phenomenon within the wider American evangelical movement, and introduce the strategies used by the missionaries to proselytise the Iranian Muslims. It is worth stressing early on that in order to understand the many dimensions which underlie and inform these religious practices it was essential to explore the everyday lives of these Iranians outside of the religious gatherings. Let us now turn to the Iranian diaspora and the events surrounding the Iranian Revolution.

Notes

1. This estimated figure is derived from M. Bozorgmehr (1998), p.5; see also V. Nassehi-Behnam (1990) and (2001).
2. See S. Bruce (1996), pp. 96–128; F. Halliday (1996), pp. 120–25; R. Mandel in D. Eickelman, and J. Piscatori (1990) pp. 153–74.
3. S. Bruce (1996), p. 97.
4. D. Eickelman and J. Piscatori (eds.) (1990), p. 17.
5. Ibid., pp. 16–17.
6. R. Wallis and S. Bruce (1989).
7. P. Bhachu (1985), V.S. Khan (1979); for criticisms see J. Eade (1994) and A. Brah (1996).
8. F. Barth (1969).
9. A. Brah (1996), p. 241.
10. See G. Bottomley (1998) and R. Miles in A. Brah (1996).
11. R. Grillo (1999), pp. 167–87.
12. Ibid., p. 176.
13. See Margaret Thatcher quoted in the *Daily Mail*, 31 January 1978; For a discussion of Powell's 1968 speeches on immigration see M. Barker (1983), pp. 1–53; see N. Murray (1994).
14. For discussions that focus on the writings of Enoch Powell, the *Salisbury Review*, and Winston Churchill MP see R. Levitas (1986), S. Verotvec and C. Peach (1997), pp. 3–11.
15. G. Seidel (1986).
16. Powell presented three speeches which laid the foundation for the new racism. On 9 February 1968, his speech was centred on a critical discussion of immigration statistics. He used an example of a case of a white girl all alone in a class of immigrants. His second speech, presented on 20 April, discussed 'the ordinary fellow-Englishman', and claimed that in 15–20 years, 'black man will have the whip hand over the white man'. Powell's third speech, given in November 1968, discussed cases of 'harassment' by blacks. The last line of the speech was as follows: 'I do not believe it is in human nature that a country such as ours, should passively watch the transformation of whole areas which lie at the heart of it into alien territory' (Powell in Smithies and Fiddick, (1969), p. 39).
17. N. Murray (1986), pp. 1–19.
18. See T. Modood in P. Werbner and T. Modood (1997).
19. See C. Peach (1992), and S. Vertovec and C. Peach (1997), pp. 8–9.
20. Ibid.
21. See Muslim statistics from 2001 census on http://www.muslimnews.co.uk
22. F. Halliday (1992).
23. A. Ahmad (1999).
24. Guardian Unlimited: Special Report
http://wwww.guardian.co.uk/religion/story/0,2763,739312,00.html

25. S. Vertovec and C. Peach (eds.) (1997), p. 8.
26. See E. Poole (2002), and S. Vertovec and C. Peach (1997), p. 8.
27. See S. Huntington (1993), pp. 22–49.
28. E. Poole (2002), p. 99.
29. See the Runnymede Trust Commission on British Muslims and Islamophobia (1997).
30. S. Vertovec (1997), pp. 32–33.
31. B.S. Turner (1994), p.21.
32. See C. Taylor (1994); S. Vertovec and C. Peach (1996); J. Nielsen (1992).
33 . See A. Brah (1996).
34. J. Nielsen quoted in S. Vertovec and C. Peach (1997), p. 11.
35. N. Yuval-Davis in P. Werbner and T. Modood (1997), pp. 193–208.
36. G. Baumann (1996), p. 24.
37. P. Werbner in P. Werbner and T. Modood (1997), p. 17.
38. A. Çaglar in T. Modood and P. Werbner (1997), p. 172.
39. See P. Gilroy (1987); S. Hall in E. Carter et al. (1995), pp. 63–73.
40. See also H. Bhabha in E. Carter J. Donald and J. Squires (1995), pp. 3–28.
41. Ibid.
42. S. Hall quoted in N. Papastergiadis (1997), p. 275.
43. A. Çaglar, (1997), p. 72.
44. J. Eade (1994), p. 2.
45. P. Werbner (2001), p.134.
46. P. Werbner (2001), pp. 146–52.
47. D. Kandiyoti (1996), pp. 16–17. See also Soysal's writings which also stress the importance of recognising new patterns of exclusion and inclusion. She argues that universalistic discourses, entitlements of personhood and strategies are increasingly being employed by groups and in turn transforming 'national' rights and the categorical dichotomies which underlie them. Y. Soysal (1994).
48. Gellner quoted in R. Hefner in P. Heelas (1998), p. 153.
49. E. Gellner (1983) and (1992).
50. See S. Zubaida (1995).
51. For example, J. De Groot (1996); J. Eade (1995); D. Eickelman (2002); D. Eickelman and J. Piscatori, (1990); M. Fischer and M. Abedi (1990); M. Gilsenan (1990); R. Hefner (1990); Mir-Hosseini (1999); R. Tapper (1991); A. Salvatore and A. Hofert (2000); S. Zubaida (1996);
52. T. Asad (1993), p. 53.
53. See S. Zubaida (1993).
54. J. Eade (1994b), pp. 377–94.
55. S. Zubaida (1995), p. 106.
56. M. Humphrey (1999), p. 16.
57. E. Hobsbawn (1983).

1

The Iranian Revolution and the
Subsequent Waves of Emigration

An estimated one million Iranians left Iran in response to the political struggles leading up to the establishment of the Islamic Republic and the repressive measures used to indoctrinate and implement the revolutionary discourse. The diaspora consists of Iranians from a range of political, socio-economic, religious and ethnic backgrounds, including those tied to the Shah and the royal family; intellectuals and skilled professionals; political activists; members of ethnic and religious minority groups, including Zoroastrians, Armenians, Assyrians, Anglicans, Pentecostalists, Catholics, Baha'is and Jews; feminists; families fearing the military draft for the Iran–Iraq war; and many others who felt they were negatively affected by Khomeini's attempt to Islamise Iran.

Iranians mainly emigrated to the U.S.A., Canada, Germany, Sweden, Britain, France, Norway, Australia, Israel and Japan. By about 1990, some 637,500 Iranians were accounted for in official national censuses of these ten countries.[1] Most of those who left Iran intended to return to their homes when the circumstances permitted. On the whole, there has been relatively little research done on the Iranians living outside of Iran. The bulk of the material is based on those living in America, particularly in Los Angeles, who make up nearly half of the Iranian population living outside Iran. A field of research is emerging on various aspects of the Iranian Diaspora in Germany, Sweden, Norway, France, Canada, Japan, Australia and Turkey.[2] The following description of the central movements and dynamics of the events that led to the revolution provides a background to the variety of orientations and patterns of association found among Iranians living outside of Iran. The settlement experience for Iranians in different countries depends on many variables, including specific immigration policies and varying historical, socio-economic and political relations between Iran and the particular nation-state. At the same time there are also similar patterns that can be detected among Iranians across different locations which are largely due to both the transformations taking place in Iran, common channels of communication and the emergence of transnational socio-economic, political and religious networks in and between the diaspora itself and Iran.

A Brief Look at the Iranian Revolution

As a result of the February 1979 Iranian revolution Mohammad Reza Shah and the Pahlavi dynasty were forced from power and replaced by the Islamic Republic of Iran, headed by Ayatollah Khomeini. There was an increasing dissatisfaction with the Pahlavi dynasty, leading up to the revolution, with the intensification of dependence on the West, over-rapid rural–urban migrations, increased income disparities and other socio-economic problems. The purpose of this chapter is not to present a full, detailed account of the political and socio-economic climate leading up to the Iranian revolution but to provide an overview that serves to illuminate the orientations and dynamics of the various groupings that left Iran.

The Pahlavi Dynasty (1924–1979)

Reza Shah set out to transform Iran into a modern, secular and independent nation-state. He established many institutions including a standing army, a modern judiciary, a national bank and an educational system.[3] The vigorous consolidation of power through the implementation of his modernisation policies stripped much of the accustomed power and authority away from the religious sphere, the tribal chiefs and the landed aristocracy.[4] Reza Shah also carried out several measures in his attempt to modernise Iran's image. For example, he changed the country's name from Persia to Iran in order to link the country with the so-called Aryan race; he glorified Iran's pre-Islamic history; and he used the achievements of the ancient Persian Empire to construct a modern national identity. A law was passed in 1928 enforcing a Western dress code for men and women, which eventually led to the banning of the veil for women in 1936. The clergy were forced to register officially with the government in order to be allowed to wear a turban and frock. The government banned religious *ta'ziyeh* [passion plays] and the media condemned popular religious practices.[5]

A new professional class emerged in order to organise and implement the new reforms. According to Amanat, 'persian nationalism helped restore a sense of pride and self-confidence of Iranians whose contact with the West had revealed the extent of their own country's backwardness. The upwardly mobile and educated Iranians saw themselves as inheritors of a civilisation at one time superior to that of the West'.[6] Nationalist pride led to the resentment of British officials and missionaries, and the subsequent closing down of several British institutions, including schools and orphanages. The implementation of Reza Shah's modernisation policies required religion to be practised at home. Rahnema writes: 'While newspapers attacked the clergy and popular religious practices, religious mourning sessions [*rozeh khâni*], remained as, if not more popular, than before. While Reza Shah basked in the glory of the secularization of Iran, the people had adjusted themselves to a double life of public secularism and private religiosity.'[7]

The repressive rule of the Pahlavi dynasty, for the most part, left very little space for organising political opposition groups. The exception was during the Second World War, when the Allies occupied Iran in 1941 and deposed Reza Shah, in favour of his son, Mohammad Reza Pahlavi.[8] The post-Reza Shah period was dominated by the emergence of numerous political parties, many of which have had a lasting influence on Iranian politics. These included the development of the Marxist–Leninist Tudeh Party of Iran; Dr Mohammad Musaddiq's National Front, which was made up of a coalition of nationalist and constitutionalist parties; religious nationalists, including supporters of Ayatollah Kashani; an Islamic radical group named *Fadâyin-e Islam*; and the parliamentary royalist group, the People's Party.[9] Press activity enormously increased during this period, with 47 newspapers in Tehran in 1943 and 700 newspapers by 1951.[10] The collapse of the political system also provided the space for the clergy and pious Muslims to once again openly perform customary religious practices.[11]

With the support of the National Front, the Tudeh Party and groupings of religious nationalists inspired by Ayatollah Kashani, Musaddiq became Prime Minister, and Iranian oil was nationalised in 1951.[12] The charisma and the popularity of Musaddiq's government led to British and American frustration and provoked the CIA-inspired coup d'état on 19 August 1953, which reinstated the powers of the Shah. In 1957, with the help of the CIA, the Pahlavi government then proceeded to expand the security agencies and created the Shah's secret police, SAVAK [*Sâzmân-e E'telâ'ât va Amniyat-e Keshvar*].[13] The Shah's power base repressed any oppositional political organisation and activity.

Mohammad Reza Shah and Uneven Socio-economic Development

In 1963 Mohammad Reza Shah introduced new policies, referred to as the 'white revolution' which included land reform; a new election law including women's suffrage; the nationalisation of forests; a national literacy corps; and a plan to give workers a share of industrial profits.[14] In the 1970s the policies appeared at first to be successful, with large increases in oil revenues in 1973. The Shah claimed that Iran would become one of the world's top five powers in the twentieth century. The programme of modernisation was driven by an image reconstructed by the state which glorified the ancient Persian Empire. The lavish anniversary celebration of 2,500 years of empire, held in Persepolis in 1971, is symbolic of the image that the Pahlavi dynasty wished to convey to the rest of the world. The socio-economic development of the 1960s and 1970s was successful for some sectors of the population, like the bankers and industrialists who serviced the Shah and the royal family. However, for the majority of the people in Iran, the economic and social developments were uneven and contradictory.

The land reforms between 1965 and 1973, for instance, changed land titles and established new institutions that removed village men and landlords from village affairs. The landlords, who owned a large amount of the best land in the country, were allowed to continue to farm the land as long as they used mechanised farming.[15] Thus, land reforms ultimately disfavoured the peasants and continued favouring agribusiness and the landlords. The expanding urban economies led to rural–urban migration and it soon became obvious that the benefits of industrialisation and land reform of the 1960s were not 'trickling down'; income distribution, both in urban and rural areas, became unequal. The effects of high levels of inflation and of state expenditure led to unfavourable social consequences. The rural–urban migration led to over-crowded slums in south Tehran and other urban areas, and levels of infant mortality, illiteracy and provision of health services remained ominous. According to Keddie, by 1977, 'an economic recession, inflation, urban over-crowding, government policies that hurt the bazaar classes, glaring income gaps, and conspicuous Western style consumption by the elite and the lack of political freedom or participation were all widely felt and belied the numer-ous official predictions that the "Great Civilisation" was just around the corner'.[16] The following section briefly discusses the growing Shia modernist movements and the secular opposition groups which developed in light of the unfavourable socio-economic conditions and political repression.

The Religious and Secular Opposition

The ulema, or religious scholars, have held an important position in Iranian society since the establishment of the Safavid dynasty (1501–1722), perform-ing roles such as preaching, administering justice and organising charitable religious endowments.[17] Historically the ulema had remained autonomous of the state. While they enjoyed established channels of communication with ordinary people they also possessed economic and ideological power in alliances with various groups.[18] They depended on the voluntary contri-butions of rich merchants and traders in the bazaar, who in turn relied on the intervention of the clergy to protect them against the state.[19] The intelli-gentsia, who were aware of the influence that the ulema and the bazaar had over the masses, frequently formed alliances with them in pursuit of reform. The modernisation policies implemented by the Pahlavi government took much of the power and authority away from the ulema. The religious sphere remained separate from the political sphere in the 1940s and 1950s. How-ever, in the 1960s religious figures began actively to participate in political opposition by promoting various brands of Shia modernism designed to repel anti-clerical trends and free Iran from foreign domination. As we shall see, the innovation and radicalisation of Shia thought started with the oppo-sition to the Shah's reforms and eventually led to the construction of an Islamic government and the concept of *Velâyat-e Faqih.*

The most important Shia thinkers that stepped on to the political stage in the 1960s and 1970s were Ayatollah Ruhollah Khomeini and, in a very differ-ent vein, a layman, Ali Shariati. Although their approaches differed, they were both dissatisfied with the weak position of Shiism in relation to the Pahlavi state and its policies. Khomeini, who had long been active against anti-clerical trends and Western influence in Iran, emerged from among the ulema in 1962, and became the leading religious opposition figure representing both the clerics and *bâzâri*'s.[20] He wrote and preached against the Shah and the implementation of the series of reforms listed above, particularly denouncing the new electoral law allowing women and non-Muslims the right to vote.[21] In 1962 he coordinated bazaar religious groups and organised the Bâzâri Coalition of Islamic societies, where he actively promoted the necessity for an Islamic government.[22] On 5 June 1963 – the anniversary of the martyrdom of Imam Hussein – Khomeini rallied thousands of people onto the streets to denounce the Shah's dependency on the United States, and the new reforms.[23] His arrest led to further demonstrations and a bloody uprising against the regime. Khomeini was exiled in 1964 and spent the next thirteen years exiled in Iraq, where he developed his doctrine *Velâyat-e Faqih* in 1970. The principle of *Velâyat-e Faqih* stems from the 'Twelve Shia' belief in the Hidden Imam – the last of the twelve infallible descendants of the Prophet who went into hiding in the ninth century. Khomeini argued that in the absence of the 'Hidden Imam' it becomes necessary to appoint a supreme ruler who has complete knowledge of Islamic law and total justice in its implementation. During his time in exile he also wrote more than 610 sermons, messages and political pronouncements.[24]

Throughout the 1960s several Islamic movements emerged in order to denounce the Shah's policies. On 17 May 1961, Mehdi Bazargan, Ayatollah Taleqâni and Yadollah Sahabi formed the Iran Freedom Movement [*Nehzat-Âzadi-e Iran*] which set out to modernise Shia ideology and institutions.[25] The Iran Freedom Movement (IFM) declared, 'we are Muslims, because we refuse to divorce religion from politics and because Shia Islam is an integral part of popular culture; Iranians because we respect our national heritage, Constitutionalists because we want political freedom and the separations of powers and Musaddeqists because we intend to free Iran from foreign exploitation'.[26] The IFM attracted wealthy and educated professionals who felt that the secular outlook of the National Front had alienated the clerical masses. They supported Khomeini's view that women should not be allowed to vote.[27] They enjoyed political freedom until the uprising in 1963, when the leaders were arrested and political debates were forced to be carried out in clandestine underground organisations or in exile. News of Khomeini's campaign, the arrival of IFM on Iran's political stage and the renewal of the National Front reached many politically minded students, such as Ali Shariati, who were studying in universities abroad at the time.[28]

Ali Shariati was instrumental in popularising the idea of returning to Islam as a way of life and attracting mass support among the youth and intelligentsia for the establishment of an Islamic government.[29] Rahnema writes: 'Given his belief in the Iranian-Islamic heritage, Shariati had no misgivings in combining the stature of Musaddiq as the nationalist leader of the movement with that of Khomeini as the religious leader.'[30] Shariati was educated at the University of Paris in the 1960s, and he applied his knowledge of Western ideas to Shiism and the teaching of the first Imam, Ali. He popularised a nineteenth-century saying: 'Every place should be turned into *Karbalâ* [a chief holy city of Iraq, and centre of Shia Muslim pilgrimage], every month into *Moharram* [the first month of the Islamic calendar], and every day into *Ashurâ* [tenth day of the month of *Moharram*; anniversary of the martyrdom of Hussein, the grandson of Muhammad].'[31] Shariati argued that Shiism was inherently just and democratic, as opposed to Western democracy which was corrupt and exploitative. He and many other members of the Iranian intelligentsia were strongly influenced by contemporary Marxism. Rahnema writes: 'Implicitly claiming the right to exercise *ejtehâd*,[32] he used the traditional religious framework and tool-box to cast religious principles, concepts and practices in the revolutionary and modernist mould he desired'.[33] In the second half of the 1960s Shariati's influential socio-political message of religion was probed by a wide-ranging audience, including the Iranian Left which comprised several secular and Shia opposition groups and contained a number of varying ideological stances to contemporary Iranian society.

A relatively small number of the disillusioned members of the opposition groups such as the Tudeh Party and the IFM formed radical, underground groups after the 1963 uprising and the political repression that followed.[34] The members became inspired by the ideas stemming from Leninism, Maoism and Castroism, to take up armed struggles in order to fight against the Pahlavi dynasty.[35] The two main guerrilla organisations that started to take form in the early 1970s were the Mujahedin-e Khalq and the Fadâyin-e Khalq. Although the two groups were anti-capitalist and anti-imperialist, they differed in their view of Islam and on strategies involved in international politics, due to the varied relationships to communist regimes in the Soviet Union, Cuba and China.[36] Although the leaders of the Marxist groupings initially objected to the unscientific and metaphysical nature of Shariati's ideas, they maintained a channel of communication with him and his followers during the anti-Shah campaign.[37] Though Shariati was not officially affiliated to revolutionary groups, his teachings were famous and attracted many recruits to political activism and armed struggle.[38] Throughout the 1960s and 1970s the leftist movement struggled clandestinely and staged armed attacks. As Paidar points out: 'The ideological unity of guerrilla organisations resulted from their common criticism of the Shah as "the puppet of American imperialism" and of his regime as the instrument of Western economic and cultural imperialism in Iran, and also from their common conviction that armed struggle was the only route to the overthrow of the Shah and the salvation of Iran from imperialism.'[39] The political activity of the guerrilla organisations led to widespread arrests, trials and executions. It is worth pointing out that public lectures and writings by Shariati and others increasingly drew parallels between the martyrdom of the revolutionaries and that of Imam Hussein at the battle of Karbalâ.[40]

The Revolution

In March 1977 the Shah's human rights record was criticised by the Carter administration, and he was pressured to release hundreds of political prisoners.[41] The release of the prisoners intensified political opposition on the streets and universities. Instead of rallying under their organisation's name, however (whether it was the Mujahedin, Fadâyin-e Khalq, IFM and so on), many campaigned under the banner of the Islamic Student Organisation and through Ayatollah Taleqâni's office.[42] Taleqâni's office was an ideal base for accommodating a range of political groupings, due to the measure of financial and organisational autonomy it had from the regime, Taleqâni's openness to notions of social justice and left-leaning ideals, and the fact that he was known to be trusted by Ayatollah Khomeini.[43]

On 7 January 1978 an insulting article about Khomeini was published in a daily newspaper. This led the local clergy to organise a series of mass demonstrations and strikes in the main urban centres, which were backed by the bazaar.[44] While the protests were spreading all over the country, the Pahlavi government tried to smooth things over by measures such as granting amnesty for opposition groups abroad, promising to observe strictly Islamic traditions, and announcing freedom of the press and political associations. The Shah's attempt failed, however, when, in September 1978, over one million people participated in a religious procession for Ramadan, in Tehran, which turned into a political protest. This was followed by the imposition of martial law and a series of strikes. In December, the government had no choice but to allow street activities to mark the Shiite festival of *Âshura*. Paidar states, 'Nearly 1 million people marched in the streets of Tehran and demanded "freedom, independence and Islamic Republic". Banners demanded the overthrow of the Shah, the destruction of American power in Iran and arms for the people.'[45] The Shah left Iran on 15 January 1979 and placed Shapour Bakhtiar, who was previously a National Front leader, as the Prime Minister of Iran.

The Bakhtiar government, however, was discredited for its negotiations with the Shah and the American government. Khomeini triumphantly returned to Iran on 1 February 1979 and was greeted by an estimated three million people in Tehran.[46] He called for Bakhtiar's resignation and announced the formation of a Council of Islamic Revolution, with Mehdi Bazargan as head of a provisional government. The IFM, the National Front, the Tudeh Party, the Mujahedin and (eventually) the Fadâyin organisation gave their support to the new council. On 11 and 12 February 1979 armed civilians gained control of government buildings, leading to several arrests and forcing Bakhtiar, several of his aides and the remains of the Pahlavi government to flee the country.

Between February and November 1979 the Council of Islamic Revolution and Mehdi Bazargan proceeded to form the new government. The plans to restructure the economy and establish a Western-style parliamentary democracy were challenged by militant clergy members and the radicalised left, who wished to prevent or postpone the consolidation of Bazargan's government. The militant clergy were organised around the Islamic Republican Party (IRI). They fought for an Islamic leadership based on Khomeini's doctrine of *Velâyat-e Faqih*. Bazargan's inability to control the situation peaked on 4 November 1979, when a group of students seized the U.S. embassy and its staff. Khomeini's support of the students holding the embassy and the hostages, helped the radical clerics in their struggle for power.

From 1979 to 1981 the Iranian political scene went through a revolutionary transition that was dominated by power struggles between various, and changing, political forces. The lines were drawn between the Revolutionary council and the provisional government within state power, and political parties and groups outside of state power. These latter groupings included the Mujahedin; the Fadâyin-e Khalq; the Tudeh Party; National Front parties; the IFM and other Islamic trends; the National Democratic Front; and a range of human and women's rights groups. Many of the groups went through radical changes and schisms as they defined and redefined their range of political and ideological views, particularly their position on the future of Islamic leadership. In 1980 the Fadâyin-e Khalq split into a minority faction, consisting of those who opposed the Khomeini regime, and a majority faction, which supported the Tudeh's position that Khomeini's government should be supported for its stand against imperialism.

Khomeini's proclamation on reveiling women and the abolition of the Family Protection Act led thousands of women protestors to march on the streets for International Women's Day, which fell on 8 March 1979.[47] Behrooz writes:

> This phase was one of relative freedom for the opposition, in which newspapers were published, political meetings were held in the open, and opposition to the IRI was, for the most part, political. The scale of these political freedoms, however, became more limited as events came to a head in June 1981. Among the important social and political issues in this phase were the rights of national minorities, the nature of an Islamic state, the rights of women, the American hostage crisis and the Iran-Iraq war.[48]

The hardline clergy secured their power base by eliminating the opposition forces by closing down newspapers and forcing various groups, such as the National Democratic Front, the Mujahedin and the Fadâyin-e Khalq, underground. Universities were closed down and many of the educated elite were forced to leave their academic positions. Many other skilled, Western-educated professionals were dismissed from their jobs. The Tudeh Party supported the Islamic government until it started to question repressive measures. It was declared illegal by the government in 1983.

In 1980 the independent candidate Bani-Sadr was elected President, followed by the Majlis [parliament] selecting Mohammad Ali Rajai as Prime Minister. A power struggle between Bani-Sadr and Rajai (who was supported by the hardline clergy) ensued until June 1981, when Bani-Sadr was dismissed from his position through parliamentary procedure. This was followed by pro-Bani-Sadr demonstrations on the streets of Tehran, which led to violence and mass executions of members of the Mujahedin along with sundry Royalists, Baha'is, Jews, Kurds, Baluchis, Arabs, Qashqayis, Turkomans, National Front, Maoists, and Marxists.[49] Ayatollah Ali Khamenei became president in October 1981. The mass arrests of both the Tudeh Party and majority Fadâyin in 1982 marked the end to all active opposition to the Islamic Republic; with all opposition shot, imprisoned or forced into exile or underground.

Although 'legitimate' religious minority groups, namely the Ahl-e Ketâb [the People of the Book] which include the Zoroastrians, Jews, Sabeans and Christians, were guaranteed religious freedom in Article 13 of the Constitution of the Islamic Republic, they were often accused of being linked to foreign countries, such as Israel, Britain and America.[50] They suffered varying degrees of harassment and discrimination, particularly in the areas of employment, education and public accommodations.[51] During the first four years of the newly established Islamic regime Khomeini adopted a radical rhetoric for religious groups that were not among the protected minorities in Iran. Baha'is and Christian converts have been referred to as *najes* [ritually unclean] and have been killed, imprisoned, and deprived of jobs, pensions and education opportunities. According to the World Directory of Minorities and the official Baha'i statistics, nearly two hundred Baha'is had been executed by the Islamic regime by 1985.[52]

The Islamic Republic and the Nationalisation of Islam

After internal political opposition was eradicated, Khomeini and the Islamic Republic continued their anti-imperialist campaign and the Islamisation of Iranian society, through violence and the use of populist rhetoric, both of which proved to be effective tools in constructing a new national identity.[53] The war with Iraq played an essential role in keeping the momentum of the revolution alive and mobilising Iranians around Shia ideology. In claiming that their political and social ideas derive directly from the original source of Islam, the Koran and the Sunna (the tradition and practice of the Prophet), the Constitution of the Islamic Republic legitimised the primacy of Islamic law and the dominance of the clergy within the state. Borrowing from many of Shariati's lectures, Khomeini and the Islamic Republic pragmatically transformed Islamic themes to suit the task at hand. Whether it was the theme of martyrdom and sacrifice or a reference to the Golden Years of Islam, religious symbols and ideas were used to draw strong communal boundaries and create social insulation.

The principle of the *Velâyat-e Faqih*, which was later amended by Khomeini, established a Supreme Religious Jurist whose main responsibility was to make certain that all laws that passed in Parliament conformed to sacred law.[54] Zubaida writes: 'Khomeini's privileging of the *Faqih* is very much within a Shia tradition regarding the centrality of a *marja'-e taqlid*[55] for every believer to follow. Its novelty, however, is in postulating a supreme *marja'-e taqlid* as the head of government and an Islamic ruler.'[56] It is also worth noting Abra-hamian's and Zubaida's argument that although the Islamic Republic political discourse is expressed in religious terms, with no reference to Western ideas or ideologies, it is embodied by a constitution based on the French Fifth Repub-lic model and borrows many concepts, such as 'revolution' and 'Republic' from modern political vocabularies.[57] It is interesting to add how, despite claims of Islam's universalism, only the Shia faithful and Iranian nationals are eligible to hold the position of the Iranian President and *Velâyat-e Faqih*.[58]

Gender relations were central to the political ideology of Khomeini and his supporters in their attempts to adapt their Islamic discourses to day-to-day practices. Changes in the policies concerning women's legal status, appear-ance and behaviour were important instruments used to mark the boundaries of the Islamic community. As Paidar states: 'Two years after the Revolution, hejâb was in full force; women had lost the right to initiate divorce and have child custody; they had been barred from becoming a judge or a president; they could not attend school if they were married; they could not study and work in a range of subjects and jobs; and they had been totally subjugated to male power.'[59] Various manifestations of popular culture and religious beliefs and practices were also transformed or banned in order to conform to the newly constructed 'original' Islamic project. For example, Sufi Orders, pri-vate mixed-sex religious gatherings, *rozeh* (gatherings concluding with a moving story of Imam Hussein and Karbalâ), and women's gatherings called *sofreh* and *jaleseh*, were either 'purified' or dismissed by the regime as being 'heterodox' and distinct from the so-called scriptural religion of the Islamic government. We shall see in the following chapters the changing relationship between the State and popular religious practices.

The Iranian Diaspora

On the whole there has been very little research done on the range of Irani-ans who were forced to leave Iran. When I started this research project no research existed on the Iranians living in Britain.[60] The vast majority of research on Iranian immigrants is based on the Iranians livings in America, particularly in Los Angeles, who make up nearly half of Iranian population living outside Iran. A growing body of work is developing on the Iranian populations in Germany, Sweden, Norway, France, Canada, Japan, Australia and Turkey.[61] Before turning to the material I have gathered on Iranians liv-ing in London, the literature that has been written on the Iranian diaspora at large will be highlighted. I shall start by discussing the material that touches upon the political opposition groups in the years following the revolution and then turn to the bulk of the research, which primarily concentrates on the for-mation of Iranian cultures and communities outside of Iran. To a great extent the following descriptions of the Iranian diaspora at large reflect the social and political patterns that I found in my research carried out in London.

Political Opposition Groups

Most of the information that has been written about the activities of the Iranian political opposition has been produced by the groups themselves, in newspapers, journals and pamphlets and on web sites. The few academic projects that have concentrated on Iranian political opposition groups in exile have generally provided an account of the political activities directly after the revolution, put forth the dilemmas of political communication among the Iranian exiles, and discussed the depoliticisation of Iranians living outside of Iran.

Monarchists

The first wave of Iranians left Iran in February 1979 during the formation of Bakhtiar's government and the fall of the monarchy. It consisted mainly of those who prospered from the socio-economic developments and their political positioning in the Pahlavi era, such as the members of the government, the military and the bankers who worked for the Shah and the royal family.[62] Although many of the first wave of exiles live in various locations in Switzerland, Austria, Britain and France, the majority have settled in Los Angeles.[63] According to Sreberney-Mohammadi and Ali Mohammadi in 1987, the political activity of the monarchist elements outside Iran has been pragmatic and fragmented.[64] Although the royal family has financed publishing houses and radio stations, and has attempted to create cohesion between various monarchist political splinter groups, such as the Âzadegân [The Free People)]; the Babak Khorramdin Organisation; the Front for the Liberation of Iran (FLI); the Movement of National Resistance; and the Kaviyani Banner of Iran, it has not been able to create an effective unified political voice.

The various monarchist tendencies have organised some unsuccessful overt and covert political operations in order to overthrow the Islamic government. For example, in 1984 Shapour Bakhtiar (the Shah's last Prime Minister)[65] and Ali Amini (the Prime Minister of the Shah from 1960 to 1962) organised a demonstration against Khomeini in north Tehran. As Sreberney-Mohammadi points out: 'A substantial turn-out of cars in north Tehran managed to block a section of the city for some time, perhaps constituting the only demonstration actually conceived and orchestrated from exile.'[66] The divergent political activities of the various splinter groups in support of a monarchy, however, have lacked a concerted social base from which a system of support could coalesce. The fragmentation was intensified when it became publicly known that various monarchist politicians were receiving funding from countries such as Iraq and the U.S.A.[67]

For the most part the Iranian royal family's handling of the ex-Shah's investments and holdings and their personal lives have been of more interest to Iranians living both inside and outside of Iran than their political activities. It is important to note, however, the increasing amount of attention that Reza Pahlavi and the monarchists have received since 2000. A number of press releases, along with changing attitudes among a number of my contacts in London, indicate that he and the monarchists' activities have gathered a small degree of momentum.[68] This could be due to a number of reasons, such as the apparent increasing rapport between Reza Shah and the Bush administration in the U.S.A., and the jaded mood of many Iranians who expected faster results from Khatami's programme of reform.

National Council for Resistance

After being forced out of the country in June 1981, the former President, Abolhassan Bani-Sadr, and Massoud Rajavi, the former Iranian leader of the Mujahedin, fled to Paris where they formed the National Council for Resistance (NCR). The NCR was founded in October 1981 as a provisional government of the Islamic Democratic Republic, and declared itself ready to take control after the overthrow of Khomeini, with Bani-Sadr to be reinstated as President and Rajavi as head of the provisional government.[69] It was a broad coalition of some fifteen opposition groups, including the Mujahedin; the Kurdish Democratic Party of Iran (KDPI), led by Abdo Rahman Qassemlou; the National Democratic Front, led by Hedayat Matin-Daftari; and several leftist groups.[70] In 1981 members of this group declared an armed struggle against Khomeini's regime, which was followed by a series of violent incidents in Tehran, mainly between the Mujahedin and the Islamic revolutionary guards. The string of violence led thousands more Iranians into exile. Rajavi and Bani-Sadr made the unpopular decision to build their political relationship through the marriage of Bani-Sadr's daughter to Rajavi, shortly after Rajavi's first wife was killed in the political operations in Tehran.

The marriage did not last long, however, as in March 1984 Bani-Sadr and others left the NCR, reportedly due to differences with Rajavi over alliances with Iraq and reservations surrounding his previous relations with the ruling regime.[71] In 1985 Qassemlou and the KDPI were expelled from the NCR for suggesting that the council should try to negotiate with the Islamic regime.[72] The NCR had to leave France in 1986, due to agreements between France and Iran, and relocated its headquarters in Baghdad.[73]

Massoud Rajavi then married Mariam, who was the Deputy Commander-in-Chief as well as Secretary General of the Mujahedin. While in Iraq, she temporarily took over his role as President of the Mujahedin until August 1993, when Mrs Rajavi was elected Iran's first future president by the NCR. As of 1996 there were 560 members on the Council (half of whom were women representing the Mujahedin) with eight people in the NCR who have the power of veto.[74] Although members of the council have argued that Massoud and Mariam Rajavi and the Mujahedin do not control the NCR, the provisional government is considered as the political front of the Mujahedin. The spokesperson for the NCR in the United States, Soona Samsami, stressed during an interview in *C-Span* (a Washington Journal), on 20 October 2002, that the NCR consists of groupings with an array of political ideologies. She also said that her *motjahed* [a qualified Jurist] was Mariam

Rajavi. The interview (during which she made the mistaken claim that the Islamic Republic would be removed from power within the month) indicates that the NCR campaign is organised and continuing its opposition efforts.

The Mujahedin's exact numbers are not recorded but most estimates say there are 'thousands' of members, coming from middle-class, traditional Shia Muslim backgrounds.[75] The members of the Mujahedin are not tied to one location but are often assigned to travel around the world, depending on the project at hand. Their main headquarters is in Iraq and the organisation has established communal housing in many major cities around the world. It is worth noting that there are many Iranians who oppose the Islamic regime and support the Mujahedin's political campaign, but who do not fully dedicate their lives to the cause.[76] Following the revolution they were known to be the most organised Iranian opposition group and were successful in generating support and funding from several Western governments and notables: for instance, the American government provided support until 1997,[77] Lord Avebury spoke on their behalf, along with several French intellectuals and wealthy and famous Iranians, including the well-known singer Marzieh.[78] In 1997 the United States defined the Mujahedin as a 'terrorist group'. Also in 1997, Mariam Rajavi was barred from entering Britain in an exclusion order, which was based on the grounds that her organisation contained a large faction of terrorists. These decisions run parallel to the time of Khatami's presidency and his efforts to build relations between Iran and some Western countries.

Although political activism has declined among other Iranian groups, the Mujahedin have maintained a persistent political presence. The vast majority of Iranians living outside Iran, however, are not sympathetic to their political campaign. Many find fault with the Mujahedin's political ideas and denounce their ongoing relationship with Iraq. Several Iranians have said to me, 'nobody who is not a Mujahedin likes a Mujahedin'. The *Independent* newspaper quoted an Iranian as saying: 'If there was any threat of them [the Mujahedin] coming to power, most sensible Iranian exiles would take the side of the mullahs against them. We would be just swapping one tyranny for another and the Mujahedin tyranny would probably be more efficient.'[79] According to Srberney-Mohammadi: 'The Mujahedin have never gained the support of Iranian moderates because their outlook was often considered extreme, and secular elements were wary of even the Mujahedin's version of Islamic modernism.'[80]

Other Leftist Groupings

The Tudeh Party, Peykâr and the Fadâyin-e Khalq, who were all active in the overthrow of the Shah's regime, are the central leftist parties organised outside of Iran.[81] The political divisions that existed between the leftist groups have continued in exile and there have been many schisms within the parties.[82] The Fadâyin-e Khalq has split into several groups due to disagreements concerning both their affiliation with the Mujahedin and different strategies for armed struggles in Iran.[83] The Marxist group who left the Mujahedin in 1975, called The Organization Struggling for the Freedom of the Working Class (Peykâr), have not been successful in linking up with the working classes or building alliances with the other leftist groupings. The limited research conducted on Iranian political opposition outside Iran indicates some of the organisational difficulties they have faced in coming to terms with both the political situation in Iran and their lives in exile.

Many of those who were politically active, with perhaps the exception of some members of the Mujahedin, have moved away from politics and have become more concerned with immigration, welfare issues and their Iranian cultural identity outside Iran. Very little information has been collected, however, concerning the changes of the various groups in terms of ideology, organisation and finances, media and communication networks, goals, strategies, and survival in relation to the diaspora and the political and social climate in Iran. Further research undertakings on the implications of politically charged events and campaigns, such as the Mykonos trial,[84] and the Berlin conference on 'Iran After the Elections' held on 7 and 8 April 2000,[85] would throw light on the ramifications of Iranian political activity outside Iran.

The On-going Process of Settlement

The majority of the research and writings on the Iranian diaspora covers a range of topics, from different disciplines, that focuses on the adaptation and the re-creation of identity and culture in light of the dominant host culture.[86] For the most part the writings separate Iranian migration into two phases, the first being the period from 1950 until the revolution and the second, the post-revolutionary years. The first phase mainly consisted of students from middle- to upper-class families who were sent overseas, primarily to West Germany, Britain, France and America, for higher education. According to Modarres, West Germany, Britain and France received a major portion of Iranian students until the 1960s when the U.S. started to attract a greater portion.[87] Most research has focused on Iranian migration to the U.S. due to the events surrounding the revolution. Similar to my findings in Britain, the length of time away from Iran and the continued presence of the Islamic regime have led to the realisation that their time away from home is more than temporary. These factors advanced the desire to maintain and cultivate Persian culture and language.

The settlement experiences for Iranians around the world depend on many variables including specific immigration policies and different historical, socio-economic and political relationships between Iran and the particular nation-state. Regional differences and other demographic qualities within nation-state borders must also be taken into consideration. There are also parallels and similar patterns among Iranians stretching across nation-state boundaries, which are largely due both to the transformations taking place in Iran and the emergence of transnational socio-economic, political and religious networks and industries. These are expressed and facilitated through pathways and exchanges of communication in and between the diaspora and Iran.

In 1998 Bozorgmehr provided an overview of the emerging field of Iranian–American studies. He organised the existing research on Iranians under the following headings: 'Immigrants vs. Exiles; Economic Adaptation; Ethnicity and Ethnic Identity; Gender; Assimilation; and the 1.5 and the Second Generations.'[88] Since most existing studies on Iranians in America were based on the first generation, Bozorgmehr points out that analysis of the '1.5 and second generation' is greatly needed to assess the patterns of settlement.[89] High levels of education and professional qualifications are distinctive features of Iranians living in the U.S. and other parts of the diaspora.[90] In the U.S., Bozorgmehr writes, 'Iranians are ranked third in terms of educational attainment and percentage in professional specialty occupations after Asian Indians and Taiwanese; and again third in rate of self-employment, after Koreans and Greeks in the U.S. in 1990.'[91] According to the 2000 census more than 20 percent of Iranian Americans have higher degrees,[92] many of them Ph.Ds. Note the need for more research on unemployed and less affluent Iranian groupings.

The U.S.-based studies frequently note that Iranians living in the United States have had to contend with negative stereotypes, shaped by the 1979 hostage crisis, which was a media spectacle in the United States. We are still waiting to see the extent of the political and social repercussions for Iranian-Americans since the 11 September attacks in New York and Washington D.C., particularly in terms of immigration policies for Iranian passport holders. Although barriers exist the studies indicated a growing importance for Iranian-Americans to maintain and find levels of coherence between their Iranian and American cultural identities. There has been a mushrooming of novels, poetry, internet sites, autobiographical writings and conference panels that delve into the themes of exile, return, exploration of identity, belonging and difference.[93] This is exemplified by a documentary entitled, 'I Call Myself Persian: Iranians in America' made by Tanaz Eshaghian and Sara Nodjoumi, which touches on the Iranian experiences since the September 11 atrocities and how the event has brought the Iranian community together. A number of organisations have also started to emerge in order to promote an Iranian-American civic consciousness and aptitude for active citizenship.[94]

Iranian cultural patterns in the United States indicate the specificity of the hybridisation of Iranian culture and traditions with national configurations of the United States. For example, an Iranian celebration for the arrival of autumn, *Jashn-e Mehregan*, has become an important and celebrated holiday for many Iranians living in the U.S.[95] According to Naficy, 'Jashn-e Mehregan, which was a minor celebration in Iran of the coming of autumn, has gradually assumed a more prominent role in Southern California, partly due to its proximity to the American Thanksgiving'.[96] It is interesting to add that *Jashn-e Mehregan* is not seen as an occasion for big celebrations among Iranians in Britain.

The substantial numbers of the many Iranian religio-ethnic groupings in the U.S., which include Muslims, Armenians, Assyrians, Baha'is, Jews, Zoroastrians and Kurds, is a dimension that greatly shapes the research coming from California. Bozorgmehr, Sabagh and Der-Martiosian's writings on the highly diverse Iranian communities in Los Angeles coined the sociological term 'internal ethnicity' and called for more nuanced studies that stay away from lumping together Iranian nationals in one uniform group.[97]

Naficy's research on Iranian television in Los Angeles shows how the internal ethnic and political identities are contested, reformulated and expressed via television production.[98] At the same time, he writes: 'Music videos and their allied television and music industries are means of the dominant culture with which Iranian exiles have buttressed themselves in the new land both economically and symbolically.'[99] Naficy also incorporates into his analysis the changing situation in Iran and the host society, which are inevitably involved in the reformulation of Iranian-American identities in California.

Along the same lines as Naficy, Michael Fischer and Mehdi Abedi examine the many ways in which Iranians, who are coming to terms with their situations outside Iran, hold on to their Iranian identities by remaking and reinterpreting aspects of Iranian cultural and religious traditions in relation to their present situation.[100] Only a small amount of research has been conducted on Iranian Muslim religious practices in locations around the U.S. According to Bozorgmehr: 'Since immigrant Iranian Muslims in Los Angeles are highly secular – itself a function of their pre-migration religiosity – religion has not served as a major force against the pressures of assimilation.'[101]

Research in the U.S. is much further along in developing a foundation for studies than other parts of the diaspora. Writings on the wider Iranian diaspora point towards similar settlement trends. In France, for instance, Nassehi-Behnam writes: 'During the first years of the exodus, the Persian community on the whole withdrew into itself due to post-revolutionary trauma and political disputes. Since the mid-1980s, the desire to maintain and partake in their ethnic identity has encouraged them to develop cultural associations.'[102] Similar patterns are reported by Hesse-Lehmann's study on Iranians in Hamburg, Germany. While taking into consideration the differences between Iranian immigrant communities due to the specificities of national configurations, there is a need for future studies to analyse the developments and exchanges between Iranian transnational socio-economic, political and religious networks and industries.[103] The extent to which Iranians abroad reposition themselves in relation to Iran's changing political backdrop, particularly since the election of President Khatami, is also a crucial consideration.

Notes

1. M. Bozorgmehr (1998), p. 5.
2. J. Bauer in A. Fathi ((1991); S. Bafekr and J. Leman (1999), pp. 95–112; L. Harbottle (2000 and 1995); K. Hesse-Lehmann (1992); Z. Kamalkhani (1988); V. Nassehi-Behnam (1990 and 1991); M. Sanadjian (1995), pp. 3–36; A. Sreberney (1998).
3. See E. Abrahamian (1982).
4. Ibid.
5. A. Rahnema (1998), p. 4.
6. M. Amanat in R. Kelley (1993), pp. 12–13.
7. A. Rahnema (1998), p. 5.
8. S. Zubaida (1993), p. 58.
9. P. Paidar (1995), p. 120.
10. These figures are quoted in A. Ansari (2000), p. 32.
11. A. Rahnema (1998).
12. See A. Ansari (2000), p. 34.
13. J. Bill (1988), p. 98.
14. See N. Keddie (1981).
15. S. Bashiriyeh (1984), p. 89.
16. K. Keddie (1981a), p. 188.
17. H. Afshar (1985), p. 220.
18. See S. Zubaida (1993) and P. Paidar (1995).
19. H. Afshar (1985), p. 220.
20. See B. Moin (1999).
21. See E. Abrahamian (1993), p. 10 and P. Paidar (1995), pp. 142–43.
22. B. Moin (1999), pp. 78–79.
23. P. Paidar (1995), p. 146.
24. E. Abrahamian (1993), p.12.
25. A. Rahnema (1998), p. 96.
26. See E. Abrahamian (1989).
27. H. Moghissi (1994), p.73
28. A. Rahnema (1998), p. 96.
29. See A. Rahnema (1998) and S. Zubaida (1993), pp. 20–34.
30. A. Rahnema (1998), p. 113.
31. Cited in E. Abrahamian (1993), p. 29. Khomeini then adopted this saying.
32. The concept *ejtehâd* means independent judgement on a decision concerning a moral or legal issue based on one's knowledge of the Koran, hadiths and the Shari'a.
33. A. Rahnema (1998), p. 300.
34. Ibid. p. 193. Rahnema points out that many students at universities in Iran during the 1960s were not politicised. Many were enjoying Western lifestyles provided by the Pahlavi regime.
35. Ibid. p. 193.
36. P. Paidar (1995), p. 170.
37. A. Rahnema (1998), p. 319.
38. Ibid. p. 320.
39. Ibid.
40. A. Rahnema (1998), pp. 277–78.
41. 700 political dissidents were released in 1977. The trend continued throughout 1978–79 when 1,386 were freed. E. Abrahamian (1989).
42. Ibid.
43. S. Zubaida (1993), pp. 61–62; A. Ansari (2000), p. 44; H. Moghissi (1994), p. 171.
44. The series of mass demonstrations included a series of religious gatherings on the fortieth day of previous riots; June 1978, a general strike to commemorate the fifteenth anniversary of the June 1963 riots against the Shah's White Revolution; riots in retaliation for the hundreds killed in a fire at a cinema, SAVAK was blamed; September 1978, riots in response to

thousands of men, women and children who were shot at a peaceful gathering, known as 'Black Friday'; strikes in Tehran oil refinery, the Abadan refinery and in several other industries.

45. P. Paidar (1995), p. 196.
46. M. Behrooz (1999), p. 178.
47. H. Moghissi (1994), p. 140–41.
48. M. Behrooz (2000), p. 103.
49. E. Abrahamian (1993), p. 131.
50. See E. Sanasarian (2000).
51. Country Reports on Human Rights Practices for 1994.
52. See *The Baha'is* (1994), a publication of the Baha'i International Community.
53. Khomeini's populist rhetoric can be read in the Constitution of the Islamic Republic (1979–80) and R. Khomeini (1981).
54. E. Abrahamian (1993), p. 34.
55. A *marja'-e taqlid* is a recognised living religious leader who is qualified to decide the outcome of moral and legal issues.
56. S. Zubaida, (2002), p. 16.
57. See E. Abrahamian (1993); A. Ansari (2000), p. 45; M. Moslem (2002); and S. Zubaida (1995).
58. A. Ansari (2000), p. 46; E. Sanasarian (2000), p. 17.
59. P. Paidar (1995), p. 232.
60. Since then the following two projects have emerged: A. Sreberney (1998) and L.Harbottle (1995).
61. J. Bauer in A. Fathi (ed.) (1991); S. Bafekr and J. Leman (1999), pp. 95–112; L. Harbottle (1995); K. Hesse-Lehmann (1992); Z. Kamalkhani (1988); V. Nassehi-Behnam (1990, 1991, 1998, 2000) and M. Sanadjian (1995), pp. 3–36.
62. It is important to note that not all who left just prior to and shortly after the revolution started were connected to the Monarchy, but left because they were against the revolution. It is estimated that Iranians have brought between thirty and forty billion dollars to the U.S., and twenty-five billion of that has been brought into the Los Angeles area. See R. Kelley (1993), p. 247.
63. The majority of the opposition leaders, varying from the extreme left to the extreme right, fled to Paris throughout different periods of the revolution. See Nassehi-Behnam. in Fathi (1991).
64. A. Sreberney-Mohammadi and A. Mohammadi (1987), pp. 108–21.
65. Bakhtiar founded the National Iranian Resistance Movement (NIRM) nine months after his exile. Members of the NIRM and supporters of the National Front are constitutional monarchists and republicans. They publish two newspapers in France and have one radio station. Bakhtiar was murdered in his home in Paris on 6 August 1991. See V. Nassehi-Behnam in Fathi (1991).
66. A. Sreberney-Mohammadi and A. Mohammadi (1987), p. 114.
67. Ansari (1992), p. 146, and Sreberney-Mohammadi and Mohammadi (1987), p. 120.
68. M. Eskandari-Qajar 'Consider the Facts: Prognosis For a Return of Kings', *Iranian.com*, 28 December; A. Moaveni and A. Zagorin (2002). *Time* 15/4, vol. 159, Issue 15: 8, 1p, 1c. 'Just Don't Call Him "King of Kings"'; M. Rubin (2001) 'A Return of Kings? Alternative Outcomes for the Middle East', *Telegraph*, 11 October.
69. See E. Abrahamian (1993); 'Background paper on Refugees and Asylum Seekers from Iran' (1995); and A. Sreberney-Mohammadi and A. Mohammadi (1987), p. 112.
70. Their joint platforms called for such measures as the nationalisation of foreign trade and industries, land reform and rights for minorities, and had special provisions for lower-middle classes. See A. Sreberney-Mohammadi and A. Mohammadi (1987), p. 112.
71. See 'Background paper on Refugees and Asylum Seekers from Iran' (1998).
72. Qassemlou, on his own, arranged a meeting with the regime where he was shot and killed by the negotiators sent by the Islamic Regime. Information obtained from an interview with Hedayat Matin-Daftari (19 November 1996).

73. V. Nassehi-Behnam in Fathi (1991).
74. Interview with Hedayat Matin-Daftari (19 November 1996).
75. See E. Abrahamian (1989).
76. Due to the number of infiltrators the organisation has made it extremely difficult to become a 'full-time' member. The formal initiation is a long process which begins in Iraq by putting the prospective member in quarantine. Family life for the Mujahedin is an area of contention. When the headquarters in Iraq were developed they created a boarding school and crèche facilities for the children of the members. However, it reached a point when family life created so many problems for the organisation, that Massoud Rajavi asked every member to choose between a political life within the organisation or a family life outside. Many members left, others divorced. Members are not allowed to marry outside of the organisation for security reasons. Therefore, members have to marry between themselves which is difficult because there are many more men than women. Men and women live communally together. (Personal interview with Hedayat Matin-Daftari, October, 1996).
77. In June 1995, in a letter to President Clinton, 202 U.S. legislators urged the administration to give Mujahedin assistance to overthrow the Islamic Regime. Congress approved nineteen million dollars for opposition groups, including the Mujahedin. See Tarack (1996), p. 159. In 1997–98, America defined the Mujahedin as a terrorist group.
78. A. Sreberney-Mohammadi and A. Mohammadi (1987), p. 114.
79. *Independent*, 'Exile press West towards Tehran spring' 21 June 1996.
80. A. Sreberney-Mohammadi and A. Mohammadi (1987), p. 114.
81. See 'Background paper on Refugees and Asylum Seekers from Iran' (1998); V. Nassehi-Behnam in Fathi (1991); A. Sreberney-Mohammadi and A. Mohammadi (1987).
82. See Behrooz (1999).
83. V. Nassehi-Behnam in Fathi (1991).
84. A German court convicted four Iranians of killing three KDPI leaders and their interpreter in a Berlin café in 1992, and accused the Iranian political leadership of ordering the murders. Bani-Sadr testified against the Iranian government, claiming that at least twenty opponents of the regime had been murdered in Europe since 1979. Bani-Sadr believes the verdict greatly damaged the reputation of the government which subsequently triggered opposition groups in exile to act. He is convinced that he and his supporters will hold power again in Iran. (Information obtained from an interview with Bani-Sadr at his home in Versailles, 3 May 1997).
85. Six prominent Iranian intellectuals: Mehrangiz Kâr, a women's rights advocate; Shahla Lahiji, publisher of women's books; Akbar Ganji, a journalist; and Ali Afshari, a student leader; Ezzatollah Sahabi, a former minister; and Hamid-Reza Jalai-Pur, an editor, were arrested and later released on bail for being witnesses to scenes of sexually provocative behaviour organised by anti-regime opposition.
86. See Asghar (1991); A. Ansari (1988); Z. Kamalkhani (1988); L. (Harbottle 1995); J. Cowen (1993); E. BiParva (1994), pp. 369–404; M. Chaichian (1997), pp. 612–27; R. Kelley and J. Friedlander (1993); A. Sreberney (1998).
87. According to Modarres, the number of Iranians who were given temporary entry to the U.S. started to grow in the 1960s, due to the dynamic socio-political conditions in Iran. In the early 1960s, one thousand Iranians arrived in the U.S. as temporary visitors. During the late 1960s the number approached ten thousand per year. See A. Modarres (1998).
88. M. Bozorgmehr (1998).
89. Ibid.
90. Although it is difficult to quantify, statistics gathered by the United Nations Development Programme in 2001 found approximately 240,000 Iranians who hold higher education degrees. See Human Development Report 2001, United Nations Development Programme (UNDP), Oxford University Press.
91. M. Bozorgmehr (1998), p. 19. See A. Portes and R. Rumbaut (1990) *Immigrant America: A Portrait*, 2nd edn., tables 4, 7 and 9.
92. M. Bozorgmehr, *Encyclopaedia Iranica*.

93. See for example, G. Asayesh (2000); T. Bahrampour (1999); D. Ardavan (1996); A. Sullivan (2001).
94. See A. Negar (2000).
95. F. Adelkhah (2001), p. 23.
96. H. Naficy (1993).
97. For a wider discussion of the strong role that internal ethnic and religious identity plays among Iranians, see M. Bozorgmehr, (1997), pp. 387–408; M. Bozorgmehr et al. (1993), in Kelley and Friedlander (1993); Bozorgmehr and Sabagh in Fathi (1991), pp. 121–44; F. Shashanah in R.S. Warner and J.G. Wittner (1998), pp. 71–98.
98. H. Naficy in Fathi (1991); H. Naficy (1993) and (1998), pp. 51–64.
99. H. Naficy (1998), p. 63.
100. M.M.J. Fischer and M. Abedi (1990).
101. M. Bozorgmehr (1998), p. 18; See G. Sabagh and M. Bozorgmehr (1994), pp. 445–73.
102. V. Nassehi-Behnam (2000).
103. See, forthcoming, K. Hesse-Lehmann and K. Spellman's research on Iranians' transnational religious networks in London and Hamburg; see F. Adelkhah (2001).

2

Iranians in Britain

Iranians affect and are affected by socio-economic and political processes in Britain in many different ways. The aim of this chapter is to shed light on some of the underlying conditions informing the social and cultural transformations that bear on Iranians during the process of migration. Since there was no prior research on Iranians living in Britain, it was necessary to conduct an exploratory preliminary study in order to become familiar with various facets of the Iranian diaspora in London. It is important to recognise that the purpose of this preliminary study was not to map out a single Iranian community or make all-encompassing and sweeping claims about Iranians' lives in London. I wish instead to emphasise some of the underlying political and socio-economic currents that Iranians have come across during their time outside of Iran, that have in turn influenced their activities, intentions and interpretations in London. I have found that three historical conjunctures – the revolution, Khomeini's death in 1989 and Khatami's presidency – and the way in which they have intersected with the particular situation of different groupings of Iranians living in London, have been important in shaping and reshaping the cultural, political, economic and religious practices of Iranians in London. In order to examine this process in greater detail the following chapters will show the links between various Iranian religious practices in London and socio-economic and political processes presented below.[1]

Demographic Information

Demographic material on the Iranian population in Britain is limited. The lack of information could be due to a number of reasons, including the relatively small number of Iranians in Britain; the fact that Iranians do not live in a concentrated area as many other minority groups in London do; many do not appear in census records because they have obtained British citizenship; and, because they are not a group that poses social problems for British society, therefore they do not draw the public eye. The first Iranians recorded in Britain were a few diplomats sent by Fath Ali Shah in the nineteenth century to secure the ratification of an Anglo-Persian Treaty.[2] In the twentieth century a relatively small number of students from mainly affluent backgrounds came for university study. The vast majority of Iranians came to Britain after the 1979 revolution. The first source of demographic characteristics comes from the 1981 population census, which found a total of 28,617 who were born in Iran and living in Britain, with 18,132 males and 10,485 females. Figures based on a research paper published by Refugee Action stated that the population of Iranians in Britain increased from 8,205 to 28,608 between 1971 and 1981. Between 1979 and 1984, eight thousand Iranians arrived in Britain, generating the largest percentage of asylum seekers in the country.[3] In the 1991 census Iranians were classified in the 'Other-Other' category, which was made up of 290,000 people (0.5 percent of the population in Britain) from a number of ethnic groups.[4] Iranians were not independently distinguished in the census classification, but with North Africans and Arabs they made up 22.5 percent (58,720) of the Other-Other category.[5] Other figures from the 1991 census indicated that there were 32,262 Iranian nationals residing in Britain, 16,856 of whom were living in inner and outer London. The figures listed above did not include the children born to Iranian parents, nor those whose immigration status was unclear.

The Home Office have also released figures in 1998 estimating that from 16,000 to 20,000 temporary visas have been given every year since 1990 to Iranians. If this estimation is right, there are many more Iranians in Britain than those indicated by the census data.

According to the Iranian consulate in London, approximately 75,000 Iranians are living in Britain, half of whom are living in the London area. The consulate also reported that around 35,000 Iranians are actually registered with it.[6] It is worth adding that in 2001 alone there was a 300 percent increase in the number of Iranians seeking asylum in Britain. The mid-term results of the 2001 census revealed the population of the United Kingdom to be 58,789,194.[7] It recorded that 40,767 Iranians live in England and Wales. As a result of the Census (Amendment) Act 2000 it is the first time since the 1851 Census that a question on religion has been asked. The Census White Paper argued that an enquiry on religion was needed to supplement data to identify ethnic subgroupings, particularly from South Asia.[8] The ethnic question, which was included in the census for the first time in 1991, was revised. It now allows people to describe themselves as, for example, 'Black British' or 'Asian British'.[9]

The estimates of the Iranian population in Britain that I heard among Iranians were greatly varied and usually much higher than the numbers recorded by the census. The estimates commonly fell in the unlikely range of 100,000 to 500,000. Iranians in London are listed as living mainly in the following boroughs: Brent, Barnet, Ealing, Hammersmith and Fulham, Kensington and Chelsea, and Westminster in inner London. Research projects have shown the difficulties in obtaining statistics with regards to the distribution of the Iranian population. For example, in 1986 to 1987 the Iranian

Community Centre wrote to several councils asking for any information regarding the number of Iranians either in London or in their particular boroughs.[10] Many of the boroughs, including Bexley, Barking and Dagenham, Ealing, Harrow, Havering, Hillington, Hounslow and Redbridge, were not able to provide such information. Ealing, which is a borough that is thought to hold one of the largest populations of Iranians, for example, sent the following reply to the Iranian Association: 'I regret to tell you that we do not have any information about the number of Iranians living in this Borough.'[11]

Research Methods

The preliminary study included unstructured interviews with Iranian men and women of different ages and from diverse political, social, ethnic and religious backgrounds; visiting Iranian ethnic and political centres, libraries and schools; observing a range of Iranian religious gatherings; attending Iranian concerts, discos and celebrations, most notably the New Year celebrations, *noruz,* attending Iranian academic lectures and conferences; and attending Persian language courses. I was also introduced to a number of informal networks through being invited by Iranians from different backgrounds to their homes for dinners and private parties. I travelled to Iran in 1999 and 2003, which gave me the opportunity to meet many of the relatives and friends of my contacts in London.

Although there are clusters of Iranian businesses and restaurants in areas such as Olympia, Kensington and Ealing, for the most part Iranians do not reside in one particular area of London. At the start of my research project, in an attempt to learn more about the orientations of Iranians in London, I asked every Iranian I came across to map-out (the majority would draw on a piece of paper) the various groupings of Iranians in London. I found this method to be very useful because it illustrated how individuals conceived the fragmentation of Iranians in London and where they placed themselves on the map. It was interesting because the vast majority of mappings were identical: linking the Monarchists to Knightsbridge and Kensington; the Professionals scattered throughout London; the Mujahedin living in the Hendon area; the Leftists scattered throughout, although many living in Ealing; and the Intellectuals, writers and poets, scattered throughout the London area with many living in north-west London.

I also found this exercise worthwhile because it was a good way to start up conversations with people whom I had never met before, and who were curious (and often suspicious) as to why a white American would be interested in Iranians living in London. I did not start the interview with personal questions, such as 'Why did you leave Iran?'; 'What is your occupation?'; 'When did you leave Iran?'; or questions that were directed at particular groupings, such as 'Do you visit any of the Iranians' community centres?'; 'Are there many Baha'is in London?'; 'What can you tell me about the Mujahedin?' Instead I started on more comfortable ground by opening a space for them to describe the way in which they envisaged Iranians living in London. I found that people enjoyed explaining to an outsider the backgrounds and circumstances of Iranians in London and their experiences of living in Britain.

Throughout the many stages of my research project I was better received by Iranians, especially when I telephoned people for interviews, if I was personally introduced or given a phone number by a fellow like-minded Iranian. I would often send a note of thanks (usually written half in English, half in Persian) to people with whom I spoke. I felt that this was a positive gesture in building up good relationships with new contacts. Although there were many occasions when I was frustrated that I could not speak fluently and understand the Persian language, I gained the impression that my efforts in struggling to speak the language were highly regarded and earned me much respect from my Iranian contacts. I also found that once I broke through the initial barriers,[12] people were at ease talking to me because I was an outsider and detached from the dynamics in and between the various political and religio-ethnic groupings. Generally speaking, I found that Iranians in London are both interested in and suspicious of other Iranians. Being an American conducting research in London was also advantageous, in that many of my contacts did not hold back from making comments about aspects of British society. It is worth adding that there is a great need for specific studies which focus on intergenerational considerations. The pattern of adaptation is different for first-generation Iranians, their children who were born in Iran and those who are born in Britain.

Iranians in London during the 1980s

The first Iranians who arrived in London just prior to and at the time of the revolution were part of the wider wave of emigration (see Chapter 1). This consisted mainly of those who, in varying degrees, were affiliated to the Shah and/or benefited from the socio-economic developments in the Pahlavi era. Many were familiar with the lifestyle in London, and the English language, before their departure from Iran. They live in many affluent quarters, including Kensington, Chelsea, Knightsbridge, Richmond, Hampstead and Swiss Cottage. The beginning of the Iran–Iraq war and the persecution of organised political groupings and religious and ethnic minority groups in the early 1980s, led to the second wave of Iranians seeking asylum and settlement in Britain. The influx of the number of Iranians to London, who were also from a range of (often weaker) socio-economic backgrounds, led to the array of political and sectarian affiliations found among Iranians in London. This is characterised by the dispersal of Iranians throughout the London area, and also evident in the proliferation of analogous community centres.

Due to the sensitive political situation in Iran during the 1980s, the social pressures in London, the divisions and mistrust between the various Iranian networks and the Iranians' self-perception of being sojourners, there was little effort made to maintain an Iranian cultural identity in the British context in the years following the revolution. Locating good schools and jobs in London was a priority.

Two central themes can be drawn from my preliminary research regarding the immediate years following the revolution. First, many reported that, although they were living in Britain, their thoughts were absorbed in the situation in Iran and they lived with their 'suitcases packed' waiting for the political scene to change so they could return to Iran.[13] Many described their feelings of remorse, frustration and helplessness during the 1980s, as the Islamic regime was establishing and forcibly implementing its discourse of Islamisation. Reports of widespread political arrests, ghastly tortures of political and religious prisoners, economic decay due to the war and national isolation, staggering numbers of soldiers being killed in the war, and the redefinition of women, to name a few, continued to shock Iranians in London. Their minds were preoccupied with many worries, including the general outlook for the future of their country; the safety of family and friends in Iran; the future of their jobs, businesses and professions in Iran; and the state of their homes and properties. Many continued to adhere strongly to the particular political view they had held in Iran. Although some found jobs in London (in many cases temporary) they mainly socialised in fragmented groups based on political, social, economic, religious and ethnic networks; spoke in Persian; and would read and write about the changes in Iran.

Another theme which surfaced during the first years in the U.K. was the desire of some Iranians to immerse themselves in British society and maintain low Iranian and (for those from Muslim backgrounds) Muslim profiles. I was told in numerous discussions with both the first and, particularly, the '1.5 generation', how they would downplay their Iranian identities in public life in order to disassociate themselves from negative pictures of Iran, usually linked to terrorism, radicalism, black chadors and Ayatollahs. Several reverted to half-hearted jokes when expressing their disbelief that they hold such an unpopular passport.

Many reported that they made a conscious effort to stay away from Iranians they didn't know and to build up groups of non-Iranian friends. As a 42-year-old woman (a teacher) points out: 'Iranians placed and continue to place a great emphasis on "fitting into" the British society. Marrying a European spouse,[14] speaking English with the right accent, securing a job or a place in a good British University (especially Oxford), and not being seen as an Iranian were all indicators of success.' I was told that if a group of Iranians went to a restaurant or club and found other Iranians inside they would choose to go to a different place. Some Iranians, particularly non-professionals, said that they have been obliged to change their Iranian name to a Western name in order to get a job. For example, many 'Bahrams' identify as 'Barry', 'Mohammads' as 'Mike', and 'Alis' as 'Al'.[15] One of my informants, Ali, who is a mini-cab driver, said that when he arrived in London in the mid-1980s people associated him with terrorists and radical religion. His Iranian friends told him he would have to change his name in order to get a job in Britain, so he has changed his name to Marco and tells his place of work and his customers that he is Italian.

Several Iranians expressed that existing negative stereotypes linked to the Pakistani population in Britain, damaged and created barriers for their chances of social and economic acceptance in London. The Salman Rushdie affair and Khomeini's February 1988 death fatwa (religious ruling) sanctioning the killing of Salman Rushdie were often referred to and led to a mixture of reactions depending on social and political orientation. The secular and liberal-minded Iranians, who represent the majority of Iranians in London, argued for the freedom of speech. Others found Rushdie's writings offensive, but were critical of book burning and other methods used by members of the South Asian population and leaders to condemn Rushdie, and accused them of overreacting. Several discussed their incredulity of Khomeini's decision to issue a fatwa and were angry and embarrassed by its negative ramifications for relations between Iran and Britain. The Salmon Rushdie affair also made Iranians in London realise that they had no spokespersons or figures of authority to represent their various viewpoints.

I was told repeatedly throughout the course of my research that many believed that Khomeini, with his powerful character and incredible popularity, was the pillar of strength behind the success of the Islamic Republic, and that the government would inevitably weaken and fall after his death. The resilience of the Iranian government and the Iranians' continued absence from Iran, however, led to the shift in self-perception, from being sojourners to settlers, and the desire to maintain and recreate Iranian culture, social circles and cultural events in London.

The first Iranian institutions to develop in London were community centres and religio-ethnic organisations, established in the mid-1980s, in order to inform Iranians of their rights in Britain and to assist in immigration, welfare, housing advice and other issues involved in the process of resettlement.[16] The religious and ethnic subgroups, including the Baha'is, Zoroastrians, Jews, Armenians, Assyrians and Kurds, either turned to the religious and social bases that had already been established prior to the revolution or created new religious and/or ethnic centres.[17] The number of Iranian educational and cultural institutions mushroomed in London after Khomeini's death in 1989.

Iranians in London during the 1990s

Many Iranians living in London realised that their stay was unlikely to be temporary due to the unchanging political situation in Iran after Khomeini's death in 1989. Many reported that the Islamic Republic's lack of policies and the negative attitudes toward Iranians abroad after the revolution and during the Iran–Iraq war, convinced them that it was not safe for them to return. Visits to the Iranian consulate to renew passports and to make general enquiries (particularly regarding military service) were repeatedly described to me as dreadful experiences that reinforced many people's decisions to live outside of Iran. Namazi (1998) writes about attitudes that some sections of the Islamic regime expressed towards Iranians outside of Iran: 'One camp labels them

[Iranians abroad] as a group of traitors comprised of a potpourri of officials of the ancient regime, "Westoxicated" Iranians, members of the oppositions, and cowardly individuals who fled to escape defending the country's borders against the Iraqi aggression. Needless-to-say, this camp has shown no interest in attracting the expatriate population back to Iran.'[18] These attitudes slowly started to change, however, after the end of the Iran–Iraq war and the period of reconstruction that followed. In 1991, the then president, Rafsanjani, extended an invitation to the exiles to return to Iran. Several informants reported that although they were promised good salaries, cars and houses by institutions in Rafsanjani's government and big corporations, they were not entirely convinced it was safe to return. While many found they were not willing to live under repressive social and political restrictions, a few started to travel back and forth between London and Iran.

Although many Iranians have become absorbed within their new milieu, many also realised that they did not wish to give up their sense of being Iranian and made great efforts in maintaining Iranian cultural forms and the Persian language. There was an increasing awareness among Iranians of the need for facilities and figures of authority to cater to Iranian customs and religious traditions, such as wedding ceremonies, significant dates on religious calendars and funeral arrangements. I was told by numerous Iranians, from a variety of backgrounds, how they worried that their children were becoming more and more British and were forgetting about their Iranian heritage; many were particularly concerned about their Persian-language skills.

These factors have led to a tremendous increase in Iranian educational, socio-cultural and business venues and activities in London, with much less emphasis placed on political matters.[19] It is important to note that Iranians tended to socialise within their political circles. There has been a growing number of cultural celebrations (particularly for the Iranian New Year), media centres, Persian-language centres, religious associations and gatherings, poetry readings, contemporary and classical Persian music concerts, films, comedy shows and discos. There has also been an increasing number of Iranian restaurants, Persian video and music shops, grocery stores, carpet and handicraft stores, hairdressers and many other businesses that have developed throughout London. The way in which Iranian identity is expressed through the range of media and cultural forms is based on many interrelated factors, including their 'information capital',[20] gender, religion, ethnicity and economic backgrounds. The following sections will bring to light some processes involved in identity construction and introduce a few of the spaces in London where Iranians express these identities, and participate in the diverse local and global Iranian scenes.

The Reinvention of a 'Pure' and 'Authentic' Past

One of the ways that Iranians have tried to come to terms with their displacement has been to draw on positive representations of the Iranian past, in order to transcend the political situation in Iran and the negative sentiments towards

Iranians and Muslims in Britain. Research projects in America have similarly shown this tendency to promote elements of the Iranian past. For example, Hamid Naficy's research on the Iranians in Los Angeles discusses the process of 'syncretic rearchaization', which is the attempt to invoke a period in one's history before it was 'contaminated' by another. He examines the ways in which Iranians in exile have tried to construct an Iranian past that attempts to revitalise either the pre-Islamic time or the pre-revolution period through their popular culture and televisual productions.[21]

Many have promoted a brand of Persian nationalism, identifying Iran with pre-Islamic symbols and glorifying the achievements of the ancient Persian Empire. Several Iranians told me that there is no 'real' culture in Iran because they lost their true Persian culture when the Islamic religion was established. I have also observed, which concurs with Naficy's analysis, the way in which many Iranian elites in exile have undergone a similar process, by construct-ing tragic and paralysing representations of the present while idealising a secular past.[22] Reverting to an ideal religious past, which will be examined more carefully in the following chapters, is also a pattern that emerged for some Iranian networks.

Internal Religious and Ethnic Identities

The organisation of internal ethnic and religious networks, with the develop-ment of Muslim, Jewish, Armenian, Assyrian, Protestant (Anglican and Pentecostal), Zoroastrian, Kurdish and Baha'i centres, provides Iranians with other markers of identity to turn to in London. I interviewed several Iranian Armenians, for example, who identify more strongly with their Armenian Christian roots than their Iranian national identity. Many reported that they speak Armenian in their homes, their children attend the Armenian culture and language Saturday school and they hope their children will marry fellow Armenians. I found that Armenians often felt superior to other Iranian group-ings. These observations are similar to Bozorgmehr's work on religio-ethnic diversity among Iranians living in Los Angeles, which found Armenian and Jewish Iranians retaining their ethnicity more than other subgroups.[23]

I spoke to many Iranian adherents to the Baha'i faith[24] who said that when they arrived in Britain they were able to join local 'Spiritual Assemblies' which were already developed by British Baha'is. Many said that having such contacts enabled them to integrate smoothly into British society because it was easier to make British friends, they had help finding jobs and received advice about living locations and school districts. Many reported, however, that differences in socio-economic and educational backgrounds made it diffi-cult to merge with the established British Baha'i community.[25] According to the Baha'i London Office of External Affairs, after the revolution 4,600 Iran-ian Baha'i refugees arrived in Britain. Most of these refugees then went to Canada, United States and Australia. According to their figures 42 percent of all Baha'is in Britain are Iranian (or with Iranian parents) with approximately 1,450 Iranians between the ages of 10 and 21.

I became particularly interested in the ways in which religion and popular forms of religiosity have been vehicles used by some Iranian Muslims to deal with their displacement and make sense of their lives outside Iran. I spoke to Iranians involved in various Muslim religious associations and gatherings in London: Sufi Orders, religious charity groups, private mixed-sex religious gatherings, *rozehs* (gatherings concluding with a moving story of Imam Hussein and Karbalâ), mosques and schools financed by the Iranian government, and Iranian Christian Churches (consisting of former Muslims who are now born-again Christians). The following chapters are primarily concerned with the way in which these religious networks have developed in London. This examination involves a historically grounded political sociology that explores the ways in which religious traditions are reinvented or shaped in relation to the conjunctures delineated in the foregoing analysis. It is important to note that a great deal of research is needed on the internal ethnic and religious identity and group affiliation among Iranians in Britain, which could only be mentioned above.

The Media Environment

A great number of mass media forms are aimed and marketed at various socio-economic, political, religious and ethnic networks in London.[26] The main Iranian newspapers in London, *Kayhan, Nimrooz* and *Etelâ'ât,* carry mainly political, social and economic news from Iran, they also advertise for Iranian businesses, services, entertainment and cultural events around the diaspora. Most of the publications are in the Persian language, although a few print in a Persian/English bilingual format, and some, mainly aimed at the second generation, are published entirely in English.[27] I was often told by Iranian men and women that in the years following the revolution they were eager for news from Iran and preoccupied with news in Iranian newspapers, political journals, magazines and pamphlets;[28] however, as time passed and the Islamic government was being consolidated, they were forced to divert their energies to re-establishing their lives in London. The number of publications decreased and the subject matter opened up to articles which discussed the Iranians' physical, psychological, spiritual and intellectual dislocation, and questions surrounding acculturation and maintaining an Iranian identity. Magazines and newspapers, such as *Banu, Niazmandihah, Nameye Digar, British-Iranian Business News* and *E-run,* focused more attention on the problems and issues that Iranians faced outside Iran as well as circulating information about Iranian cultural events such as musical concerts, comedy shows, discos and poetry readings.[29]

An Iranian television programme called *Rangarang* is available on satellite television, and it has been possible since 1999 to receive a 24-hour television channel, supported by the Islamic regime, via satellite. In 2000 Zia Atabay started National Iranian Television, which is a Los Angeles-based television station that broadcasts to Iranians around the world via satellite. There are over twenty Iranian radio programmes, many of which are Persian speaking, based outside Iran.[30]

The Internet is a very important forum for communication and identity construction for many Iranians.[31] There are four different ways that Iranian sites can be accessed on the Internet. Information is posted on the World Wide Web by Iranian political groups (such as the Fadâyin-e Khalq, Mujahedin and the Islamic Republic), religious and ethnic groups (such as Armenians, Assyrians, Evangelical Christians, Jews, Baha'is, Sufi Orders and Kurds), social, professional and economic organisations, and families and individuals (including Iranian pop stars and artists). An on-line magazine called *The Iranian* (http://www.iranian.com), was set up in the U.S. by Jahanshah Javid in 1995, and has become a popular site for posting articles on culture, politics and those dealing with identity conflicts. Second, there are roughly fifteen different Iranian newsgroups which are designed for interactive discussions between Iranians around the world. Newsgroups, such as soc.culture.iranian, provide a space for Iranians to write about a range of topics, including music, sports, jokes, news, politics, music, poetry, marriage, sex, immigration laws and so on. In the past three or four years, as the Internet has become more popular, the newsgroups have become highly politicised and the dialogue is often aggressive. Third, numerous Internet chat rooms have developed via Internet Relay Chats (IRC) or the World Wide Web. The rooms have been designed to provide a space for Iranians to converse with each other in real time. It is possible to play backgammon and other games, and the rooms have been used to relocate friends and relatives. Fourth, it is possible to receive the latest information concerning Iran and the Iranian diaspora, channelled through various specific topic-oriented mailing lists. This includes book clubs, dating clubs, and up-to-date news articles taken from Reuters, Agence France Press, the BBC and others.

Many men and women, particularly from the younger generations, said they regularly logged on to Iranian pages on the Internet. I was often told that the Internet is ideal because, although they do not like to attend Iranian cultural events, they like to keep up to date with Iranian politics and events. Many prefer to talk anonymously in chat rooms about topics such as dating, sex and family difficulties. It is also an important medium for political opposition groups to organise and express their views to cohorts living around the world. For example, Bani-Sadr, the ex-president of Iran, said that he completely depends on e-mail and web pages to organise and maintain contact with his opposition party. He uses it as a forum to publicise his newspaper and to discuss latest political developments. He stressed the importance of having access to information and communication links on the Internet for someone in his position, who rarely leaves his home due to security problems.[32] We shall also see the importance of the Internet for religious organisations in the next chapters.

The Iranian New Year

The Iranian New Year, *noruz*, which falls on the first day of spring, is the only calendrical occasion that is acknowledged by Iranians from all backgrounds. The following section highlights the celebratory customs and activities surrounding *noruz* whilst demonstrating the increasing importance of an Iranian national tradition; the socio-economic, political, ethnic and religious boundaries that divide Iranians in London; and the way in which these various boundaries have shifted over the years.

The *noruz* tradition and the activities that surround it have become increasingly popular amongst Iranians in London during the 1990s. I heard several explanations as to why Iranians did not attend the few organised *noruz* activities during the 1980s. Many said that although they met with friends and family for *noruz*, they were not in the mood for such celebrations, especially during the Iran–Iraq war. Others said they stayed away because they suspected members of the Iranian government would be present at the organised events. Many reported that they weren't aware of any Iranian *noruz* activities. *Noruz* activities have become the most important Iranian tradition for Iranians to observe. This is not only because it is historically the most celebrated custom in Iran, but also because it is 'neutral', in that it is detached from religion and the many other internal divisions engraved in Iranian society. Many said that they enjoy introducing the traditions of *noruz* to non-Iranian friends and that the growing events are starting to make a wider impact on London's cosmopolitan landscape.

Preparations for the Iranian New Year celebrations begin several weeks before the day, with thorough cleaning of homes, sending out *noruz* cards to family and friends, baking pastries, finding new outfits and, around 11 March, planting wheat seeds and lentil seeds in order to sprout green by the New Year's day. A few days before *noruz* the following symbolic items (called *Haft Sinn* – the Seven S's), each beginning with the Persian letter *sinn,* are placed on a tablecloth or *sofreh*: *Sabzi* [sprouts], *samanu* [a sweetmeat made of germinated wheat], *seeb* [apple], *senjed* [a dried lotus fruit], *sir* [garlic], *somâq* [sumac], and *serkeh* [vinegar]. Several other items, such as coins, a bowl of eggs, a goldfish, a flask of rose water, a significant book (usually the Koran and/or poems by Hafez), and sometimes a mirror, are placed on the *sofreh*. I have been told a number of different meanings of the various symbols, but mostly it is believed that each *Haft Sinn* item symbolises the seven angelic heralds of life-rebirth, health, happiness, patience, joy, light and beauty. Families have their favourite ways of setting up their *Haft Sinn* table; many made the comparison to Christmas trees.

The activities surrounding the Iranian New Year, which is on the first day of spring and is based on the calendar of pre-Zoroastrian Persia, begin on the last Wednesday of the year, called *Châhârshanbeh Souri,* and end on the thirteenth day of the new year (*Sizdah Bedar*). Throughout these twelve days Iranians visit friends and families, with the younger family members calling on the older ones first. The number of people attending the increasing number of organised events grew in the 1990s. Internal divisions (based on socio-economic backgrounds, religion, political affiliation and ethnicity) were evident in the organisation and participation of the various events. I've attended private and public *noruz* parties since 1995. The following schedule is taken from my field notes of the *noruz* activities (not including the private parties) I attended in 1997:

Noruz

1376 [The New Year] began on Thursday March 20, at 14:54:46

Events:

25 February – University College, University of London: Persian student's *noruz* Party.
13 March – City University: Persian student organisation, party hosted by the Khayyam Society, 7:00–10:00.
15, 16, 17 March – Kahrizak Annual *noruz* bazaar (charity) – Montagu Square.
15, 16 March – Charity for Tajikistan: Zoroastrian centre and Ismaili centre.
18 March – Châhârshanbeh Souri – Mill Hill East, Pursley Road NW7.
18 March – Châhârshanbeh Souri– Alexander Palace (organised by the Rostam School).
18 March – Châhârshanbeh Souri– organised by the BBC Persian centre for employees at BBC World Service.
19 March – Kânoon-e Iran community centre (Leftists) Conway Hall 25 Red Lion Square. 7:00 – (£8 entrance fee).
19 March – Zenith disco 8:00pm Park Royal.
19 March – Le Palais – concert.
20 March – Jâmeh-e Iran community centre (Tudeh) 7:00pm Hammersmith town hall (£12 entrance fee).
20 March – Shahmaghsoudi Sufi Order 1:00.
21 March – Mujahedin – Kensington town hall 7:00.
21 March – Iranian Pentecostal Christian Church – 7:00.
21 March – Kânoon-e Iran (Monarchists) 8:00 Marriot Duke Street.
21 March – 1001 nights Ballroom disco 9:30 Holland Park Avenue.
22 March – Baha'is: Holland Park School, Campden Hill Road
Airlie Garden, 7:30.
23 March – Arizona nightclub 9:00.
23 March – le Palais – concert.
23 March – party hosted by Iranian Embassy.

Each year I made a point of showing my *noruz* party schedule to Iranians from different backgrounds in order to observe their reactions. For example, when I discussed other *noruz* events while I was at the party organised by the community centre, Jâmeh-e Iran (where I met mini-cab drivers, shop keepers and restaurant employees, several of whom were unemployed and many of whom had recently arrived from Iran), I heard many criticisms of the Monarchists' parties at expensive hotels, which charge £100 for a ticket to enter, and I was warned to stay away from both the Mujahedin's party and the Iranian Embassy's party. When various Iranians at the *noruz* party held at the Marriot (where I met mainly professionals and (ex)-Royalists) looked at my schedule, many were surprised that so many events had been organised. I was repeatedly told to stay away from the Mujahedin's party and the Embassy. At the Mujahedin's event, I was told the dangers of having any sort of meeting with the Iranian Embassy. They said it was best not to attend any of the other events as they were infiltrated by members of the Iranian government. Most of the Iranian intellectuals and elites were not as interested in attending publicly held celebratory *noruz* events. Some reported they attend *noruz* dinners in support of Iranian heritage foundations and charity groups.

The internal divisions between Iranians have lessened at popular cultural events such as concerts, sporting events, comedy shows and discos. It is at these events (organised not only at *noruz*, but throughout the year) that the old divisions become less pronounced and other identity markers, such as language, culture or Iranian national identity are prioritised. A case in point was a concert tour in 2001 of Iran's most beloved pop star, Googoosh. Singing after decades of silence while living in Iran, her emotionally charged tour stirred the memories and hearts of tens of thousands of Iranians around the world. It was striking to witness, at one of her London concerts, thousands of people crying as they sang along to her familiar songs. Many were holding up their mobile phones so their friends and family in Iran could listen.

Since the late 1980s Iranians in London have moved towards the maintenance and reformulation of Iranian culture in London. As shown above, what Iranian culture is and how it is best expressed is highly contestable. There is a great need for research on the '1.5 generation' of Iranians living in London. Young Iranians have been highly successful in obtaining good degrees and professional positions in British society. Many speak of the importance of finding and maintaining a creative balance between their Iranian and British cultural identities, and wish actively to contribute to both British and Iranian societies. A number of young British-Iranian film and documentary makers, academics, comedians, fashion designers, poets and musicians are increasingly expressing their hybridised identities both innovatively and creatively.[33]

President Mohammad Khatami's presidency and the changing political climate in Iran have created a new set of circumstances through which Iranian identity is constituted and contested.

Khatami's Presidency

Mohammad Khatami's May 1997 Presidential Election victory over conservative opponent Ali Akbar Nateq-Nuri was a crucial event, both for Iranians living in Iran and those abroad, in the history of the Islamic revolution. His election victory, which was largely due to the votes of women and the young, was widely interpreted both inside and outside Iran as a turning point in Iran's political climate, from the repressive and conservative nature of the revolutionary rhetoric to a more moderate platform of reform. He successfully tapped into the Iranian population's general frustrations with the ruling elites and their policies, marked by a number of dissatisfactions: the deteriorating economic situation; isolation from the international community; the discriminatory legislation concerning women and personal status; the prohibition on gender-mixing in social settings; and the harassment received for improper hejâb. His promises of change within the Islamic system, however, have not convinced many critics who question the cleric's reforms in light of the continued role of Ayatollah Khamenei and the concept of Velâyat-e Faqih [a divinely ordained position], unremitting violations of human rights, unfair trials, the rising number of political executions, and the unending persecution of religious minorities. Whether one is an opponent or supporter of Khatami's cabinet, his popular rhetoric of reform and the polemical debates that have developed between Iran's different factions, have created a new political context for Iranians in Iran and abroad, and have led the international community to rethink their attitudes and positions towards the Iranian government.

Khatami's presidency has revealed the complex balance of power in Iranian politics, between those who advocate the basic tenets of the revolution and an array of reformists who are fighting against corruption and for many different shades of freedom of expression and democracy. An apparent series of political and social developments since Khatami's victory, including the period of mushrooming pro-reform newspapers printing real news; women's magazines that touch on women's issues and draw attention to the regime's shortcomings; the development of public Internet facilities; the relaxation (although sporadic) of rules on gender-mixing in public spaces; and a shift in foreign policy, have all led to a number of clashes between the political factions. The conservative Council of Guardians, for example, has continued its endeavours to increase its power through testing the 'Islamicity' of prospective candidates for presidential and parliamentary elections, while Parliament creates barriers by passing laws which counteract Khatami's cabinets reforms.[34] Conservatives have increasingly been cracking down on reformists in high-profile conflicts. The banning of pro-reform newspapers and the arrest of several leading reformist politicians has contributed to their campaigns against the reformers.[35]

Khatami and the 'Dialogue among Civilisations'

Despite the domestic power struggles, Iran's worsening economic situation has given the Iranian government little choice but to reform the revolutionary laws that forbade foreign investment. As Roy pointed out: 'Iran is in dire need of foreign investments ... The business milieu in Iran, including the bâzâris and clerical holding like the *astân-e qods* (which owns the sanctuary of Imam Reza in Mashad), have undergone a radical shift in thinking, and are now advocating foreign investment'.[36] Although Khatami's economic restructuring programmes are considered to be vague, he has been striving to establish a stable and optimistic political, economic and social image of Iran in the international community, with hopes of rebuilding diplomatic ties and attracting foreign investors. Khatami's approach to the accommodation with several Arab and Western states is based on a positive dialogue promoting Iran's commitment to a revised foreign policy of democracy and justice. Since becoming President he has spoken effectively at a number of public and far-reaching forums: the summit meeting of the Organisation of the Islamic Conference (OIC), hosted by Iran in December 1997; an interview directed at the American people on Cable Network News (CNN) International, on 14 December 1997; and an address to the general assembly of the United Nations in September 1998, where he called for 'a dialogue among civilisations' and advocated measures such as 'the rejection of force, and the promotion of understanding in cultural, economic and political fields, and strengthening of the foundations of liberty, justice and human rights'.[37]

Khatami has also used the forum of public speaking to send positive signals to Iranians living abroad. For example, in a speech given on the Iranian New Year, Khatami sent his greetings to Iranians living abroad and added, 'the beloved Iran belongs to all Iranians who long for sublimation, independence and progress of the country' and asked them to continue to make an effort to preserve their Iranian heritage (Namazi 1998). The ex-president, Rafsanjani, repeatedly invited the educated and successful Iranians living outside of Iran to return home and contribute to the reconstruction of Iran's economy and society. Although recruiters from government institutions and Tehran's big corporations (who promised good salaries, free housing, cars and other benefits) convinced some Iranians to return, many were still unsure about their safety in Iran's unsettled and unpredictable environment.[38] Khatami has put forth stronger initiatives in order to break down the general mistrust by creating a number of new policies and programmes. These include issuing temporary visas for men who have not fulfilled the mandatory military service; foreign-residing Iranian men being allowed to buy their mandatory two-year military service; Iranian Embassies and Interest Sections being instructed to treat expatriates amicably; the tough requirements involved renewing passports being relaxed; the cost of a passport reduced; and the declaration of one's religion on passport forms no longer being required.[39]

A new section in the government attending to the cultural affairs of Iranians abroad has also been created. According to Darbandi, the present Director General, the Iranian government was not able to institute the proper policies regarding Iranians abroad, in the years following the revolution and war with Iraq, because they were forced to divert all of their attention to stabilising and rebuilding Iran. He discussed the policy on Iranians abroad in a letter written in May 1999:

> Presently, the unified policy by consensus in regards to Iranians abroad is that countrymen abroad are considered a part of this nation's body that for different reasons left the country. In this view these countrymen are not considered Westoxified foreign agents nor as cowards who fled the country in order to run away from war. It is the natural and basic right of any human being in the

search of better conditions and opportunities to choose a good place to live. We will never tell this generation to pack their suitcases and return to Iran forever; he has the right of choice. But we will surely invite him to try to travel to Iran anytime he find the chance to do so, and to see Iran up close.[40]

Darbandi stresses in his letter that the Department of the Cultural Affairs of Iranians Abroad is not trying to benefit from the financial standing of Iranians abroad, but is instead striving to create the conditions in which Iranians living abroad are able to maintain their Iranian culture and language.

Responses to Khatami's Reforms

The economic, political and cultural fields of articulations that are being constructed anew, in accordance with Khatami's programme of reforms, and the struggles being waged between different political forces have generated many different responses among the international community and the various networks of Iranians living outside of Iran. Khatami's diplomatic efforts have been hailed by many political leaders as the beginning of the long-awaited change in Iran's political climate. Several European countries have welcomed the moderate tone of Khatami's reforms and have implemented a number of diplomatic and trade initiatives with hopes of restoring normal relations. For example, Austrian President Klestil, the first European head of state to visit Iran since 1979, made a two-day visit to Tehran in late September 1998 for a business delegation. Khatami's visit to France from 13 to 15 October 1999 was deemed successful by both the Iranian and French governments. According to France's foreign minister, 'Khatami has proved in his dialogue among civilisations that he was willing to improve the status of Iran in the international arena, under such conditions, our absence from Iran would be a mistake'.[41]

During the 1999 United Nations (UN) General Assembly meeting in New York, Britain and Iran agreed to exchange ambassadors for the first time in twenty years. Morteza Sarmadi was made Iranian ambassador to Britain. The upgrade in diplomatic relations was made possible by the Iranian government's decision to remove the death sentence placed on the writer Salman Rushdie after the publication of *The Satanic Verses*.[42] Additional turning points between Iran and Britain have been visits by Foreign Secretary Jack Straw to Iran, and several phone conversations between Prime Minister Tony Blair and Khatami.[43] The diplomatic relations between Iran and Britain went through a rough patch in February 2002 when Iran turned down David Reddaway, Britain's preferred nominee for its ambassador to Iran. Reddaway was rejected due to his alleged former activities at the British Secret Service (MI6) and was labelled in right-wing Iranian papers as a 'Jewish spy'.[44] The British government defended Reddaway and said that the decision was not justified. Richard Dalton has since been named the next British ambassador to Iran.

The 11 September 2001 attacks in New York and Washington D.C., and Iran's inclusion in Washington's 'axis of evil', has damaged the series of signals indicating a softening in relations between the U.S. and Iran. These signals included the loosening of the trade sanctions in April 1999 and the removal of Iran from the list of major drug-producing countries in December 1998. Furthermore, in response to Khatami's proposal of a cultural exchange with America, the American government and Iranian authorities have jointly organised a programme sending a group of American scholars to Iran for Persian-language studies.

The manner in which Iranians abroad, who are interwoven into the social and cultural fabric of their adopted societies, come to be (re)positioned in relation to Iran's new political context is a matter for particular research projects. Khatami's government has certainly stimulated a renewed interest in the political, economic and social situation in Iran among the various Iranian networks in London. During the course of my research I have come across several and varied shifts in opinions and attitudes towards the Iranian government since Khatami's victory. Generally, discussions have centred around whether or not Khatami is, in fact, a democratic reformer locked in struggle against the 'hard-liners' or if he is a just another Mullah, firmly committed to the clerics' monopoly on power. Many who were categorically opposed to the Islamic government have been warming – more so economically than politically – to aspects of the Iranian government. I have been repeatedly told that Khatami and the reformists are in opposition to the Islamic regime and that Khatami has the potential to transform Iran into a politically moderate state.

Changes in participation of Iranian cultural events in London also indicate changes in many Iranians' attitudes towards the government. For example, I have spoken to a number of Iranians at events organised by the Iranian embassy, such as the *noruz* party (which have been more frequent and elaborate since the government has established facilities for attending to the cultural affairs of Iranians abroad) who in the past would have refused to attend events sponsored by the Islamic government. There has been a large increase in the number of Iranians who travel back and forth between Iran and London.[45] It is important to add that many Iranians abroad expected faster results from Khatami and have become increasingly sceptical of his programme of reform.

The steps towards rapprochement with Iran have come under attack by many critics who accuse Western governments and many Iranians living abroad of 'selling out' to the regime and succumbing to pressures by major companies, who are eager to reap the benefits of Iran's newly opening economic markets. They have also been accused of side-stepping a number of issues, including the Berlin court's charge that Iran's leaders were involved in political assassinations on German soil in 1992; the series of brutal murders of political dissidents in 1998, including the nationalist politician Dariush Foruhar and his wife Farifteh; the arrest of Iranian intellectuals and writers who attended the Berlin conference on 'Iran After the Elections' held from 7 to 8 April 2000; the arrest of Mohammad Khordadian in June 2002, a folk dancer based in Los Angeles, who was accused of corrupting youth during a visit in Iran; and ignoring recent data collected by organisations such as the United Nations Human Rights Commission, *Iran Monitor* 1 and Amnesty

International, which document the continuation of the number of systematic violations of human rights in Iran, including the increasing number of arbitrary arrests, secret and unfair trials, torture, stoning and public executions.[46]

There have been several events that illustrate the conflicting views among Iranians abroad regarding the Iranian government. For example, the organisation of the academic conference entitled, 'Ayatollah Khomeini and the Modernisation of Islamic Thought', which was held at the School of Oriental and African Studies (SOAS) on 15 October 1999, generated a highly charged debate in Iranian newspapers, on Radio Spectrum and various Internet sites. Iranians from many different backgrounds condemned the SOAS for jointly organising the conference with the Institute of Islamic Studies, which has been criticised for being closely involved with the reactionary parts of the Iranian regime.[47] Some SOAS academics offered an invitation to Ayatollah Araki, who was known to be the London representative of Khamenei, the supreme leader, to speak at the conference. Several different groupings of Iranians protested by boycotting the event and picketing in front of the SOAS. A number of leaflets were passed out that denounced the SOAS academics for associating with the Islamic regime and for commemorating the centenary of the birth of Khomeini.

Academics, business leaders, and students attended the conference. Many said they, too, were against the repressive elements of the Iranian government, but argued that everyone should have a right to speak their opinion in an open forum. A number of members of the Institute of Islamic Studies insisted that it had no political role and regretted that the protesters would not discuss their opinions in an academic environment. Debates among Iranian networks became more heated when the SOAS announced that they had accepted £180,000 worth of donations for fellowships from the Iranian Ministry of Higher Education and the Islamic Centre of England.[48]

Despite protests against elements of the Islamic Republic and their continued violations of human rights, the re-establishment of Iran's profile from a rogue state to a regional power in the international community will inevitably continue due to its strategic and economic importance.[49] However, the inclusion of Iran in President Bush's designation of the 'axis of evil' has certainly slowed progress. The pace at which relations are mended will be largely determined by the way in which the reformists deal with the domestic struggle for power. Nevertheless, Khatami's political platform of moderation and reform, along with social factors, such as Iran's participation in 1998 World Cup and the success of Iranian filmmakers, have all contributed to a new juncture in which Iranians living outside of Iran are reassessing or reconfirming their attitudes towards the present situation in Iran.

Conclusions

Since there was no existing background information on Iranians living in London I carried out a preliminary study, which was not meant to describe and explain the Iranian experience in London in its full social complexity, but to provide a better insight into the basic social, economic and political processes in which the various networks of Iranians in London have come across in Britain. I have organised the material I gathered around three historical conjunctures, namely, the Revolution and its aftermath, Khomeini's death, and Khatami's presidency, which have played significant roles in the way in which Iranians continue to position themselves in relation to both the British and Iranian societies. I have tried to point out some of the ways Iranians have constructed their identities anew in accordance with the changing circumstances, and introduced some of the means and mediums through which they are being expressed.

The focus of following chapters narrows in order to explore the ways in which religious traditions have been used by Iranians in order to make sense of their lives outside Iran. Building on studies that have shown that religion is often compounded by changes that occur during the process of migration, I examine several Iranian religious networks in order to demonstrate how religious discourses and practices are not constant, but are reinvented, shaped and rejected in relation to the social and political processes discussed above.

Notes

1. This approach has a lot in common with Bourdieu's field analytic framework which encourages a researcher to identify the way in which individuals are mediated through the underlying conditions of struggle that shape cultural production. A social field, Bourdieu writes, 'can be described as a multi-dimensional space of positions such that each actual position can be defined in terms of a multi-dimensional system of co-ordinates whose values correspond to the values of the different pertinent variables'. P. Bourdieu and L. Wacquant (1992), pp. 2–59.
2. See D. Wright (1985).
3. The Iranian Community Centre annual report for March 1988, London.
4. The 1991 British Census was the first census to gather information on the socio-economic characteristics of the main ethnic groups in Britain. It found that just over 3 million of the 54.9 million people living in Britain wrote a description of their ethnic identity in the census. Nearly half of the ethnic minority population was made up of individuals of South Asian origin, followed by 870,700 people classified as 'Black-Caribbean'. Based on these responses the census office created 35 ethnic-group descriptions. These were then classified into groups of four: White, Black, Indian/Pakistani/Bangladeshi, and Chinese and others. They were then broken up into groups of ten: White, Black Caribbean, Black African, Black Other, Indian, Pakistani, Bangladeshi, Chinese, Other-Asian, and Other-Other. This was followed by a full listing. In the four fold classification Iranians have been placed in the Chinese and Others groupings. Once the Chinese and Others classification was broken down to Chinese, Other-Asian and Other-Other, Iranians were accounted for in the Other-Other category, along with North Africans, Arabs, Mixed Asian/White, British ethnic minority, British (no ethnic minority indicated), Other Mixed Black/White, Other Mixed Asian/White, Other Mixed-Other. As Peach points out, the heterogeneity of the Other-Other category obscures the diverse range of ethnic groups. See C. Peach (1992) and D. Owen (1992).
5. OPCS/GROS (1993) and C. Peach (1992).
6. Iranian consulate (December 1999).

7. See www.statistics.gov.uk and G. Vidler, Research Paper, House of Commons Library, 9 March 2001.
8. Ibid. The voluntary question on religion is written as follows: 'What is your religion? (This question is voluntary; Tick one box only), None; Christian (including Church of England, Catholic, Protestant and all other Christian denominations); Buddhist; Hindu; Muslim; Sikh; Jewish'. See G. Vidler (2001), p. 12.
9. See www.statistics.gov.uk
10. The Iranian Community Centre (ICC) 1985 newsletter.
11. Iranian Association newsletter, London, 1986.
12. For example, when people agreed to meet for further interviews; when I was warmly received by community centres and associations; and when I was invited to dinners and parties.
13. Research projects conducted in other countries reported similar reactions. See, for example, H. Naficy (1993); V. Nassehi-Behnam (1991); K. Hesse-Lehmann (1993).
14. Research is needed on the dating and marriage patterns of Iranians in Britain. Through my observations and discussions I learned that a number of Iranian men and women married non-Iranians during the 1980s. Many of these marriages are rumoured to have ended in divorce. *Khâste-gâree*, the formal introduction of potential marital partners for daughters and sons, arranged by parents and their family and friends, is a tradition that is practised by many Iranian networks. I have had several discussions with Iranian men who have arranged marriages with Iranian women in Iran. Many said that they want to speak Persian with their spouse and children and to maintain their Iranian culture in London. I asked about finding Iranian spouses in London, and I was given responses such as: 'it's possible, but by the time you find an Iranian woman who you are compatible with political, socially, religiously and so on, there are not many to choose from'; 'most Iranian women in London expect too much … they're high maintenance. It's hard to make them happy because they're complex, complicated. They want rich men and a glamorous lifestyle'. Many said they preferred 'simple', 'nice' and 'traditional' women from Iran.
15. See B. Blair (1991).
16. For example, Kânoon-e Iran was founded in 1982 and is registered as a non-political, non-profit making charity. It provides many services including Persian language courses, organises lectures on aspects of Iranian culture, produces Persian language textbooks and it hosts numerous Iranians festivities throughout the year. Another community centre, also referred to as *Kânoon-e Iran,* was set up in 1983 with funding from the Greater London Council and London Borough Grants Units. It is reputed to be associated with left-wing politics and is located in North London. They assist Iranians with immigration, welfare, housing and education problems. They have a women's section which specialises in classes and social and cultural events for women. They organise a number of activities, including a New Year party, seminars and summer trips. Another central community centre is *Jâmeh-eye Iranian* (the Iranian Association), which was established in 1984 and funded by various sources, such as the London Borough Grant Unit (LBGU) and the Urban programme, sponsored by the London Borough of Hammersmith and Fulham. It was originally located in West London, and in 1987 it moved to Palingswick House, King Street, London W6. I met with a representative from *Jâmeh-e ye Iranian* who said the organisation is politically independent; however, it is reputed to be affiliated with the Tudeh Party. They are involved with similar services as *Kânoon-e Iran.* The Rostam School was one of the first Persian-language Saturday schools to open in London (1981). It is privately funded and provides Persian training at many levels of comprehension, including pre-school, secondary, GCSE (General Certificate of Secondary Education), 'A'-level (Advanced level), Persian for adults and private tuition. It also organises extra-curricular activities.
17. Research is needed on the religious and ethnic Iranian subgroups, such as Armenian and Assyrian Christians, Jews, Baha'is, Kurds and Zoroastrians. I interviewed Iranians from all of these subgroups and found that I was gathering too much material for this research project.
18. Namazi goes on to say that Mohsen Nourbakhsh, the Governor of the Central Bank, was forced to resign from his post for showing an interest in a policy that would attract skilled expatriates back to Iran. S. Namazi (1998).

19. The 'full-time' members of the Mujahedin were always noted as the exception to the move away from politics and towards the evolving needs of the Iranian exile community. The Mujahedin can often be seen campaigning on the streets of London, with poster-size pictures of Mariam Rajavi, presenting scars from the torture they received from the Iranian revolutionary guards, and asking for financial support to assist the downfall of the Islamic Republic. They have established their own community centre and school in North London and they organise their own cultural and social events. One of their largest events was held at the Earls Court arena on 21 June 1996, entitled 'Women, Voice of the Oppressed'. The event was advertised to the general public as an international celebration of women's unity, with a line-up of speakers and entertainers: Nawal El Saadawi, Lord Avebury, Marzieh (a famous Iranian singer), Willhelmenia Fernandez and Mariam Rajavi. Mariam Rajavi spoke for one hour in Persian, her many followers were screaming, chanting and brought to tears by her words. The Mujahedin claimed that 25,000 tickets were sold for the event, which is an overestimation.

20. A concept coined by Bourdieu (otherwise known as 'cultural capital') to describe non-economic skills such as, educational qualifications, general cultural awareness and verbal facility. He suggests that holding such skills can become a power resource. See P. Bourdieu and L. Wacquant (1992), pp. 2–59.

21. H. Naficy in R. Kelley (1993).

22. Naficy looks at a number of prominent Iranian artists and writers, such as Sa'edi, Amirshahi and Kho'i who write about 'being neither here nor there', expressing feelings of sadness and remorse about their lives in exile. See H. Naficy, in A. Fathi, (1991) p. 130.

23. Bozorgmehr (1997), pp. 387–408.

24. The Baha'i faith emerged from messianic movements in the nineteenth century in Iran. They believe that a man named Baha'u'llah was the latest of the divine messengers (following such teachers as Krishna, Zoroaster, Moses, Jesus and Muhammad). Members of the Baha'i faith have faced discrimination in Iran for the past 100 years. The persecution of the 250,000-member community became more systematic after the Islamic Revolution in 1979, with more than 200 reported executions. The Baha'i faith is one of the fastest growing of world religions with a reported five million followers in over 200 countries. See M. Momen (1997).

25. I interviewed several people at the Baha'i National Spiritual Assembly in London. I attended the national Baha'i three-day conference in Scarborough and some Baha'i gatherings (which they call 'fireside chats'). Whereas the Iranian Baha'is I came across were primarily from educated and affluent backgrounds, the non-Iranian Baha'is were generally from middle-class backgrounds, carrying different 'information capital'. It was interesting to observe how some non-Iranian Baha'is would exalt Iranian Baha'is because they are from Iran and speak the language of the prophet.

26. The newspapers and magazines can be bought around London at various Iranian/Middle-Eastern shops grocery stores, newsagents, and book stores. The library for Iranian studies, located in Ealing, was formed in 1991 as an independent association. It holds all the newspapers and a number of publications from Iran.

27. See A. Sreberney (1998).

28. There has been a number of journals and magazines that are (or were) available in London. For example, the *Mujahedin* publish a number of magazines and pamphlets under various names, such as *Women's Voice*, and pamphlets for the Women's Human Rights International Association; a political journal, *Ruzegâr-e No*, academic journals such as *Iranian Studies* and satirical magazines.

29. There has been a much greater interest in Iranian political news since the many changes in Iranian politics marked by Khatami's presidency.

30. For a full listing see www.irannet.com. Research is needed to explore the political and cultural significance of Iranian radio and television.

31. H. Nazeri (1996) and H. Naficy (1998).

32. The Internet has also provided Iranians with a measure of power and authority. For instance, a radio presenter in California made some discriminatory remarks about Iranians on her radio show. These remarks were taped by an Iranian listener who subsequently broadcasted the derogatory comments to the many Iranian channels and links on the Internet. I was, for example, able to download the radio show and listen to the discrimatory remarks, via my computer in London. An Iranian lawyer in America then drafted a petition and demanded an apology for the Iranian-American communities, and asked that some disciplinary action be taken against the radio announcer. The manager of the radio station proceeded to post an apology on the Internet and noted that he fired the announcer.

33. To name a few examples: Omid Jalili has become a well-known British comedian whose routine draws from his experiences living in Britain as an Iranian; his show about living as an Iranian in the post-September 11 was warmly received by critics; Shappi and Peyvand Khorsandi (the children of Hadi Khorsandi who is a famous Iranian writer and comic who founded the journal *Asqar Âqâ*) are also comedians in London; Parisa Taghizadeh and Marjan Safinia made a TV documentary about Iranians in London called 'But You Speak Such Good English'; Taghi Amirani and Amir Amirani are well-known film and documentary makers; Mimi Khalvati is a respected poet whose books include *The Chine* (2001), *In White Ink, Mirrorwork* and *Entries on Light*; her *Selected Poems* was published by Carcanet in 2000.

34. O. Roy (1998), pp. 38–41.

35. The internal clashes of power reached boiling point in July 1999 when a group of students at the University of Tehran demonstrated in front of the university campus, against the closure of the pro-Khatami daily newspaper *Salâm*, and Parliament's proposed amendment to the Press Law, which would further restrict the freedom of speech. The peaceful protests were violently broken up by law enforcement forces/vigilantes. Students have been arrested and tried in secret trials, while no action has been taken against the vigilantes.

36. O. Roy (1998), pp. 40–41.

37. Quotes taken from U.N. HQ, New York, 21 September, and transcript of Interview with Iranian President Mohammad Khatami, CNN interactive, 7 January 1998.

38. See *Economist*, 'Come home, almost all is forgiven' 2 May 1992.

39. S. Namazi (1998), p. 16.

40. A translated letter written by Darbandi in May 1999 in response to Namazi's 1998 article in the *CIRA Bulletin*.

41. Interview with Vendrine on Radio France Inter, 24 August 1998.

42. The bounty on Salman Rushdie's head still stands informally and was recently increased to£1.8 million ($ 2.8m). Rupert Cornwell, 'Britain names Ambassador to Tehran', *Independent* (London) 5 May 1999.

43. J. Muir, 'Straw Heads For Iran Talks', 9 October 2002, BBC News.

44. Ibid. and 'Tehran-London ties on brink of collapse', 11 February 2002, the Dawn Group of newspapers.

45. I have observed this among the Iranians involved in my research project. A woman who works in the Iranian consulate also said that the number of Iranians travelling back for the first time since the revolution has greatly increased since the policies have changed. She said that exact numbers are not available.

46. See *Iran Monitor* 1, 18 June 2002, and K. Nejat (1999).

47. The Institute of Islamic Studies was established in Maida Vale by Iranian clerics in 1997 in order to improve awareness of Islam in Britain.

48. J. Grimston (1999).

49. O. Roy (1998), p. 41.

3

Sofreh: a Shia Muslim Religious Ritual for Iranian Women

I first heard about *sofreh* gatherings being held outside Iran from a university student who was relieved to hear that a good family friend, living in Germany, organised a women's religious gathering in order to put forth a special wish for him to pass his university exams. This prompted me to ask Iranians to describe their religious practices in more detail, and subsequently I learned about a number of religious gatherings, such as *sofreh* and *jaleseh* gatherings for women, mixed-sex private religious gatherings, Sufi Orders and various religious charity organisations. This chapter concentrates on *sofreh* gatherings: the central aim is to unfold the continuities and changing forms and practices of a Shia Muslim religious tradition in London.

It is very important to emphasise that Iranians who are from Muslim backgrounds, and living in London, hold a wide range of orientations and views towards religion. For example, the majority of Iranians I spoke to considered themselves to be 'culturally' Muslim. It was often stressed how threads of Islamic traditions are unconsciously woven into their daily practices and vocabularies, and provide the framework for ceremonies such as weddings and funerals. Many expressed a discomfort with organised religions and believed that religion should be a private matter. I was frequently told that the essence of Islam is beautiful and tolerant, but it has been manipulated and tainted by the Islamic regime in Iran and by other political extremists. It was often made clear to me that Iranians are Shia Muslims and should, therefore, not be regarded in the same light as, or compared to, Sunni groupings in London, such as Pakistanis. The outlooks and sentiments towards religion were certainly diverse.

Early Shiism

There are two main branches of Islam: Sunni – the majority faith – and Shiism. These two branches share fundamental beliefs, such as the centrality of the prophet in the religion and the five basic ritual obligations.[1] The two branches are divided over the succession of the leadership in the Muslim community after the death of the Prophet Muhammad in A.D. 632. The origins of Shiism lie in those who believed that the Prophet Muhammad's cousin and son-in-law, Ali (d. 661) should have succeeded the Prophet to the Imamate (leader of a community) and that the succession should then be reserved for the direct descendants of Muhammad, through his daughter Fatima and her husband Ali. This direct line of true Imams, stemming from Ali and Fatima, are considered to be pure and without sin. Opponents of Ali, however, obstructed him from taking power and placed the Prophet Muhammad's companions, Abu Bakr, followed by Omar, then Uthman, as the caliphs. Ali did attain the Caliphate for five years until he was murdered in A.D. 661. Thereafter the Caliphate passed to Muawiya, who was a member of the Ummayyad clan, who was known for his late conversion to Islam, and hostility toward Muhammad in his early days in Mecca.[2]

Following the assassination of Ali, people joined together in opposition to the Caliphate by the Ummayyads. They aimed at achieving their leader's political goals under the banner of Shiism. This period is marked by an event at Karbalâ which has subsequently played important and various roles in Shia devotions. Supporters of Ali urged his son, Hussein, to lead a revolt against Yezid, who is reputed to have been a tyrant and a pleasure-seeking wine drinker. Imam Hussein left for Kufa to lead a rebellion against the Ummayyad caliphate with a small group of followers, including his wives, children and friends. At Karbalâ, near the River Euphrates, his entourage was intercepted and surrounded by the forces loyal to Yezid. From the second to the tenth day of the month of *Muharram*, Imam Hussein and his followers endured the attacks by Yezid's army. On *Âshura*, the tenth day of *Muharram*, Hussein was killed.[3]

Hussein's martyrdom is central to many Iranian legends and rituals such as: *ta'ziyeh* [passion plays]; *hey'at mahalleh* [neighbourhood associations]; *dast-e azâdari* [ritual funeral processions]; and *sofrehs*, the Shia women's ritual.[4] Shia Muslims also commemorate the martyrdom of other holy personages, like the twelve Imams. Although such manifestations of popular religion, which are often centred on saintly lineage, magic and ceremony have been an important devotional practice in Shia Islam, they have often been ignored or dismissed as unimportant and lacking theoretical interest. They have, for example, been labelled by secular nationalist projects and Islamic political movements as 'pre-modern', 'backward' and/or 'heterodox'.[5]

Popular or folk religion is often discussed as being distinct from the orthodox and urban religion of the Ulema. This distinction has often been depicted by theorists in terms of Weber's concept of 'elective affinity'[6] and has been considered as unchanging historical categories of conflicting traditions – orthodox beliefs connected to scriptural and puritanical practices, on the one hand, and popular beliefs and rituals connected with the lives of Islamic figures, attendance at tombs and shrines, Sufism, prayer gatherings, evil eye beliefs and vows, on the other hand. Islamic belief and ritual have been used as researchable entities in order to analyse the historical and contemporary essence of 'Muslim society'.[7] Other research, however, has challenged this framework of analysis and has shown evidence that the boundary between popular religiosity and orthodoxy has not always been tightly drawn and it is, therefore, problematic to assume that each category has fixed meanings and sociological constants.[8] Another of my objectives is to demonstrate that adherence to 'orthodox' forms of Islam can not always be clearly distinguishable from 'popular' forms, therefore making it necessary to examine a wide range of activities in order to recognise the complexities and social significance of Muslim practices.

There has been a tendency to attach fixed meanings or roles to religious symbols or ritual events, often claiming that the essence of Shiism provides a clear social, political and moral code for the actions undertaken by its adherents. For example, there is a popular explanation that Shia Islam doctrine is inherently revolutionary, stemming from the belief of Imam Hussein, his revolt against the oppression of Yazid and his death at Karbalâ.[9] This line of thinking, which sees a religious essence embedded in Iranian culture, has been used to explain the dynamics of the Iranian revolution and why it happened only in Iran and not other countries faced with similar discontents.[10] Similar types of argument have been made by writers such as Del Vecchio-Good and Good, who maintain that the traditions that revolve around the events of Karbalâ organise a prototypical view of the *qam-o-qosseh* [sadness and grief] entrenched in Iranian culture.[11]

Several studies have challenged such interpretations by demonstrating the various ways in which the events at Karbalâ have been reworked to suit the task at hand. Hegland, for example, points out how the role of Hussein is sometimes an intercessor for individual believers, while at others is politicised as revolting against injustices.[12] According to Zubaida: 'Shias throughout the world have been celebrating these rituals of mourning over the centuries without realising any necessary political implications, except on the occasions in which political interpretations are explicitly constructed in relation to contemporary struggles.'[13] I would like to build on such work that argues that cultural or religious practices cannot be explained in general and all-encompassing paradigms that are embodied and reinforced in ritual. I argue against such theories that attach fixed beliefs and meanings to religious doctrines and practices. The following examination of Iranian women's religious gatherings considers how familiar links to the past are reworked and serve as spaces of convergence, in which some Iranians made sense of their predicament in the early stages of the process of migration. I hope to show how these different religious traditions can be seen as possible springboards to orientate pathways of participation into wider public spheres.

Sofreh Gatherings in Iran

Sofreh, which can literally be defined as a 'table cloth', becomes a part of a
Shia Muslim women's ritual when it is spread with food offerings to holy
figures and fairies [*pari*] who are invoked through prayers and stories, and
asked to help with tasks, problems and crises.[14] It has been customary in Iran
for the devout to gather in (usually) gender-specific groups for religious
instruction and practices. Whereas Iranian men's ritual events are usually
held at mosques or local shrines, women's ritual events are usually held privately, in the women's homes, or in front of mosques in order to give food to
the poor.

Zoroastrians and Sofrehs

According to Fischer, Jamzadeh and Mills, the ritualised form of *sofrehs*
derives from the Zoroastrian religion, which was Iran's state religion before
the Muslim conquest in A.D. 642.[15] Zoroastrians' faith, based on the teachings
of the ancient prophet of Iran, Zarathustra, posits the doctrine of individual
moral choice in a world where there is an ongoing struggle played out
between the Good Creation of Ahura Mazda and the Evil Creation of Ahriman.[16] In order to bring about the eventual downfall of the Evil Creation of
Ahriman individuals and the community are expected to advance the cause
of good by adhering to doctrines such as Good Thoughts, Good Works and
Good Deeds. They are also expected to participate in a number of ritualised
calendar events in order to preserve a healthy physical and mental state.
These events include festivals such as the bi-monthly *Goehambar* feasts of
thanksgiving, the feast of All Souls [*hamaspathmaidyem*], New Year or *noruz*
celebrations, pilgrimages to shrines with animal sacrifices and personal rites
such as initiation, marriage and death memorials.[17]

Jamzadeh and Mills believe the importance placed on the ritual *sofreh* is
directly related to Zoroastrian doctrine which stresses worldly well-being and
the preservation of the community's health. The cosmological doctrine
emphasises the joyful tone of Zoroastrian religious feasts. Most Zoroastrian
ritual occasions require the formal display of the *sofreh* cloth, upon which food
and certain other religiously significant objects are laid. After the blessing and
consecration of the food by group prayer and liturgical recitation led by a
priest, the whole congregation enjoys eating the food together. It is important
that the food is not wasted or burned. Shares of the consecrated food of the
goehambar feasts are sent to the homes of all those who were not able to attend
the ceremony, which reinforces the pancommunal nature of the feast.[18]

The celebration of Zoroastrian *sofrehs* are a part of the Zoroastrian calendrical cycle and the manner in which they are celebrated is based on the
themes of the unity of the Good Creation.[19] There are seven basic categories
of Ahura Mazda's Good Creation. Jamzadeh and Mills discuss how the religiously significant objects, placed upon the *sofreh* to be consecrated, represent
the basic seven categories of Ahura Mazda's Good Creation:

The particular objects placed on the *sofreh* have specific symbolic values, though the selection of items varies in local practice ... For Iranian Zoroastrians, essential items for the *sofreh* include a mirror, a small fire for incense (especially for burning the seeds of wild rue, whose Persian name, *esfand*, also means holy), fresh warm bread, fresh water, greens and fruits and nuts called *lork*. If the ceremony is a death memorial, a portrait of the deceased is present; on a non-funerary *sofreh*, a portrait of Zoroaster may appear. *Sofrehs* relating to initiation and wedding ceremonies have additional, special, constituents. For instance a pair of scissors displayed is said to ward off evil, sugar moulded in the shape of a cone stands for the sweetness of life, a green scarf symbolises good fortune and stability, and a needle and green thread are emblems of the mending and solving of problems. Thyme leaves mixed with rice are placed on the wedding *sofreh* for the priest to scatter over the couple for blessing. The colour green, reiterated in this array, has retained a general connotation of auspiciousness in arid Iran, as in the expression *sabzibaxti*, 'green' or good fortune.[20]

All community members are required to attend the *sofrehs* and it is obligatory, for those who can afford it, to host a feast. Although Zoroastrian *sofrehs* are a communal religious duty, they often take place in private homes. Jamzadeh observed that sexual segregation is not pronounced in Zoroastrian *sofrehs*: both men and women who host the feast share in the preparations. According to Jamzadeh and Mills the symbolic *goehambar* feast, celebrated by both males and females, plays a strong role in the Zoroastrian ideology of unification.[21] They go on to say that although Zoroastrian women do occasionally resort to votive *sofrehs* in situations of personal need, Zoroastrian *sofrehs* are predominantly non-votive and pancommunal. Jamzadeh writes: '*Sofrehs* in orthodox Zoroastrian contexts developed neither the themes of female exclusiveness nor the emphasis on votive and patron-dependent relationships that characterised the ritual among Muslims' but instead 'a *sofreh* expresses the unconditional membership of all believers in a unified, good cosmic order'.[22]

Michael Fischer's observations of Zoroastrian *sofrehs* differs on this point. He stresses Zoroastrian women's involvement with votive procedures and claims they are in many instances virtually identical to Muslim *sofreh* ritual procedures and texts.[23] Whereas Jamzadeh and Mills emphasise the link between the Zoroastrian cycle of communal *goehambar* feasts and *sofreh* gatherings, Fischer links a different aspect of Zoroastrian religious practice to the *sofreh* ritual. He focuses on the women's monthly pilgrimage cycle, instituted in order for women to visit various shrines and prepare a kind of *sofreh*. The following extract is from the procedure at *Pir-Vameru*, a shrine visited on the second day of the monthly pilgrimage cycle. It is worthwhile quoting it at length in order to show some of the parallels between the Zoroastrian and Muslim practices.

The shrine room contains five oil lamps. Four of which are set on white bricks at the four corners of the *sofreh*. On the *sofreh* are donations of roasted chickpeas, sugar ball sweets, dried fruits and nuts, fresh fruit, sugar cones, myrtle, cypress twigs, and an incense holder. On the walls are hung dolls of men and women, called *bibi kuk*, which are placed there by childless women in hopes of conceiving. Tea and oil bread are made by people who have vowed to do some act of charity, and stew is cooked for lunch. As at any shrine the form of worship is individual prayer, reciting favourite sections of the *Avesta* such as the Bahram Yasht, the appropriate *Yasht* for the day, and so on. But in mid-morning everyone attempts to squeeze into the room to listen to the recitation of the story done by an old lady. The fresh fruit on the *sofreh* is quartered, one piece placed in each corner. The reciter then tells the story in flat sombre tones while gazing into a mirror. A second woman beats a slow rhythm with a spoon on a bowl of water and punctuates the recitations with soft *balehs* ('yes ... yes'). When the recitation is finished, the mirror is passed around and people line their eyes with the ash of pistachio or walnut which is supposed to give energy and general health. The bowl of water is passed around and the water is poured into one's hand. Sweets are passed around. People then break up into more informal groups outside the room. Some clean roasted chick-peas; others serve stew; others just chat, read palms, and relax.[24]

Fischer argues that Zoroastrian and Muslim community rituals were variations of a pattern and the votive procedures were an important element of Zoroastrian women's religious lives. It has been argued by the Zoroastrian religious establishment that the votive *sofreh* is not a proper expression of Zoroastrian piety and is a borrowing from folk Islam.[25] According to Fischer, Boyce's work acknowledges, but de-emphasises the mutual borrowings between Muslims and Zoroastrians (that local shrines have Muslim names, and *sofrehs* are similar among Muslims and Zoroastrians). Boyce does not, however, acknowledge that the Muslim and Zoroastrian legends are transformations of one another.[26]

Iranian Shia women were often surprised when I asked about the similarities between the Muslim and Zoroastrian religious practices. Many stressed how *sofrehs* are firmly rooted in Islam. It is worth noting a conversation I had with a Mullah at the Holland Park mosque about votive *sofrehs*. He was not familiar with the similarities between the ritual form of Zoroastrian *sofrehs* and the Muslim *sofrehs*. He went on to say that directing wishes towards a holy figure is a legitimate shortcut for asking Allah for help, but the symbolic inferences and rituals that women attach to *sofrehs* are more traditional than religious.

Although the boundaries between such confessional religious gatherings are seen as distinct, the purpose of this brief section on the Zoroastrian tradition of *sofreh* demonstrates how practices can transcend religious boundaries in shared cultural domains. Let us now turn to the accounts of Iranian Muslim *sofrehs* in twentieth-century Iran and see the way they have been shaped and reshaped by the development of political discourses and various historical conjunctures, and have been used by women both as spaces to construct and channels to express religious, socio-economic and political identities.

Sofrehs *and Historical Conjunctures*

In Iran during the nineteenth century a number of religious and political reform movements emerged in response to the weakness and corruption of the Qajar state (1794–1924). The culmination of these movements led to the Constitutional Revolution of 1906, which was marked by an unusual and diverse alliance between the merchants of the traditional urban bazaars, the secular intellectuals and the Shia clergy. Collectively they called for a constitution and the protection of Iran's national interest. It has been argued that the Constitutional Revolution created a link between national progress and women's progress, which diversified the positions held by women and led to the development of a women's movement in Iran. Paidar points out two consequences of the affinity between national independence and women's progress:

> First, it has made it impossible to talk about the interaction between feminism and Islam without taking into account the interaction between Islam and nationalism. Second, this has been one of the main reasons why individualistic types of feminism based on women's personal experience and individual choice, a stance commonly associated with feminism in the West, have not developed in Iran.[27]

A similar observation was made by Kandiyoti, who noted that the connection between nationalism and feminism in the Middle East has discouraged a systematic investigation of the daily lives of women and the production of gender hierarchies in relation to religious discourses and institutions.[28] According to Afkhami, the politics of women's liberation during and shortly after the Constitutional Revolution was in many ways shaped by the politics of secularisation.[29] Najmabadi makes an important point that too much emphasis has been placed, during this period, on unequivocal linkages between Iranian feminism and Western notions of modernism, secularisation and feminism. In addition to references being made to the progress of women in non-Western countries such as China, Japan and the Ottoman Empire, writings from this period indicate that a range of modernist and Islamic positions coexisted.[30]

Although there have been an increasing number of studies that are filling in some of the blind spots on women and society in Iran, from the late Qajar period to the present, relatively little has been written on Iranian Shia women's religious rituals and observances.[31] The accounts that do exist indicate that women's religious gatherings have undergone a number of changes in conjunction with broader social and political transformations. According to Bamdad, in the Constitutional Revolution the few women who emerged on the political stage turned their traditional religious and social gatherings into political meetings, where they would discuss, organise and circulate the latest political news.[32] Other studies write that in the past (and presently in Iran) *sofrehs* have been used as vehicle to create a 'women's domain' that allows for the development and expression of women's relations with other women.

The modernisation policies implemented by the Pahlavi government took much of the accustomed power and authority away from the ulema, and secular forces dominated the political stage. The Pahlavi state continued the secular nature of the early twentieth-century path (albeit in their own style) to 'modernise' the image of women and their position in Iranian society. According to Paidar, the Pahlavi state's stance on women's social position was influenced by different and often contradictory impulses: 'On the one hand, urban centres were exposed to the conception of women as sex objects through the mass media. On the other hand, state policy on the family attempted to regulate female sexuality in accordance with the Islamic *shariat* [Law]. Thirdly, in responding to the pressures of national development, the state formulated policies which contained emancipatory potentials for women'.[33] The few accounts written about *sofreh* gatherings illustrate the ways in which these different tendencies have been both embraced and rejected by various *sofreh* networks during the Pahlavi era.

For those adopting an Iranian women's emancipatory discourse, the *sofreh* ritual was associated with backwardness and traditionalism, and possibly undermining or invalidating a more 'modern' secular identity. For others, *sofrehs* continued to provide women, from a range of socio-economic and religious backgrounds, with the opportunities for social interaction and for achievement of status. Good states that, 'religious gatherings given by women of the new or old elite status groups were similarly eclectic affairs, with some women from the bazaar and bureaucratic classes present, as well as an occasional old women from the working class. The *sofrehs* of Tehran's upper classes were gatherings for the elite and excluded those who did not belong to the appropriate class'.[34] Betteridge, who wrote about women-only gatherings in Shiraz during the 1970s, stated, 'especially for those who come from more traditional families, religion offers a much needed opportunity to assemble. It is also one of the few occasions in which a sizeable amount of money can be properly spent on a women's gathering. Once a vow has been made and answered, a woman is bound to fulfil it; her family will support her in completing the obligation.'[35] Janet Bauer's study of migrant women living in poor neighbourhoods in south Tehran in the 1970s, discusses the way in which *sofreh* gatherings were also channels used by prayer leaders to denounce the un-Islamic behaviour and appearance of the women portrayed in the media and the rich women of north Tehran, and to put forth codes of conduct (which would have been defined by the particular prayer leader) appropriate for a proper Islamic woman.[36]

As discussed in Chapter 1, the 1960s and 1970s saw a rise of cultural nationalism closely linked to Islam. A few of the ulema's intellectuals became politically vocal about many subjects, including women's role in society and the importance of family life. The campaign urged the rejection of Western styles and norms that destroy family values and degrade women into nothing more than silly 'sex objects'. Instead, women were advised to restore Islamic values by embracing the new Shia models of womanhood, which represented women as mothers and revolutionaries.[37] The advocates of Shia modernism denounced the *sofreh* gatherings in the Pahlavi era as superstitious and heterodox, and as excuses to overeat and gossip. Ali Shariati, who actively promoted new models of Muslim womanhood for Iranian women, criticised the way in which the upper classes were using *sofrehs* to expose their wealth. He argued that they were 'silly ladies' parties' carried out under the pretence of religion.[38]

During the establishment of the Islamic Republic, the official women's movement, which was secular until the rise of Shia modernism in the 1970s, was placed within an Islamic framework. Large numbers of women, cutting across the political, religious and social spectrum, participated in the various activities surrounding the revolution.[39] Some of the women's religious networks became politicised and served as a conduit for the revolutionary discourse. In addition to mourning for the martyrdoms of Shia holy figures, women discussed the latest political news and mourned for the martyrs of the anti-Shah movement. According to Friedl, the religious networks were used to spread quickly and effectively the latest political reports and oppositional literature and tapes.[40]

In post-revolutionary Iran the Islamisation of women's roles led to a number of new policies, including compulsory veiling and gender segregation of public space. Torab observed, in her study of ritual discourse in a south Tehran neighbourhood, that women's gatherings had increased since the revolution, and are used to discuss current social and political issues, as well as for prayer and devotion.[41] She pointed out how, following the revolution, some speakers would conclude the women's religious gatherings with revolutionary slogans and recitations of the *salavât* in the name of political figures.[42] *Sofrehs* in post-revolutionary times are discussed by Kamalkhani, who observed that women-only gatherings are not only places for women to express their religiosity but also political and social spaces where women connect to broader spheres of political debate.[43]

Torab makes another observation, that no two rituals are exactly the same as they vary in structure and performance. She shows, for example, the celebratory and joyous sides of Shia rituals, which are often absent in explanations that tend to associate gatherings only with sorrow and grief. She also notes that in response to the gendering and marginalisation of public space since the revolution some women have turned parts of their private properties into neighbourhood religious centres.[44] The development of neighbourhood centres allows women more autonomy to explore and practice their religion as they wish. Furthermore, Torab notes: 'This is a transformation of domestic space into professional work-space, where, through their "gossip", the women could build up or demolish reputations, including those of local merchants, doctors, clergyman and politicians alike, in a play of power.'[45]

Adelkhah makes interesting observations about the rising number of neighbourhood religious gatherings being held in Iran since the revolution.[46] She argues that religious sociability can be looked at in light of the increase in structural and bureaucratic differentiation in the religious domain.[47] The proliferation and range of women's religious gatherings can be seen as part of the fragmentation of social, religious and political forces in public and everyday life in Iran. Adelkhah writes:

> Of course the regime has sought to impose its Islamic code and its prerogatives with its well known methods. But it is far from being able to control the dynamics of a country in the midst of demographic growth, reconstruction, and a

change of identity, stimulated by trade liberalisation and changes in the regional environment. The complex relationship between state and society is largely mediated through Islam, that is, through Islamic institutions, practices, intellectuals, financial resources, etc.[48]

She discusses the ways in which different levels of religious sentiment, such as popular religious practices, the Islamic Republic's version of Islam and theological writings interact at neighbourhood gatherings, and in turn intersect with everyday concerns. Both Torab and Adelkhah demonstrate how women's religious spaces in post-revolutionary Iran are differentiated spaces (in terms of gender, wealth and religiosity) and have the capacity to reinforce, question and/or ignore the Islamic government's attempts to rigidly 'purify' and indoctrinate religious symbols and ideas.

I was invited to attend a women's-only gathering to commemorate the birthday of Zeinab [*mouludi zeinab*], the sister of Hussein, at a large home in north Tehran during the summer of 1999. A few of the one hundred or so women who attended arrived at the home wearing proper hejâb, black *chadors* and stockings, while the majority wore more trendy renditions of a version of the required dress code *mânto-rusari*, meaning headscarves and over-garments. Underneath their chadors and *mânto-rusari* many wore fashionable and quite revealing dresses. A few women continued to wear headscarves inside the home. The women, who sat along the periphery of the room, conversed among themselves until the invited woman cantor [*sokhan-rân*] started to sing lively and festive songs. It was not long until the room was filled with women dancing. The cantor would ask the women to stop dancing while she sang songs with lyrics from the Koran. After one hour the cantor said it was time to pray and asked the women to be seated and for the lights to be switched off. After the cantor told stories in Zeinab's honour the women raised their arms with their palms outfaced, and started to continuously repeat Ali's name and put forth their vows, or *nazr*. Many of the women started to cry (and a few cried uncontrollably). A 15-year-old girl who was sitting next me, crying and repeating Ali's name, turned to me and whispered 'Backstreet Boys *doost dârî?*' [Do you like the Backstreet Boys?]. When I told her that I sort-of liked the Western pop group she smiled and continued to cry and repeat Ali's name.

The prayers were followed by a passion play called *arus-e Qureysh*. The hostess chose twenty-one women (myself included) to participate in the play. We were taken to a different room and were asked to put on either a red, white or green ornate gown and veil. It was explained to me that the outfits and the other items that are needed to perform a passion play can be rented at a shop. Interestingly, many of the women I asked did not know the story behind *arus-e Qureysh*. The women dressed in red portrayed the women in the Qureysh tribe who had not accepted Islam. They went on the stage, put make-up on each other, and behaved in a silly, racy and rambunctious fashion. As the women dressed in green (myself included), who portrayed Fatima and her close circle of friends and symbolised beauty and purity, walked onto the stage, the women in red were blinded by goodness and fell to the floor. The women in green lined up in rows of three, with the woman acting as Fatima sitting in front, and performed a shortened version of *namâz*. This was followed by the women dressed in white, who symbolised the wedding of Fatima and Ali, joining the women dressed in green in dancing around in a circle as the cantor threw blessed candy to us and the audience.

Several women made an analogy between the acting out of *arus-e Qureysh* and the battle between the differing lifestyles of Western women and Muslim women. It was explained to me that the women in red are like women in the West. Many said that such plays are reminders of how Islamic women should behave, and are enacted to urge women to rise above the temptations that Western women have succumbed to. Other women present, however, made it clear to me that they did not accept this interpretation. They downplayed the religious dimension of women-only gatherings, and were concerned that I was gaining an inaccurate impression of their social lives. It's worth adding that several women who attend women-only gatherings in London (and Iran) were not familiar with the interpretation of the play described above. As a group of university-aged women were asking me about college course requirements in Britain, the U.S. and Canada, they invited me to other women-only gatherings where they claimed the preachers and participants were more modern and open. It was interesting to meet women with varying social, political and religious ideas and leanings (who were often from the same immediate or extended family) at the same gathering. This account sheds some light on how complex and differentiated religious gatherings are in Iran.

It is important to add that women's religious gatherings are often intertwined with fund raising for charities and with philanthropic activities.[49] Historically, the development and management of charitable activities among women in Iran, and presently both inside and outside of Iran, can throw light on the shifting dynamics of public and private domains.[50] The intended and unintended consequences of religious charity-based activities, which are often carried out to fulfil a religious service or duty [*khedmat*], can draw attention to local societal problems, whilst providing a 'respectable' way for women to participate actively in public domains. The collection and distribution of money to the poor and needy are also linked to *khoms*, one of the two, major, religious taxes that Shias are expected to pay to chosen religious dignitaries and their administrations.[51] Women are actively involved in deciding to whom and through which, increasingly bureaucratic, channel the religious taxes should be distributed. Secular-minded women have created 'religion-free' charities both inside and outside Iran in response to the mushrooming of women's religious gathering and activities since the revolution.

This discussion of women-only religious gatherings has attempted to demonstrate how the meanings and roles attached to them have shifted across time and according to the various socio-political conjunctures. It showed how women's gatherings in Iran have been important spaces for women to sort through, manage and contest the discourses through which the state discourses and other societal issues are produced and addressed.

Sofreh Gatherings in London

Based on my field research in 1997 and 1998 this section describes various *sofrehs* held by Iranian women in London. There are different Iranian social networks in London upon which Iranian cultural forms, such as *sofrehs*, depend. The research is focused on a large and loosely-knit network of Iranian women who follow the Shia calendar of events, and who revolve around the Shia institutions (but not always the same Shia institutions) in London. The Iranian women within this loosely-knit network vary in terms of religiosity, education and wealth, and often belong to different socio-economic, religious and political groupings. What these women have in common is their attendance at various *sofrehs* held at a female prayer leader's home in Holland Park. Many women have told me that her home is blessed with special spirits and is therefore a very beneficial place for votive *sofrehs*. Grandmothers, mothers and daughters have been present at the *sofrehs* I attended. The majority of the women, however, are middle-aged or elderly, and are the first generation of Iranians living in London following the Iranian Revolution in 1979. Unlike many displaced groups who live in close proximity to each other, these women are scattered throughout various central-London boroughs. Whilst a few women arrived at the *sofrehs* after work, the majority of the women are not employed.

A woman I'll refer to as Ms. Parvizi, is the Iranian religious leader located in Holland Park. She is known by many religious and non-religious Iranians as the 'Professional *sofreh* organiser'. One interviewee stated: 'Women do offer *sofrehs* privately in their own homes in London, but it is easier and less trouble to pay [the prayer leader] to prepare and bless the food and organise everything … her house has good spirits and it is known that wishes [*nazr*] come true there.' There are three different ways in which a votive *sofreh* is offered by Ms. Parvizi. First, a weekly *sofreh* ritual is open to Shia women every Thursday. Second, women throughout the week, in order to make new vows or return the favour of successful vows made in the past, sponsor 'invite-only' *sofrehs*. Third, *sofreh* rituals are held on special days throughout the Shia calendar of events. The type of *sofreh* offered (which range from elaborate to simple occasions) will be decided either by the prayer leader, or concur with the themes running through the Shia calendar of events, or be chosen personally by the woman who wishes to sponsor (and finance) the *sofreh*.

The essential ingredients of the *sofrehs*, such as the ritual form of the various types of *sofreh* and its primary purpose of requesting personal favours, are present in all three categories of *sofrehs* offered by Ms. Parvizi. I found that the varied choice of the women's participation in the three categories of *sofrehs* depends on the religious, social and economic importance placed on *sofrehs* by the women, which in turn is related to their broader religious and socio-economic networks. For example, different types of *sofreh* are thought to be heterodox and religiously impure, while other *sofreh* are considered to be orthodox and allowed to be held in mosques. The amount of money required to sponsor one also varies from *sofreh* to *sofreh*. The next section describes in some detail the various *sofreh* rituals in relation to the three ways in which *sofrehs* are organised by the Ms. Parvizi. This will be followed by an examination of women's broader social, economic, and religious networks.

A Thursday Evening Sofreh Gathering

From 4:30 p.m. to 8:00 p.m., every Thursday, around thirty-five to forty-five Iranian Shia women meet in Holland Park in order to take part in a votive *sofreh* ritual. I was told that the Thursday *sofreh* gatherings, which are open to all Shia women in London,[52] are promoted by the prayer leader's close friends, who spread the word at social and religious events in London, and/or by telephoning the women. Many of the women who regularly attend the Thursday *sofrehs* consist of those who describe the gatherings as being their primary way of practising their religious faith. One informant stated: 'I go to *sofrehs* every Thursday, like Christians go to church every Sunday.'

Those who regularly attend the Thursday *sofrehs* make up a social network which extends outside the *sofreh* gatherings. Others who occasionally attend the Thursday meetings are divided between women who revolve around several Shia institutions and other women-only circles in London, and those who come and go according to their personal schedules. Thursday night *sofreh* gatherings not only provide a routinised local space in which to exchange, compare and discuss information concerning religious and social affairs and the ins and outs of daily life, but are also a medium through which emerging and shifting patterns of socio-economic and political differentiation and stratification are rediscovered, symbolised and expressed. Parallels can be made with research findings on women-only gatherings in Iran. For example, Adelkhah writes the following about women's religious meetings:

> They are, very classically, an occasion for exchanging precious information relating to daily life – about housing or marriage matters, for example – and for displaying one's social distinction by one's appearance, one's financial contribution or the dishes laid out on one's tablecloth; they are even occasions for trading in consumer goods brought from one of the country's Free Zones, from Dubai or from a place of pilgrimage, or in home-made works of craftsmanship produced under the compulsion of the economic crisis.[53]

Before I describe in detail *Sofreh Abu'l-Fazl*, which is the type of *sofreh* most frequently held at the Thursday meetings, it is imperative to emphasise how it was necessary to attend dozens of gatherings. As we shall see, the content of the various gatherings were unique, as they were contingent upon many variables, including the background of the participants, the internal power struggles among the women, and the current political and social conditions locally, in the wider diaspora and in Iran.

Sofreh Abu'l-Fazl

I was invited to the prayer leader's property in Holland Park to attend a Thursday night *sofreh* in the name of Abu'l-Fazl. The invitation surfaced after asking many different Iranian women if I could attend a *sofreh*. While many said 'yes', it was difficult to get a concrete invitation. Several said that only Muslims were allowed to be present during the ritual. Many women I asked who don't attend such gatherings, were shocked that *sofreh* gatherings were taking place in London, and warned me that the Iranian government was probably financing them or using them as a way to monitor Iranians living in London. Eventually I received an invitation by asking a highly regarded religious woman.

I was informed by several women, and had read in previous research projects on *sofrehs*, of the need to dress smartly and conservatively, to wear a veil (although I didn't know what 'style' of veil) and jewellery. As I entered I took off my shoes and proceeded into a large room, where an ornate table cloth was laid out on the floor and set with around thirty place settings. The following symbolic items were placed on the *sofreh* waiting to be blessed: two large candle sticks and many small candles; *halvâ* (a dish prepared from flour, sugar, butter, and saffron);[54] and *âjil-e moshkel-goshâ* (a mixture of currants, almonds, dried peas, hazelnuts, pistachio nuts, dried mulberries and small white candy),[55] and dates.[56] Specific food is prepared at the *sofreh* Abu'l-Fazl for the special purpose in the fulfilment of a vow. The dishes remain covered until after the prayers for help are finished. The sitting room where the gatherings are held is decorated with printed calligraphic inscriptions from the Koran, pictures of Ms. Parvizi's children (graduating from university) and grandchildren, and items such as china and crystal.

As the women arrived they would greet each other as they found places to sit around the *sofreh*. Each woman is handed a Koran and served tea and dates by an elderly Azeri worker from Tabriz, referred to as *Hâji Khânoum*.[57] The women were mostly dressed in black suits and black scarves; the majority of the women took off their scarves once the ritual commenced.[58] Some women were greeted with more enthusiasm and greater respect; this was followed by *târof* (Iranian convention of etiquette), where the women would persuade the higher-status women to sit in the best seats, be served tea first, and so on. As I was clearly an outsider, I offered my seat to every Iranian woman who entered the room. I believe that such gestures were very important for the acceptance of my presence at their religious gathering and helped me to be invited to more.[59] News and gossip were exchanged until the female preacher was ready to commence the ritual.

The Female Preacher

Ms. Parvizi walked elegantly into the room with a dignified demeanour, elaborately wrapped and veiled in black lace. All the women greeted her with the utmost respect as she took her reserved seat in the corner of the room. She was in her late fifties, and a mother of three children. She had gained her high position and popularity among many Iranians due to her religious, social and economic success in London. She said that she had been attracted to religion ever since she was a child and has gained knowledge about Islam, informally, throughout her life. She became skilled in reading the Koran and became a *ra'iseh-jaleseh*, one who arranges *rozeh*s for various kinds of religious meetings, and eventually specialised in *sofrehs*. She also performs wedding ceremonies for Iranian couples in London.[60] Although many Iranian women can read the Koran, only Ms. Parvizi is trusted to make *tasfir* [interpretations]. Her interpretations of the Koran, which are usually described as religiously 'moderate', generate different reactions depending on the women's backgrounds. She is a skilful communicator and storyteller, and is also known by Iranian men and women for her campaign to teach Iranians in London to learn and recite the Koran.

I have been told by many contacts that the female prayer leader is dependant on the income earned by the religious events she organises. Kamalkhani found in her research that female preachers' stipends were calculated, 'on the basis of their religious rank, their religious knowledge and their local popularity, although the economic situation of the female host and the occasion for the *rozeh* or *jaleseh* were also taken into consideration.'[61] As a woman who single-handedly built a secure and comfortable life for herself and her three children in London, Ms. Parvizi is considered to be a woman of great strength and dignity, as well as a role model for other women. She is now financially successful. Her success is seen as a reflection of her strong faith, purity of health and piousness. She also plays a central role in distributing charitable funds and arranging package journeys to Mecca and other pilgrimage sites.

The Ritual

Before Ms. Parvizi started the religious meeting she introduced me to the women, and told them I wanted to learn about Shia religious traditions.[62] She started the service by saying into a microphone *B'esm-e'llâh-e rahmân-e rahim* [In the name of God the merciful and compassionate] and then turned to the recitation of *Sura VI: An'âm*. This particular chapter of the Koran, which is often read at such gatherings, was recited both because of its familiarity and because it mentions the many different names of Allah, which is beneficial, it is believed, when praying for help. While some women chose to follow silently, others took turns reciting the verses out loud. Ms. Parvizi constantly corrected their pronunciation of the Arabic script. The women and young girls who participated were greatly encouraged by the preacher, and I was told they gain extra religious merit for their efforts. Ms. Parvizi often stopped at intervals in order to translate the Arabic passages into Persian, and to offer *tafsir* on how the Koranic verses should be implemented in the women's daily lives. The recitation of the Koran lasted two hours and thirty minutes, throughout which many of the women earnestly followed the text, whilst others would whisper amongst themselves. Afterwards, one of the women would often start the rounds of *salavât*, which is an Arabic phrase meant to greet the Prophet and his successors. Once a woman starts saying '*Allâh-eh mase-allâh Mohammad va 'âle Mohammad*', the rest of the women would join in. The salavât is usually recited several times at each *sofreh*.

The recitation was followed by putting forth the prayers for help and the vows, by turning the lights off, lighting the candles and saying '*khodâ-yâ be haq-e Abu'l-Fazl ke bâb-ol-havâ'eg ast hâjat-e mâ râ bar âwa'r'* [Oh God, I implore you in the name of Holy Abu'l-Fazl who is the gate to all wishes fulfil my request]. I asked a woman whether or not it was appropriate to ask Allah for more than one wish to be granted. She laughed and said: 'God is so great that we can make as many wishes as we want and I believe that the wishes will all come true.' The women make personal wishes, such as: 'I wish my daughter passes her exams' or 'I wish that my son finds a nice wife'. The preacher, with great skill and aptitude, then retold the story of Abu'l-Fazl 'Abâs, who is one of the great Shia martyrs and is honoured on the eighth day of *Muharram* (days commemorating individuals of *Ahl-e Bayt*).

Abu'l-Fazl 'Abâs was the half-brother and personal attendant of the third Imam Hussein – a grandson of the Prophet. He fought in the battle at Karbalâ (A.D. 680), in order to defeat caliph Yezid, and defend Imam Hussein and the wives and children. Yezid's army blocked the way to the River Euphrates leaving Hussein's party of followers to die of thirst. Abu'l-Fazl 'Abâs, without any fear, went out to search for water for the children of Imam Hussein. As he fought his way through Yezid's army, both of his hands were cut off and he was left with no choice but to carry the water-tube with his teeth to the camp, where he died in Hussein's arms.

Some women whimpered throughout the story of Abu'l-Fazl, whilst others buried themselves in their chadors and sobbed. It is important to note that at some *sofrehs* no women cried. Generally speaking, at most of the *sofrehs* I attended, there were moments of contemplation, crying, laughing and joking. At certain intervals the women simultaneously tapped their chests lightly and stood to face Mecca. This was followed by more prayers facing Mecca. It is believed that the holy figures were present at the *sofreh*. I was told by women before attending this *sofreh* that it was at this point of the ritual when the women would try to find out whether or not their wishes have reached the ear of God [*mostajâb-e do'â*]. There are various procedures, such as looking for 'signs' on the surface of the halvâ dish, or writing on eggs names of suspected people with the evil eye, and looking for signs and seeing what name 'cracks' when pressure is randomly applied. However, these practices were not carried out at this *sofreh*, and instead the candles were blown out and the blessed food was prepared for serving.

As the food was served, the pious atmosphere of mourning and devotion turned into a more social and jovial gathering. First they ate *ash*, which can be a delicious thick porridge made with lentils, noodles, flour, dried buttermilk, kidney beans and chick peas. 'Ash' is a dish that is specifically prepared for religious *nazr*.[63] *Adas polo*, a rice dish prepared with lentils, raisins and dates and served with chicken on the bone, was then served. I was surprised to see how quickly the food was served and eaten by the women. This was followed by the halvâ, the *âjil-e moshkel-goshâ* and fruit. The women take home the uneaten food as it is bad luck to waste blessed food. As we sat around the *sofreh* and ate the food the women engaged in several different conversations. Many women, in both Persian and English, directed the following questions to me: Do you like Iranian food? Who is your Persian teacher? What government is paying for your education? Are you married? Do you live with a man? Are you currently having your period? Are you becoming a Muslim? and so on. It was clear, and of course understandable, that the women were trying to ascertain why an American woman in her twenties was interested in learning about their lives and religious gatherings. I explained to them that I was conducting research on Iranian religious practices in London and that I became interested in Iran and Islam through my studies and friends I had met from Iran since my arrival in London in 1991. The questions continued the following Thursday at a gathering in the name of *Abu'l-Hassan-e Mujt'abâ*.

Sofreh *Abu'l-Hassan-e Mujt'abâ*

The structure of the *sofreh* Abu'l-Hassan-e Mujt'abâ[64] was very similar to *sofreh Abu'l-Fazl* except that the following elements were all the colour green: table cloth, napkins, candles, plates and decorations. An extremely large platter full of cucumbers and green tangerines was also placed on the *sofreh*. Many of the women wore green dresses and scarves. Green, which is the symbolic colour of Islam, is believed to be the colour of paradise, the gown of the angels and the colour in which the prophet dressed. It is also thought that the Prophet sewed green clothes for his grandsons, Hassan and Hussein, to wear. The colour green, as discussed earlier, is also central to Zoroastrian *sofrehs* as a sign of good fortune and stability.[65] Instead of telling the story of Abu'l-Fazl, the prayer leader told the story of Hassan and his forty wives. She said that although Hassan had forty wives he still died a lonely man.

A story about Hassan and Hussein lost in the desert was also commonly told at the *sofreh* Abu'l-Hassan-e Mujt'abâ. Donaldson's research from 1938 similarly describes the story, writing that when Hassan and Hussein were small, they lost their way in the desert and the Prophet found them being protected by an angel in the form of a snake. Although the manner in which the long history of women-only rituals in Iran are experienced by the participants must be examined in light of motivating forces of the participants, the following illustrates the historical continuity of the themes and the linkages between the stories of holy figures and gendered practices involving food and vows. Donaldson writes:

> Fatima vowed that if they were found uninjured, she would cook a potfull of gruel, made of rice milk, grease, sugar and cardamom seed, and that she would give it to any who would come. This she did on the desert by the roadside, so it has become a custom for women who have deep earnest desires to do this just as Fatima had done, though now they do it at home in a dark room. No man, nor boy, nor pregnant woman (for her unborn child may be a boy) should look upon it or they would become blind, and no person who was not ceremonially clean should look at it, or its power would be taken from it. Those who eat of it, however, will get whatever desire they may express, but at the time of fulfilment of their wish they must pay a money reward to their hostess.[66]

A woman makes vows at *sofreh* held in the name of Abu'l-Hassan-e Mujt'abâ, just as she would at a *sofreh* Abu'l-Fazl. If a woman's particular request is granted, she will sponsor a private *sofreh*, send money to an appropriate shrine in Iran or offer some money to those in social and economic need. I asked my informants how much money they vowed to send away if their wish was granted. One woman responded, 'If one does not have much money then £150.00 is appropriate ... I usually send around £450.00'. If a woman decides to sponsor a *sofreh* in return for the granted vow, the type of *sofreh* chosen (which ranges from simple to elaborate) will concur with the amount of money the woman is willing to spend. There are also a number of 'private' *sofrehs* scheduled at the prayer leader's house throughout the week; these require an invitation from the woman who sponsors the gathering.

'Invite-only' Sofrehs

Private *sofrehs* are held at the prayer leaders' house and are sponsored by an individual Iranian woman in order to put forth her personal wishes or to fulfil a specific vow in which the request was granted. Whereas Thursday votive *sofreh* gatherings are in theory open to all (Iranian) Shia women and are held weekly, the invite-only *sofreh* gatherings are competitive and strengthen personal networks. The Holland Park *sofreh* circuit is known by Iranian religious (and many non-religious) women in London as 'the place' to hold a *sofreh*. I have been told that is socially acceptable to pay for the *sofreh* services provided by the prayer leader in order to fulfil the Iranian woman's duty to entertain and be hospitable, which is a central and highly valued component of Iranian culture. It is ideal for women whose homes are too small to host a *sofreh*. Many women said they were accustomed to spacious homes in Iran and they simply did not have the capacity to entertain guests in the small rooms and kitchens found in London's expensive homes. Others admitted that they did not want to 'lose face' by showing other Iranians their lowered living standards. Other said that they preferred Ms. Parvizi's service because they did not wish to 'show off' their homes and be envied and in danger of the evil eye.

Women, who practise and think about their faith in many different ways, and are from varied socio-economic backgrounds, pay the prayer leader to perform the *sofreh* ritual for the individual and her invited guests. The fact that Iranians do not live in one area of London could be another practical explanation for the emergence of Ms. Parvizi's *sofreh* service. This makes it impossible for women to go on foot to a religious gathering, as is customary in Iran. The price charged by the prayer leader will depend on the type of *sofreh* the sponsor chooses. The women receiving invitations to a particular type of *sofreh* will therefore have an idea of the expenses involved. Invite-only *sofrehs* are also sometimes sponsored by Iranian women who regularly attend the Thursday night *sofrehs*. I was told that Saturday and Sundays are reserved for the wealthiest Iranian women to offer their elaborate *sofrehs*.

I was invited to a *sofreh* sponsored by a wealthy woman whom I will call Monir. She is in her early forties and occasionally attends the Thursday night *sofreh* gatherings.[68] It was held on a Saturday night at Ms. Parvizi's house. Although the type of *sofreh* chosen by Monir was *sofreh* Abu'l-Fazl, it differed in several respects. For instance, the tablecloth was beautifully and elaborately decorated with over sixty candles (each candle resting beautifully on little green leaves), large bouquets of flowers, the essential foods (*halvâ, âjil-e moshkel-goshâ, khormâ*) were placed in crystal bowls. The Sura VI: An'âm was recited; however, the prayer leader did not spend much time on the *tafsir*. Instead, more time was spent on lighting the numerous candles, requesting personal wishes, listening to the martyrdom story of Abu'l-Fazl, and eating the blessed food.

Although some of the women present at the invite-only *sofreh* were women who attend the Thursday *sofreh* gathering, most were the hostess's personal friends. This social network of women were extremely well dressed in designer suits and were educated and successful. These women do not wear hejâb or head scarves in public.

Another invite-only *sofreh* I attended was quite different from the elaborate ritual described above. Whereas Monir's *sofreh* placed an emphasis on the social aspects of the ritual, this *sofreh* stressed religious devotion and mourning. Once again *sofreh* Abu'l-Fazl was the type chosen by the sponsor. Although the distinct ritual form and terminology of the Abu'l-Fazl ritual remained constant, the practice and discourse which were prescribed to the religious symbols and ritual by this social network of women differed. This *sofreh* was held at the prayer leader's home on a Sunday at 3:00 p.m. and organised by a devout Shia woman. Some women were dressed in black suits with black veils while many others wore chadors. Despite the complete absence of males, many of the women (including myself) were covered throughout the entire *sofreh*. Women wearing chadors sat in the seats closest to the prayer leader, which are saved for the most pious women. The table was simply set with the required food items and a few candles. This network of women could pronounce and recite the words of the Sura IV: An'âm with ease and more time was spent on the prayer leader's interpretation of the Sura.

Sofreh *Hazrat-e Roqiye*

I was told that the repast of the daughter of Imam Hussein is usually offered at noon, in front of a mosque or a place of sanctity and pilgrimage. I have come across *sofreh* Hazrat-e Roqiye (and other types of *sofrehs*) at the homes of women who want to say a prayer for help and make a vow in the presence of their close friends, but do not want to organise an elaborate event. The woman who sponsors the *sofreh* offers bread and dates. I was told that a special type of bread, called *sangak*, is traditionally served at these gatherings.

Calendar sofrehs

The calendar *sofrehs* are based on the formal Shia calendar, which is lunar [*qamari*]. It consists of different legends that coincide with special days on the calendar, starting with the first of *Muharram* with the Prophet's migration from Mecca to Medina in A.D. 622. It is thought that personal wishes have a much better chance of coming true when requested on the holy days. The calendar *sofrehs* are, therefore, very crowded, with a broad assortment of women from various socio-religious networks determined to request their personal wishes. A few *sofrehs* that I attended which were associated with the formal Islamic calendar are described below.

Sofreh *Commemorating Fatima's Death*

I attended two of the three *sofrehs* organised during the calendar year to commemorate the death of the daughter of Muhammad and the wife of Ali. They were held, once again, in Holland Park. The *sofreh* was set with the same symbolic foods and items as described at the *sofreh* Abu'l-Fazl, with two exceptions. Firstly, a sweet called *shole zard* (rice, sugar and saffron) was specifically prepared in memory of Fatima.[69] Secondly, the food was catered and not home-made.[70] There was the same scrambling to find seats appropriate to the various women's status. At the arrival of one Iranian woman many women stood and excitedly greeted her. The women sitting next to me whispered: 'She is very rich.'[71] She was also the woman who sponsored the elaborately-catered *sofreh* in the name of Fatima. The ritual that followed was identical to the *sofreh* discussed above except that instead of telling the story of Abu'l-Fazl, the well-known story of Mohammad's *'abâ* [cloak] was told, which goes as follows. One day Muhammad told Fatima that he wasn't well so he was going to lie down under his cloak. Shortly afterwards, Hassan and Hussein joined their grandfather under the cloak. When Ali returned home he told Fatima that he could smell the fragrance of the Prophet and both Ali and Fatima joined their family under the cloak. The story continues with God allowing Gabriel to go to earth and join the five under the cloak. Gabriel told the five that God had chosen them and wanted them to be cleansed from all their sins. Mohammad then took an oath that special blessings would come to Shiites who gather and retell the story of 'the five bodies of the family of the *'abâ*. The prayer leader's storytelling skills, once again, captured the entire congregation's attention and stirred the women's emotions.

Moulude: Sofreh *Commemorating Fatima's Birthday*

A votive *sofreh* commemorating Fatima's birthday was held on a Thursday from 3:00 p.m. to 7:30 p.m. at the home of the prayer leader. The room was brightly decorated with flashing coloured lights. Instead of the regular essential food items (*halvâ, âjil-e moshkel-goshâ,* and *khormâ*), the tablecloth consisted of several types of Iranian pastries, cakes and candies, bright coloured candles and flowers. The women were dressed in festive and colourful clothes, including the prayer leader who wore a long, brightly coloured, sequined gown. There were more women than usual present (probably around fifty) and a wider range of ages, including more children. I recognised women from both 'invite-only' *sofrehs* and the Thursday night *sofreh* (and there were many new faces). After the Koran was recited, the candles were lit and the women made their personal requests to themselves. The prayer leader, who normally at this point retells a martyrdom story and brings the women to tears, had all of the women sing joyful and familiar songs about Fatima. She was able to keep the momentum going throughout the night. Each song was followed by candy being thrown around the room and ululating. A couple of women started to dance around the room; while several of the women clapped louder, others looked at the two women disapprovingly. Torab found in her research that,

> any form of song that departed from the *moulude* frame was unacceptable to some of the more pious or *maktabi* jaleseh women who were ever so careful to curb individual free expression. They considered singing and dancing religiously forbidden *harâm*, especially in gatherings that invoked God's name, and permitted only in a husband's presence. A compromise was usually reached, but not without some friction.[72]

During the sing-along one of the prayer leader's assistants went around the room holding an opened Koran on which women placed money.[73] After eating the Iranian sweets, a large meal was served (*adas polo bâ morgh, sabzi, panir, nân,*) and a large selection of fruits (including *khormâlu*). After dinner the women recited Sura LXVIII: *Qalam.*

Sofreh *Commemorating Ali's Birthday*
The birthday of Ali, the Prophet Muhammad's cousin and son-in-law, was celebrated with two *sofrehs* at Ms. Parvizi's property in Holland Park.[74] Both *sofrehs* were organised in the same way as Fatima's birthday *sofrehs* (above), apart from the stories which focused on Ali's mother and childhood instead of Fatima's. Many women, as at the other *sofrehs*, sat in another room throughout the *sofreh* ritual. These women claim to be menstruating and therefore can not attend the *sofreh.* (It became evident that menstruating is sometimes a convenient excuse for those who do not wish to sit through the Koran readings.) In order to learn more about the women and their lives outside the *sofrehs*, I sat and talked to them instead of sitting through the ritual. There were approximately forty-five women present at each celebration.

Although it was meant to be a celebration, the women's moods were sombre after Ms. Parvizi informed them of an accident that involved an Iranian couple in London. An Iranian man had had a heart attack and went to the hospital. His wife rushed to the hospital and had a terrible car accident on the way there. The husband died and the wife was in a critical condition. The women tried to find reasons why this terrible incident happened to such good people. They also spoke about how difficult it was for them to organise memorials and funerals in London. Several expressed their wish to be buried in Iran.

While we were eating, a woman in her early forties, named Malous, asked me about my research project. I told her that there are many misconceptions and stereotypes about Iranians and Shiism, and my research, in describing the lives of some Iranian networks in London, set out to demonstrate the diversity of Iranians' religious lives. She became very excited and said:

Yes, the West thinks we are all fundamentalists and radical. You can see how we practise our faith ... it is peaceful and civilised. The Catholics are the radical and dangerous ones. They force their children to attend Catholic schools because all Catholic schools are free. The children are never able to think for themselves. The Vatican won't even let in non-Catholics and girls who wear short skirts.

I told her about my Catholic upbringing and the ways it varied from her account. I said, for instance, that the Catholic schools I went to were quite strict but unfortunately not free. Malous's observations of Catholicism were unusual. I was often told by pious Iranians that they prefer Catholics to other types of Christians because they don't change their doctrines and principles to suit modern times. After the *sofreh* commemorating Ali's birthday a group of us walked to the Holland Park *Majma'* for another birthday celebration for Ali.

There are several other types of *sofrehs* held for holy figures, such as Sakineh, daughter of Hussein; Zeinab, Hussein's sister; and Umm Kolsum, the sister of Hussein. The following will introduce the *sofrehs* that were described to me.

Sofreh *Bibi-seshanbe*

Bibi has several meanings in Persian: it can signify the female descendants of the Prophet; refer to an honourable woman or a good hostess; or, more specifically, to *paries* (fairies) to whom women give food as a votive offering. Many of my informants refuse to attend *sofrehs* that called on the *pari* because it was considered to stand outside legitimate Islamic practices. During an interview, a Mullah at the Holland Park *Majma'* did not wish to comment on such *sofrehs*. Some of the women I spoke to, who attend Ms. Parvizi's *sofrehs*, believe that *sofreh* 'Bibi-seshanbe' is a legitimate religious practice. They mentioned that they have had the best luck with *sofreh* Bibi-seshanbe. It is not a type of *sofreh*, however, that is held by Ms. Parvizi. Perhaps this is because many of the women I asked found these *sofrehs* heterodox and impure.

There are many different versions of the *sofreh* Bibi-seshanbe, including 'Bibi Nur' and 'Bibi Hur'. A group of women who live in Kilburn described the repast. This *sofreh* is held on Tuesday, and halvâ, bread, cheese and fresh herbs are served, but the ingredients must be given by good friends to the host of the gathering. The host prays for the guests to arrive because no one is supposed to be formally invited. I was told that Bibi Hur and Bibi Nur were particularly useful to call upon when something has happened which was not truly meant to happen. For example, a woman named Nazila said that she called upon Bibi Hur and Bibi Nur when she was blamed for something that she was not responsible for. Paradoxically, women also told me that it was often used by those searching for an ideal man. Some women said they would pray to the fairies with a covered dish of halvâ on the *sofreh*. After the prayers they would uncover the halvâ and formulate their fortunes according to the imprints on the halvâ.

Socio-religious Networks in London

Let us now turn to the underlying complexities of the *sofreh* ritual and the interactions between codes of gender, class, nation and the different expressions of Islam in London. This requires an investigation of the various bases of the social networks that are represented at the *sofrehs* and extend outside the gatherings, including their connection to religious institutions and charity organisations. This will be followed by an examination of the ways in which the bases of the religious networks are shaped and reshaped by entanglements between political conjunctures and processes in both Iran and Britain. Ms. Parvizi's *sofrehs*, which are known as being 'moderately religious' and as relatively neutral territory, consist of women primarily stemming from two large, loosely-knit networks. Each network can, in turn, be broken down into smaller circles which revolve around various Shia institutions and are based on demographics, education, politics and socio-economic distinctions (usually based on fathers', and husbands', or ex-husbands' profession and status). The two networks, which I will call the Central London Network and North London Network, are by no means distinct and tend to blur during public social and religious events. They tend to have differing views on what it means to be a good Muslim, and how Shiism should determine a woman's and her family's code of behaviour. Ms. Parvizi's *sofrehs* can be thought of as a bridge between the two networks.

The Central London Network

This network consists of mostly affluent women who mainly live in Kensington, Knightsbridge, Holland Park, Hammersmith and Wimbledon. They will often wear a decorative scarf in public or no scarf at all. Many of the women are (or were) royalists, and do not want to be directly associated with the Islamic regime. We shall see how fragmentation of the Islamic government, culminating in the election of Khatami in 1997, has blurred the clear distinction between those who opposed or supported the Islamic government following the revolution. Many of these women attend Ms. Parvizi's Thursday night and calendar *sofrehs* as the primary way to practise their faith. They may also sponsor invite-only *sofrehs*. While there is a large amount of mixing of classes in the *sofreh* gatherings, the activities of the Central London Network that extends outside of the *sofrehs* can be examined horizontally according to class. Some of the wealthy women in this network are often members of a charity called 'Kahrizak' and a few are members of the Shahmaghsoudi Sufi Order. The middle-class women within the Central London Network often accused the women involved in the Kahrizak charity of social climbing, and sometimes questioned the Iranian government's involvement with the charity. The middle-class women are members of the Shahmaghsoudi Sufi Order.[75] Some of the women go to the Holland Park *Majma'* following the Thursday night *sofreh*. It would be rare to find an upper-class Iranian woman from the Central London Network at the Holland Park *Majma'*, just as it would be rare to find lower middle-class Iranian women at a Kahrizak function. What the women who make up the Central London Network have in common is that they consider themselves as moderately religious, they are opposed to the hard-line Islamic politics in Iran, and they attend Ms. Parvizi's *sofrehs*.

The North London Network

The majority of the Iranian women in the North London Network live in Kilburn, Maida Vale, Brondesbury, West Hampstead, Hampstead and Finchley Road. These women are known to be more pious than the Central London Network women, and wear headscarves and a loose overcoat or proper hejâb in public, regularly pray, fast, eat halâl foods, and travel to Mecca and to various shrines in Iran and Iraq. They are referred to by some women in the Central London Network as the 'Kilburn women' and do not regularly attend Ms. Parvizi's weekly *sofrehs*. Some will attend the calendar *sofrehs* and hire Ms. Parvizi to organise private invite-only *sofrehs*. 'Kilburn women' often complained that Ms. Parvizi's *sofrehs* are more social than religious. Others say that the location of Ms. Parvizi's *sofrehs* is too far to travel to and it is more convenient to organise their own *sofrehs*. They also hold women-only gatherings at the Al-Khoei Foundation in North London and, in different vein, the Islamic Centre of England in Maida Vale. The North London Network consists of a range of women from varying socio-economic backgrounds, and can also be divided vertically in terms of those who support the Iranian government and those who do not. Again, this is not a clear division and it fluctuates according to the changes in the political and economic scene in Iran. The women's husbands, who conduct business with the Iranian government, also blur this division.

The following section consists of my field notes of the places and events that I was introduced to by women who attend Ms. Parvizi's *sofrehs*. In order to organise my research I have created three loose categories from which my introductions to the various social and religious institutions stemmed. First, the organisers of the *sofrehs*; second, the Thursday *sofreh* gathering (which contains women primarily from the Central London Network); third, the 'invite-only' *sofrehs* and the calendar *sofrehs* (the Central London Network and the North London Network are both represented). These categories are by no means distinct and are primarily used to organise my research.

The Sofreh Organisers' Networks

Ms. Parvizi has a range of friends who assist her in organising the *sofreh* gatherings. We shall see how they associate themselves with various circles within both the Central London Network and the North London Network, covering the range of classes, levels of religiosity, political leanings and demographics found in the Iranian religious community.

Imam Hussein Mosque

A woman, whom I will refer to as Farifteh, asked me to meet her at the Imam Hussein mosque, which used to be a church, in Kilburn. When I arrived, all of the women knew about my visit and referred to me as 'the new girl'. Although I repeatedly told them, both in Persian and English, that I am a researcher wishing to learn about Iranian culture and Shiism, they continued to refer to me as a Muslim. Most of the women I spoke to were young mothers in their late twenties and early thirties and were not employed outside of the home. A couple of women told me that their Iranian husbands were in between jobs and were having a difficult time finding their way in British society.

The Iranian government bought the old church and had it renovated and adapted into a small Shia mosque. The women's section of the mosque is a small area upstairs, which at one time was the choir loft. Many of the women were dressed in chadors, while others wore loose robes and headscarves. On Saturday nights the programme was translated into English, which explains why Farifteh wanted me to attend. Several women present were British and had recently converted to Islam and married Iranian or Iraqi men. Interestingly, the women said that they converted to Islam first, and then eventually had their marriages arranged through an organisation in Oxford. The women had all changed their Christian names to Muslim names. The English women married to Iranians could all speak conversational Persian but the English women married to Iraqis could not speak Arabic.

I learned that none of the British women have attended or even heard of a *sofreh* or *jaleseh* gathering. When I described the ritual to them in some detail they thought it sounded 'dodgy' and reckoned that it was not truly Islamic. The Imam Hussein mosque was a small mosque and all the women knew each other well. Interestingly, the women who attended three or four *sofrehs* a week had never extended an invitation to the group of Persian-speaking British converts. There could be at least three possible and overlapping explanations for keeping the British women isolated from the *sofreh* circles. First, a *sofreh* gathering is an organically hybridised Iranian and Shia tradition and treated as an 'Iranian' space in London, which explains why Muslims from other backgrounds tended to question the sanctity of the ritual. Second, the *sofreh* organisers could have been wary about the British women's husbands' close connection to the Iranian embassy and the manner in which they spoke openly and positively about the Islamic Republic in Iran. Finally, there was a socio-economic gap between the middle class *sofreh* goers and the less affluent women who frequented the Imam Hussein mosque.

Several women, whom I had previously met at the pious 'invite-only' *sofreh* and from the Khoei Foundation, frequented the English session on Saturday evenings so that their British-born daughters could listen to the Imam speak in English. There was very little social interaction between the Iranian and English women. I found myself rotating between the two 'camps' of women. It was interesting to observe an Iranian woman offering bread, cheese and dates to a British woman. As the British woman would say in both Persian and English, 'I just had dinner, I am not hungry, it will only go to waste,' the

Iranian woman, in following the rules of *târof* (Iranian rules of etiquette) continually insisted that the woman take the bread. The British women became
very agitated and noted later in private that Iranians were obsessed with food
and were wasteful. The Iranian women commented, in private, how
unfriendly and cold British women were.

After the *namâz* (prayers), the Imam gave a lecture, which was transmitted
via television sets for the women to listen to and watch upstairs in the
mosque. The Mullah, who spoke in poor English, discussed how Shia Muslims must trust and be guided by their local Imams. After the sermon, Hâji
Khânoum served bread, cheese and dates to the women. The women invited
me to return to the Imam Hussein mosque, to attend the celebration for
Fatima's birthday, the following Saturday. Some of the women also invited
me to attend a celebration at an Iranian school in Kilburn.

Iranian Cultural and Educational Centre: Islamic Republic of Iran
At a later date, one of women I met at the Imam Hussein mosque introduced
me to the Iranian school in Kilburn Park. She said that the Iranian Islamic
school was held in a private home in London until 1995 when the Iranian
government bought the school ground in Kilburn Park, formerly called St.
John's. The Iranian Cultural and Educational Centre is one of sixty, independently funded, Muslim schools in Britain.[76] The Iranian school usually
has around 120, Monday to Friday full-time students;[77] a Saturday school
offering Arabic lessons; and a Sunday school of around 250 Iranian children
that teaches Persian and Islamic studies. The school teaches, in both English
and Persian, the curriculum currently being taught in schools in Iran. I was
told that government employees were expected to send their children to this
school. Iranians who frequently travel back and forth to Iran and carry out
business with the Iranian government also send their children to the Iranian
school. The school fees are subsidised by the Iranian government. Parents
pay £400.00 per year for their children's education, mini-bus transportation
and for a daily hot lunch. The school is decorated with pictures of the late
Ayatollah Khomeini and numerous other Iranian national and religious
emblems. The school is associated with the Imam Hussein mosque, the Holland Park *Majma'* (also called the Islamic Universal Association) and the
Islamic Centre of England. They provide a mini-bus service to transport the
children after school to the Holland Park *Majma'*.

The Islamic Republic designated Fatima's birthday as the ceremonial day
on which nine-year-old girls begin to take on their religious and social
responsibilities.[78] This rite of passage, called *jashn-e ebâdat*, is also carried out
by the Iranian school in London. The student body, teachers, several of the
students' mothers and the Mullah from the Imam Hussein mosque were all
present at the ceremony that I attended. When girls at the school reach the
age of nine they are considered to be capable of adhering to religious and
social rules. For example, they are required to wear hejâb, pray, fast and
adhere to rules of modesty. The ceremony consisted of singing, poetry and
storytelling, and was followed by each of the twelve girls reciting words from

the Koran and then receiving special presents from the Mullah. These included a prayer carpet [*sajjâdeh*], prayer stone [*mohre tasbih*], head scarf [*maqna'e*], a loose robe [*mânto*], a framed certificate of distinction and some sweets.[79] The ceremony was followed by girls performing *namâz* with the Mullah. I spoke to several of their mothers, whose economic situations vary and who live throughout central London. They considered the ceremony to be a very important event in their daughter's life and compared it to the first communion practised by Catholics. They emphasised how the ceremony is carried out in an identical manner in Iran.[80] I asked several mothers if they were concerned that their children were not mingling with non-Iranian children or taking a more active role in mainstream British life. They stressed the need to follow the Iranian state's school curriculum because of the likelihood of moving back to Iran. They also wanted to ensure that their children upheld the Iranian state's version of Islamic beliefs and practices. The pointed out how British schools do not recognise and/or monitor many of their key requirements, such as dress codes, adherence to prayer times, halâl food in cafeterias, and religious and national holidays.

I asked the women at the school how they celebrated *Noruz* (Iranian New Year) in London. They visit private homes and partake in the *Noruz* festivities organised by the Iranian embassy. I also asked several women (including some of the teachers) if they host or attend *sofrehs* in London. The art teacher responded: 'I will throw a *sofreh* if I have a special wish to ask for. I have been to several private *sofrehs* in Iranian homes in London. Many women, especially if their home is not large enough, will pay a woman [Ms. Parvizi] in Holland Park to hold their *sofreh*.' She has never been to a 'Holland Park *sofreh*' but she knows many women who have.

During the next Thursday *sofreh*, Farifteh asked me if I had enjoyed my visit to the Imam Hussein mosque and whether or not I planned on going every Saturday. I told her that it was very useful for my research, but that I live too far away to go regularly. I mentioned that Ekram took me to the Iranian school in Kilburn. I was surprised when she said that she was not familiar with the school. It made me wonder if she was perhaps trying to distance herself from the Iranian government. The following week at the Thursday *sofreh* Farifteh told me that she had arranged for me to attend the Saturday night gathering at the mosque. She had spoken to the Mullah and they had arranged for the mosque to pay for a minicab to transport me to and from the gathering. I told her that the offer was unnecessary but very kind, and that I already had another engagement anyway.

The brief section on the Iranian school was important to highlight because it throws light on the organisational networks and exchanges between Iranian institutions in Iran and Britain and touches on some of the methods used to articulate the Iranian state's educational system and religious beliefs and practices to Iranians living in Britain. The school, however, is numerically small and certainly does not reflect the vast majority of Iranians, including those who are practicing Muslims, who attend British schools that concentrate solely on the British curriculum.

Networks extending to 'Thursday Sofreh Gatherings'

The Kahrizak Charity

I was told by numerous Iranians (religious and non-religious) about a charity called Kahrizak. One of the women who attend Ms. Parvizi's *sofrehs* arranged for me to attend the monthly charity meetings. What follows describes the social dynamics of a few of the monthly lunch meetings. It is worth adding that during the course of my research I heard many remarks and speculations about the religious and political underpinnings of the Kahrizak charity. For example, some people said it consists of wealthy and religious women who are linked to the Iranian government, while others said it consists of wealthy women and is politically independent.

The first monthly Kahrizak charity meeting I attended was held in a large home in Hampstead, an affluent area of north-west London. An Iranian woman was seated at a table in the entrance of the house. She greeted me and asked for the £20 entrance fee and the name of the woman who had invited me. She explained that the money was collected for the 'Kahrizak Sanatorium for the Disabled and Elderly' in Iran. It is a private, non-profit making charitable organisation that was established in 1971 by the late Dr. Mohammad Hakimzadeh. The sanatorium has over 1,500 patients and provides medical care and assistance for the elderly and those suffering severe disability. This branch of the charity started at the beginning of the 1990s in London. It organises two big events a year in London, and holds a monthly lunch for its members and invited guests.

Approximately sixty beautifully dressed women, ranging from 30 to 70 years of age, were present at one of the monthly meetings. I recognised fifteen of the women, who regularly attend the Thursday 'core group' *sofreh* circle. Ms. Parvizi is a member of the charity. I knew some women from the Shahmaghsoudi Sufi Order (which is the focus of the next chapter). I also came across women from both the North London Network and the Central London Network. Through conversation it became evident that the women had their economic positions in common, and not their levels of education, piety or political opinions. The elite of several Iranian religious networks, whose religiosity and politics vary, participate in the Kahrizak charity. For example, I spoke to several highly educated and secular-minded women who circulate with well-known Iranian and non-Iranian academics, businessman, artists and politicians. I spoke to educated, and more pious, women who were involved in organising activities that correspond to the religious calendar of events for Iranians in London. Many conversations focused on the importance of the Kahrizak hospital, social events in London and news from Iran. Many talked about activities being sponsored by the Iranian Heritage Foundation, which is a non-political U.K.-registered charity that supports academic research and cultural activities on aspects of Iranian society. Several of the women were directly involved in establishing the Iranian Heritage Foundation in 1995. Books of popular religious philosophers, such as Soroush and Gomshei, were exchanged at the luncheon. Conversations were punctuated by the women viewing a video which featured the growth and progress of the Kahrizak sanatorium in Iran.

According to a 37-year-old member, although it is not overt, the charity is framed by Islamic rules. She said, for example, that the committee members (and a number of the regular members) appear in public in proper hejâb, and all of the meat served at the events is halâl. No men are allowed at the monthly meetings. There is a *Noruz* dinner for the women and their husbands, but the men and women are required to eat separately. At each meeting there is a room reserved for the women to pray. She stressed that many of the women do not necessarily adhere to the five pillars of Islam, but they wish to maintain a level of respectability. Many wish to preserve their religious traditions in London. The charity is recognised by the Iranian government, which is necessary in order for the charity money to reach the hospital, but this does not mean, of course, that the women support the Iranian state. It is also important to emphasise that many of the woman do not see the Kahrizak charity as a religious charity.

At each meeting there are tables containing various items, such as clothes, jewellery and dishes to sell to the members in order to benefit the charity. The meetings start with a lecture, on a range of subjects (such as poetry, cooking and literature), presented by an expert in the field. For example, on one occasion a lecture on Iranian carpets was given by a British woman from the Victoria and Albert Museum. An elaborate lunch with an extraordinary range of delicious Iranian food was served at each meeting.

The discussion at Kahrizak charity luncheons shows the linkages between Iranian women's religious gatherings and wider transnational fundraising for charities and philanthropic activities. The fundraising activities for the Kahrizak hospital have mushroomed around the Iranian diaspora during the 1990s. In 1999 the subsidiaries of Kahrizak, known as the Ladies Charitable Society, was recognised by the United Nations as a non-governmental organisation. The first International Conference on Aging in Tehran was sponsored by the United Nations and organised by Kahrizak and the Ladies Charitable Society, also in 1999. The development and management of charitable activities among women, historically in Iran, and presently both inside and outside Iran, can throw light on the shifting dynamics of public–private demarcated domains.[81] The religious charity-based activities, which are often carried out to fulfil a religious service or duty [*khedmat*], draw attention to local societal problems whilst providing a 'respectable' way for women actively to participate in public domains.

Shahmaghsoudi Sufi Order

Several of the women who attend the Thursday night *sofrehs* are also, regular and irregular, members of the Shahmaghsoudi Sufi Order (discussed in Chapter 4). It is important to note that although several women who attend the Thursday night *sofrehs* also attend the Shahmaghsoudi Sufi Order, the Sufi Master of the Order denounces *sofreh* practices. I have spoken to several male and female members of the Shahmaghsoudi Sufi Order who criticise Ms. Parvizi's *sofrehs* for being social and superstitious; I have spoken also to women in the Sufi Order who organise their own *sofrehs*, and claim them to be holy and legitimate.

Majma' Jahâni Islami

There are a few women who regularly go to the Holland Park *Majma'* (Islamic Universal Association) following the Thursday-night *sofrehs*.[82] The *Majma'*, (discussed in greater detail below), is frequented by Iranian Shias on Thursday nights because of the recitation of Muslim legends based on Hussein's martyrdom. The *Majma'* also provides services for pilgrimages, Ashurê, Ramadan, and funerals. Although a few women from Ms. Parvizi's Thursday night *sofrehs* attend functions at the *Majma'*, many of the women do not like the *Majma'* due to the differences in terms of class, religiosity and the closeness of the *Majma'* to the Iranian Embassy.

Networks Stemming from 'Invite-Only' Sofrehs and Calendar Sofrehs

It is thought that personal wishes have a much better chance of coming true when requested at calendar *sofrehs*, held on the holy days of the Shia calendar. Therefore, women from both the Central London Network and the North London Network often attend the calendar *sofrehs* held at Ms. Parvizi's. Women from each network also attend invite-only *sofrehs* organised by Ms. Parvizi. The following paragraphs introduce the various institutions to which I was taken by women following the invite-only and calendar *sofrehs*.

After the *sofreh* commemorating Ali's birthday, I walked with several women to the Holland Park *Majma'*. This *Majma'* attracts Shias living in London from diverse national backgrounds: Thursday evenings are known as 'Iranian night' at the Holland Park *Majma'*. The women and men are seated in unequally separated sections of the room which are divided by a curtain. The smaller, women's, section was completely full of women and children. They sat in groups talking as the men sat quietly and tried to listen to the speakers. The speakers would frequently tell the women to be quiet and the women would generally ignore their request. The young children sang birthday songs to Ali. The little girls sang on one side of the wall and the little boys sang on the other side, and they attempted to sing together. Several women made candid remarks to me about the crowds and the types of Iranians in the *Majma'*. They said that the room consisted of 'low class' Iranians. One woman, who had recently joined the Shahmaghsoudi Sufi Order, complained about the noise and the disorder, and repeatedly told me that I was not witnessing 'real Shiism'. They commented that the crowd of people present at the *Majma'* were there only for the free food and not to pray. Several women then approached the group of young women I was chatting to and asked if they were looking for a husband. They politely refused, but the women proceeded to tell us about their sons and cousins. One girl, whom I will call Nanou, became very irritated and embarrassed. Nanou was finishing her degree at the University of London. She is involved in many Iranian and non-Iranian social scenes. Her faith is important to her and she has recently started to attend the Shahmaghsoudi Sufi Order. She wants to find her own man, fall in love and then get married. She was insulted by the women in the mosque who were trying to marry off their sons and cousins. In her opinion the women were backward and low class.

Elaborate Invite-only Sofreh

Many of the women present at the elaborate invite-only *sofreh* described earlier are members of the Kahrizak charity group. I was also told by women attending this *sofreh* about private, mixed-sex, religious meetings held at people's homes on certain calendrical holy days (especially throughout Ramadan and *Muharram*).

Pious Invite-only Sofreh

As described earlier, the women who attended the second invite-only *sofreh* were devout Shia Muslims, who also take part in the activities organised at the Holland Park *Majma'*, the Khoei Centre and the Islamic Centre of England in Maida Vale. A woman who teaches Persian at the Holland Park *Majma'* was present and invited me to take Persian lessons at the mosque. I met a woman named Mina at the pious *sofreh* who rarely attends Ms. Parvizi's *sofrehs* because she finds the emphasis more on food and socialising than on prayer. She wears a chador in public and alternates between the activities at the Khoei Centre and the Holland Park *Majma'*, and she often makes pilgrimages to various shrines. Three days after Mina's father passed away she invited many friends and family to meet at the Holland Park *Majma'* to pay their respects. There is a cemetery near Harrow where many Shia Muslims are buried. I was told that Iranians meet on Thursdays because Sura Komeh is followed by a story that is conducive for making vows.

To commemorate the death of Mina's father a tablecloth was placed in the middle of the room with foods for the dead (*halvâ, khormâ*), and foods for healing (fruit and *shole zard*).[83] Many women went to pay their respects to Mina at the Holland Park *Majma'* after attending the Thursday-night *sofreh* gathering. I first spoke to several women who said that they were leaving as soon as they could because they did not like the Holland Park *Majma'* circles.

I met a lot of women, including a 26-year-old named Nazanin.[84] She was born in London and had recently received her Masters degree in chemical engineering. She did not start wearing a hejâb or become religious until she was 13. She circulates between the Khoei mosque, the Imam Hussein mosque, the Holland Park *Majma'*, and the Hammersmith *Kânoon-e Iran* [Iranian community centre]. Nazanin also attends a Koran *tafsir* [interpretation] group, every Saturday night, for young Iranian adults, organised by the Iranian community centre, and a Koran reading group in a house in North London every Wednesday. She knows Ms. Parvizi, but she does not go to her *sofrehs*. She partakes in women-only gatherings held by a different *sokhanrân* [female leader] whom I will call Nahid, in her home in Maida Vale on the first Thursday of every month. I met Nahid and was invited to the next gathering. I also arranged to accompany Nazanin to the Wednesday-night Koran reading in North London. She telephoned me the day before the Koran reading and asked if I am Muslim. When I said 'no', she cancelled our appointment and said that the Koran reading would be very boring for a non-Muslim to sit through. I did accompany Nazanin to a Shia students' organisation near Euston station, which consisted of Shiites in their twenties from various countries.

Gender and Discourse

The following section, by relating profiles and stories of various Iranian women from both the North London Network and the Central London Network, will shed light on some of the linkages between gender roles and expectations, and the various discourses of Shiism being expressed in London. There has been relatively little research interest in local and cultural specificities, such as *sofrehs*, in Iran, due to a bias in social scientific approaches towards macro-processes. According to Kandiyoti: 'The historical connection between feminism and nationalism in the Middle East has left an enduring legacy of concerns around the effects of cultural imperialism which has discouraged a systematic exploration of the local institutions and cultural processes, centrally implicated in the production of gender hierarchies and in forms of subordination based on gender.'[85] *Sofrehs* held at Ms. Parvizi's constitutes a space in London where women preserve and dispute the cultural constructions of gender generated in various Shia social and religious institutions and in the women's households. I have heard many, and often conflicting, explanations of, firstly, the rules surrounding the *sofreh* ritual and, secondly, of how an Iranian Shia woman should behave at a *sofreh*, in wider Iranian scenes in London, and in British society at large.

Purity and Pollution

Sofrehs, like other Shia rituals, have codes of pollution and rules for purification. When I first asked about *sofrehs*, some Iranian women told me that I would probably not be allowed to attend because I am not a Muslim. In some visions of Shiism, the touch of a non-Muslim is one of the items considered *najes* [ritual uncleanness]. When a pious and respected woman made arrangements for me to attend a *sofreh*, I found out later that there had been discussions regarding my proposed visit. Some women argued that a non-Muslim would pollute the ritual and negatively influence the outcome of their wishes. The pious and respected woman argued that it is a duty to educate those who are interested in Islam. Other women said that it was senseless to exclude non-Muslims from the *sofrehs* when many of their own sons were married to non-Muslims in London. The continued acceptance of my observations of their *sofreh* rituals demonstrates the transformation of a rule, traditionally applied to the Iranian cultural form by some women, under the spatial conditions in London.

Other Shia codes of pollution and rules of purification continue to be firmly attached to Ms. Parvizi's *sofrehs*. For example, in addition to the special food required for *sofreh* rituals, Ms. Parvizi's kitchen also follows Islamic dietary injunctions by serving halâl meat.[86] Whether or not the women eat halâl meat outside the *sofreh* gathering depends upon their personal beliefs and habits and/or the stance taken by the various Shia institutions with which they are associated. For example, during a *sofreh* a woman named Malous commented on an Iranian restaurant in London which served an excellent meat dish called *abgousht*. Once some of the women heard the name of the restaurant they scolded Malous for eating at a place that did not serve halâl meat. Malous and her brother told me at a later date that, although they are both practising Muslims, it would be impossible to have social lives in London and practise all the Islamic dietary restrictions.

This discussion concerning halâl meat extends outside the *sofrehs* to Shia institutions and organisations. For example, Islamic dietary laws are an issue for the members of the Kahrizak charity. Nazanin, for example, regularly attends the Kahrizak charity. She believes in God but is against all forms of organised religion (although she occasionally attends *sofrehs* to make wishes). She once brought a meat stew to a monthly gathering and they refused to serve it because it was not halâl. When I asked a pious woman who attends *sofrehs* and is a member of Kahrizak if all the women present at the Kahrizak function were religious and followed the dietary laws, she answered 'Of course!' – as if it were a stupid question. I asked other women, at the same Kahrizak function, the same question and they made comments such as: 'My family's lives are not dictated by silly rules', 'I am not caught up in dietary laws that applied in the seventh century'.

Whether or not a woman should be allowed to read the Koran whilst menstruating has also been a topic of discussion. Blood is another item in Shiism which is *najes*. According to Fischer: 'In both Islam and Judaism there are a series of graded forms of ablution and purification from the more serious and less frequent pollutions to the least serious and more frequent. Menstruation is a periodic pollution more serious than blood from a cut, and it involves a full ablution (Muslim *ghosl*) before prayer or entering a holy place.'[87] This issue is a particularly delicate subject due the varying opinions of Shia institutions that extend outside the *sofrehs*. For example, whereas the Khoei Centre expects its adherents to uphold the codes of pollution and rules for purification, the private, mixed-sex, religious gatherings and the Shahmaghsoudi Sufi Order find no fault in reading the Koran whilst menstruating and praying at the *Khaneqâh*.

During a *sofreh*, it was the turn of a girl in her early twenties to recite the Koran. An older woman abruptly interrupted her and said in Persian, 'Don't you have your period?' This was followed by a discussion between several of the women, and the girl was not allowed to continue. Afterwards I spoke to a woman named Nebe, who is in her forties and who defended the girl. She told me that although Ms. Parvizi's *sofrehs* are moderately religious, many of the women are still caught up in silly rules and do not understand what 'real Shiism' is about. Nebe is a practising Muslim and attends mixed-sex gatherings in private homes and had rejected Sufi Orders (although I learned a year later that she is presently a member of the Shahmaghsoudi Sufi Order). She believes that Shiism is a modern religion and must not be practised as if we were living hundreds of years ago. She can not understand the women who actually think God cares whether or not a woman prays while menstruating. Regardless of the opposition to the pollution law regarding menstruation at *sofrehs*, many of the women uphold the tradition.

Rules of Conduct

The rules of conduct at *sofrehs* are complicated by several conflicting notions which stem from, firstly, the varied ideas of how women in Iran traditionally behaved at *sofrehs*; secondly, the behaviour which coheres to the discourse of the various Shia institutions in London; and, finally, the social conditions in London. In order to illustrate these different roles and expectations, the 'dress code' at the *sofrehs* will be discussed.

I have asked a range of Iranian men and women from different political, social, religious and economic backgrounds their opinion about the *sofreh* ritual being held by women in London. I was told by the presiding Mullah at the Holland Park *Majma'*, that there is a 'legitimate' and 'truly Islamic' way in which *sofrehs* should be conducted, and that he was very concerned with the way in which *sofrehs* are being practised by some women in London. This is why he allows *sofrehs* to be held on some Fridays in a side room in the Holland Park *Majma'*. This is also a way to oversee the women's practices and keep the women's money within the institution. The majority of responses referred to *sofrehs* as an excuse to show off clothes and jewellery. Many of these attitudes regarding *sofrehs* may have been shaped by the type of *sofrehs* that Betteridge discusses in her research conducted between 1974 and 1976 in Iran.[88] She states:

> I attended my first ritual dinner and rozeh given in the name of 'abâs ... I was somewhat surprised when I was told to put on my best clothes and jewellery; I knew that the entire ceremony would include rozeh and had assumed that black clothes would be appropriate ...We parked the car, put on our chadors, then entered the house ... They [the women] were made up, wearing colourful suits; most of them had on printed or light-coloured veils.

The dress code at the *sofrehs* in London depends upon the type of *sofreh* held and the social and religious background of the sponsor. The way in which women dress is not only an indicator of social status but also demarcates the women's various (and often changing) levels of religiosity. The way in which women dress at the various *sofrehs* (ranging from black chadors to black leather trousers) generates a lot of discussion and gossip as to how Iranian women should dress for both *sofrehs* and for everyday life. Most of the women attending Ms. Parvizi's *sofrehs* can be categorised in the Central London Network and believe that women should dress modestly and smartly. Although a number of the women do not wear a headscarf in public, the majority of them walk into Ms. Parvizi's house wearing a headscarf. I have spoken to women who do not see the point of wearing a headscarf to walk in the door of the *sofreh* gathering. According to Laleh, who is in her forties, Shiism is a modern religion and therefore Shia rituals, such as *sofrehs*, should be modernised. Laleh finds clothes and veils irrelevant to the ritual process. Other women are influenced by the discourse stemming from the Shahmaghsoudi Sufi Order that denounces chadors.

Others, however, argued that women should wear a headscarf and dress modestly, in a long black skirt and a black blouse. A pious woman in her forties named Mariam, who occasionally attends Ms. Parvizi's *sofrehs*, is critical of the attitude towards dress among Iranian women in London. She believes that the way in which women dress at *sofrehs* and in everyday life is an important demarcation of modesty and reverence. She argues that the *sofreh*, if used correctly, is a powerful method of asking God for special favours. If the women are concerned about their clothes and make-up, then their minds are obviously not on the prayers. The various attitudes towards dress at *sofrehs* do have implications. For example, once, before a *sofreh* was to begin, a man very quickly passed by the '*sofreh* room' and ran out the door. While some of the women did not even take notice, or did not care, other women were very upset and embarrassed because they were not wearing their veil. They demanded that in the future they should be warned about the presence of men in the house.

A 45-year-old Iranian woman, who wears a decorative scarf in public, invited me to a family party in Kensington. Some of the relatives at the party are members of the Shahmaghsoudi Sufi Order, other relatives are practising Muslims who reject Sufism (these women wore decorative scarves and consider themselves as religiously moderate), and other relatives are strictly Muslim and wear proper hejâb. The way in which the women dressed determined the interaction between the men and women throughout the night. For example, two rooms in the house were openly connected by a large entryway. For the most part, the men sat on one side of the room and the women sat on the other side. The food was laid out on the floor covering both rooms. In the women's room the women wearing scarves and chadors sat together; on the other side of the room sat fashionably dressed women without scarves. One of the women wore a revealing dress and was subject to gossip by the other women. For the young men, and the women not veiled, it was acceptable to move freely between both the 'male room' and the 'female room'. I asked a woman, in consideration of the various religious attitudes present, whether or not there would be dancing after the dinner. She said that her ultra-religious relatives used to forbid dancing at the parties, but due to the pressure from the others they have no choice but to accept it. Their young daughters, however, tend to disappear to other rooms of the home when the dancing begins.

The dynamics at this party were similar to Ms. Parvizi's *sofrehs* in that the various distinctions between what is harâm and halâl, and *mahram* and *nâmahram*, are not fixed, and can be negotiated in different situations and among family members; this corresponds to behavioural expectations and relations between men and women. In order for Iranian cultural forms, such as *sofrehs*, to continue to exist in London they must rely on durable social networks which range from the mixed-sex private gatherings to the Holland park *Majma'*. Although the various networks have different notions about 'Shiism', '*sofrehs*', 'Islamic pollution laws', and 'dress codes' the space at Ms. Parvizi's *sofrehs* gives women an opportunity to compare, contrast and transform the different views on how to be a Shia Muslim outside Iran.

Why Do Iranian Women Attend Sofrehs*?*

Sofrehs, as with many other Iranian popular cultural forms, have been used as an identity-building vehicle in the process of emigration, and have been reproduced and modified in relation to the socio-political conditions in both Iran and Britain. The following section will argue that the *sofreh* networks have also been shaped by the two socio-political conjunctures introduced in Chapter 2.

As discussed earlier, many Iranians started to feel more settled in London after years of thinking their stay was going to be temporary. Many reported that although they have grown accustomed to life in London, they do not wish to give up their Iranian culture and past. In response to this, around 1990, there was a mushrooming of Iranian socio-cultural and religious organisations and events in London, many of which have been constructed as distinct from the Iranian state's political and religious discourses. There was also a con-scious effort by some Iranians to mould their identities in relation to the debates concerning the changing dynamics of structure, religion and national identity in contemporary Britain. Iranians often talked about the negative stereotypes of Muslims in Britain and beyond and did not want to be associ-ated with the radical portrayals and images.

It was the first time in their lives that many felt the absence of and need for a religious framework. At a very pious *sofreh,* I asked a 26-year-old woman, named Nazanin, if the thirty or thirty-five women present at the gathering had always been practising Muslims. She (discreetly) pointed at each indi-vidual and said: 'She started practising three years ago; Fatima eight years ago; Mariam went to Mecca about a year ago, before that she was drinking in night clubs; Sara a long time ago, Fati three or four years ago', and so on. I asked many woman when they became practising Muslims. They often associated their increasing interest in religion with dreams. Women often talked about the supernatural and the divine, and their everyday lives, through dreams. Several said that their lives had no real meaning until they were convinced by friends to travel to Mecca, where they were spiritually blessed. For example, Farifteh and her family lived in Dubai after the revol-ution and moved to London three years ago. Farifteh has always believed in God, but was never a practising Muslim until she went to Mecca five years ago. She now wears a headscarf in public and prays. According to a woman in her forties, named Malous, it became a trend for her network of friends to go Mecca and return wearing a scarf. She said that her friends spent the 1980s in nightclubs and casinos, then travelled to Mecca and had spent the 1990s at *sofrehs* and charity functions. For these women, *sofreh* gatherings developed as a popular form of religious practice in London. As Malous noted, it became popular to become religious. She said that the women who are now involved in the religious networks used to be anti-regime, they used to drink, go to casinos, etc. She said that they have turned around 180 degrees. She thinks that many women are hypocritical because they are act-ing religiously in order to increase their family status. Malous travels back and forth from Iran to London. She said that in Iran, her social circles rarely talk about religion. She stressed how her friends in Iran would find it hard to believe that she was sitting in a restaurant in London with a young woman from the U.S. talking about *sofreh* Abu'l-Fazl!'

When I asked women why they attend *sofrehs*, the majority of the women said they needed to ask God to guide them and their families through troubles and crises. The active behaviour in asking for help at religious gatherings empowers the women, gaining them a sense of personal control over themselves and their families. Zubaida considers the social significance of religion from two perspectives, instrumentality and solidarity:

> In the context of instrumentality, religion represents a set of resources for the fulfilment of particular objectives to do with health, wealth and happiness. This is where popular culture appears as a bricoleur, constructing remedies from various elements to suit the task at hand ... Religion in another perspective is the sphere of social solidarities based on common belonging, with specific institutions and rituals of worship which identifies the believers and separates them from the practitioners of other faiths.[89]

The instrumental use of *sofrehs* to serve individual ends does not stop at the initial procedure. Some women said that big wishes take longer than small wishes to come true. Other women said that one must ask the same wish several times in order for it to come true. I asked Malous if her wishes ever came true. She showed me a notebook filled with pages of wishes that she has asked for at the *sofrehs*. She had a system in the notebook which indicated the wishes that had come true, those that had almost come true, those that needed to be asked for again, etc. When I asked women why some wishes never came true they said it is possible that someone could be a victim of *nazr*, or evil eye. Instead of feeling helpless, *sofrehs* enable women to 'push God' in their favour. On one occasion there were two Iraqi women who attended the calendar *sofreh* who told me that I was in the wrong place to learn about 'true Shiism'. They described the *sofreh* ritual as 'Iranian' and 'pagan'. I asked them, if that was the case, why they attended and they replied that they had difficulties and needed to pray for extra help.

Throughout my research the importance of both retaining an Iranian identity in London and successfully integrating into British society were stressed. Many Iranians do not want to be associated with the negative images of some of the other Muslim groups in Britain. The *sofreh* gatherings, whilst providing women with a private Muslim–Iranian space in London, allowed women to lead anonymous public lives. *Sofrehs* are also a place in London where women can speak Persian and exchange information concerning births, marriages, deaths, illnesses, graduations, news from Iran, Iranian cultural events in London, gossip, and so on.

The second socio-political conjuncture that has influenced some Iranian women's religious patterns is the Islamic Republic's apparent move towards a politically moderate Iranian state. As discussed in Chapter 2, due to several factors, such as Khatami's presidential victory, changing policies towards Iranians outside of Iran, and the mending diplomatic relations between Britain and Iran, there have been more Iranians formerly in opposition to the regime that have been slowly warming (more so economically than politically) to elements of the Iranian government. These processes seem to explain some of the difficulties in making sense of some of the women's religious networks in relation to their political affiliations. For example, I spoke to women who are royalists and denounce the regime, and women who are sympathetic with the Iranian government, at the same *sofreh* gathering or charity event. I was told that building new social relationships has been necessary in order to do business in Iran.

According to Nazila and her mother (both are/were royalists, are currently members of the Shahmaghsoudi Sufi Order and attend *sofrehs* on occasion), it is no longer possible to make clear-cut divisions between the supporters of the regime and the opponents of the regime: they are shaded by business and religion. Religious and cultural gatherings in London are used to discuss the changes in Iran and become familiar, aligned or realigned with the various strands of religious and political thought currently being debated in Iran. When these women travel, which is often to Iran, Dubai and Los Angeles, many of them attend *sofrehs* and other women's gatherings.

Conclusions

This chapter has argued that in order to understand the diversity of Islamic practices it is necessary to examine popular religious manifestations, such as *sofreh* gatherings, and the ways in which they have been subject to transformations in relation to particular conditions and discourses. By taking a close look at *sofreh* gatherings in London I have tried to show the ways in which they have been used by some Iranian women as an identity-building vehicle in the process of emigration. *Sofrehs*, which were often described as a direct method that empowered women to 'push God' in their favour, have become one of the social and religious bases used by women to help come to terms with their lives outside Iran, as well as to maintain and negotiate their Iranian and Muslim identities in London. The research projects which focus on women's religious gatherings at different points during the twentieth century in Iran illustrate the many and changing meanings and roles of the *sofreh* performance, and the ways they have been used as channels to express religious, socio-economic and political identities.

During the 1980s and the beginning of the 1990s, Ms. Parvizi's *sofrehs*, which were usually described as religiously moderate, tended to attract older Iranian women who wanted to stay clear of the religious perspective of the Iranian government. It provided a centrally located domain for women who live dispersed throughout several London boroughs, to meet together, to pray, and exchange information concerning births, marriages, illnesses, news from Iran, Iranian events in London, and so on. Performing the *sofreh* ritual provided an Iranian/Shia space for women to reproduce and reshape an

Iranian tradition that was consistent with their present situations. For many of these women, attending Thursday night *sofrehs* has become a part of their weekly routine. Sponsoring a Thursday night *sofreh* or paying Ms. Parvizi to conduct an invite-only *sofreh* service are also ways for women to fulfil their duty of being hospitable. The invite-only *sofrehs*, which are more overtly competitive than the Thursday night *sofrehs*, provide a forum for women to promulgate their social, economic and religious status, and strengthen personal networks by choosing who is invited, the type of *sofreh* to be held and the expenses involved in the food and display.

At the various *sofrehs*, I came across many, often conflicting, definitions of what it means to be an Iranian Shia Muslim in London, which reveals the uncertainty of religious practice and representation, and the ways they are contested and negotiated. This process is particularly apparent during the process of migration, when it is unclear how one should live as an Iranian Muslim outside Iran. During the years that followed the revolution there was a clear distinction between those who supported and those who opposed the brand of Islam implemented by the regime. This became more and more shaded and complicated when Khatami became President of Iran in 1997. My investigation of the women's wider social networks illustrated many levels of religiosity that articulate a number of distinct discourses and assume the role of determining what a valid or invalid practice is for Shias living in London. My examination of the different Shia institutions, such as the Holland Park *Majma'*, the Kahrizak charity organisation, the Shahmaghsoudi Sufi Order, the Imam Hussein mosque and the Islamic government's elementary high school, demonstrated how they relate to the various women in relation to demographics, education, political standing and socio-economic distinctions. The *sofreh* service provided by Ms. Parvizi bridged together women from a range of religious, social and economic backgrounds and has become a place where they sort through the different religious interpretations and views generated in the different social and religious associations, their households, workplace and so on.

During the period 1996 to 1998 I regularly attended weekly *sofreh* gatherings. Since then I have maintained contact with Ms. Parvizi and several other women, and periodically attend gatherings. It is fascinating to see how the socio-religious networks have crystallised over the years. Contingent on one's socio-economic background, level of religiosity, and positioning to the Iranian political scene it is now much clearer which female preacher, religious facility, wedding organiser, or Sufi Order, one would seek out for religious and special occasions.

Notes

1. The five pillars are: the attestation of faith; prayer; almsgiving; fasting during the month of Ramadan; and a pilgrimage to Mecca.
2. D. Pinault (1992), pp. 4–6.
3. The succeeding Imams assumed the role of supreme religious leader of the Shia community and lived for the most part peacefully in the Abbasid caliphate. Although the Shia com-

munity were allowed to develop into a sectarian community with its own forms of theology, law and ritual, the Imams and their followers were kept under close surveillance because Shia legitimism posed a threat to the Caliphate. It is from this movement, Shiism in the ninth century, that the doctrine of twelver Shiism developed. This doctrine, which was affirmed in A.D. 873–74, further depoliticised the sect by developing the disappearance of the infant twelfth imam, Mahdi, who is thought to return someday. This doctrine, therefore, had resolved the numerous Shia revolts headed by various persons who laid claim to the Imamate while not violating the principle that the Imam must always exist. See D. Pinault (1992).

4. G. Thaiss (1972), p. 352.
5. See D. Kandiyoti (1996); N. Tapper and R. Tapper (1987), pp. 69–92; A. Torab in A. Ansari and V. Martin (2002), p. 152.
6. See M. Weber (1978), p. 245.
7. E. Gellner (1992); J. Hall (1985); M. Mann (1986).
8. See F. Adelkhah (1999), p. 111; S. Zubaida (1995), p. 151–88 and (1993), p. 103.
9. The events at Karbalâ, for example, were used in this fashion by both Khomeini and Shariati. See A. Rahnema (2000), pp. 315–16.
10. For a discussion of the political interpretation of mourning rituals see M.M.J. Fischer (1980), pp. 12–31 and 170–80. For a statement of this view see B. Lewis (1985), pp. 7–10.
11. M. Delvecchio-Good and B. Good (1988), pp. 43–63. For a critique of this type of approach, see A. Torab (1998).
12. M. Hegland in N.R. Keddie (1983), pp. 218–35.
13. S. Zubaida (1993), p. 60.
14. For a discussion on *sofrehs* and other women's gatherings, see F. Adelkhah (1999); Torab in Ansari and Martin (2002); Torab (1998); L. Jamzadeh and M. Mills in C.W. Bynum (1986); M. Afkhami and E. Friedl (1994); A. Betteridge in N. Falk and R. Cross (1989), p. 154; M.M.J. Fischer in L. Beck and N.R. Keddie (1978), pp. 222–31.
15. For an account of the history of Zoroastrianism see M. Boyce (2001 or 1995). See also, M.M.J. Fischer (1978), pp. 222–31; and L. Jamzadeh (1986).
16. L. Jamzadeh (1986), p. 28. See also M. Boyce (2001).
17. Ibid.
18. Ibid.
19. See L. Jamzadeh and M. Mill (1986) for a full account of Zoroastrian cosmology.
20. Ibid., pp. 29–30.
21. Ibid., p. 34.
22. Ibid.
23. M.M.J. Fischer in L. Jamzadeh and M. Mills (1986), pp. 29–30.
24. M.M.J. Fischer (1978), pp. 202–3.
25. See M. Boyce in L. Jamzadeh and M. Mills (1986), p. 52.
26. M.M.J. Fischer (1977), pp. 294–99.
27. P. Paidar in D. Kandiyoti (1996), p. 52.
28. D. Kandiyoti (1996), pp. 1–28; See also, J. de Groot (1996), pp. 29–59; A. Najmabadi (1998), pp. 59–84; and P. Paidar (1996) pp. 51–68.
29. M. Afkhami (1994), pp. 5–18.
30. A. Najmabadi (1998), p. 75.
31. For descriptions and analysis of Iranian-Shia women-only gatherings see F. Adelkhah (1998); A. Torab (2002), pp. 143–68 and (1996), pp. 235–52; Z. Kamalkhani in H. Afshar (1993), p. 85–86. For a brief summary of writings by and about Iranian women since the revolution see Z. Mir-Hosseini (1999), pp. 283–85.
32. B. Bamdad (1977), p. 14.
33. P. Paidar (1995), p. 158.
34. M. Good (1974), p. 486.
35. A. Betteridge (1980), p. 153–54.
36. J. Bauer (1985a).
37. P. Paidar in D. Kandiyoti (1996), p. 57.

38. A. Shariati (1990).
39. See H. Esfandiari (1997).
40. E. Friedl in M. Afkhami and E. Friedl (1994), p. 163.
41. A. Torab (1996), p. 235.
42. Ibid., pp. 115–16.
43. Z. Kamalkhani in H. Afshar (1993), p. 85–86.
44. Ibid., pp. 148–49.
45. A. Torab (2001), p. 149.
46. F. Adelkhah (1999), p. 109
47. Ibid., pp. 105–38.
48. Ibid., p. 116.
49. There is a great need for more research on the way in which local and transational Islamic charities and trusts are organised in Britain. There are more than 1,000 Islamic trusts and charities set up in Britain, with a total income of £42 million. See, J. Wilson (2002).
50. For further discussions on the significance of the charity field in Iran after the revolution, see F. Adelkhah (1999).
51. According to the Islamic Centre of England and the Holland Park *Majma'*, khoms is the one-fifth tax, according to which all adult Muslims who are financially viable and have surplus profit contribute 20 percent of their annual savings, commercial profits and property after the deduction of daily expenditure. *Zakât* is a tax which must be paid on certain kinds of agricultural produce and livestock, and on gold and silver.
52. They say that the *sofrehs* are open to all Shia women; however, very few non-Iranians attend. I met two Persian-speaking Iraqi women at the *sofrehs*. They quietly told me that *sofrehs* are not really Islamic, but an Iranian tradition. I asked why they were present at the *sofrehs*, and they responded that they had important requests to ask God. I regularly asked non-Iranian Shias about *sofrehs* at mosques and other religious events. The majority of the women are not familiar with the practice. They often make comments such as 'Sounds very Iranian, any-thing to do with food is Iranian' or 'it doesn't sound Islamic'.
53. F. Adelkhah (1999), p. 110.
54. Halva is a dish cooked for merit. It is cooked for Abu'l-Fazl, in memory of Hussein and for the dead.
55. *Âjil-e moshkel-goshâ* was described to me as the 'problem-solver' and should not be wasted after the *sofreh*.
56. I was told that dates were Muhammad's favourite food.
57. Hâji Khanoum is an Azeri from Tabriz and is a well-known figure amongst the Iranian religious networks. She rotates between Parvizi's *sofrehs*, the Imam Hussein mosque, Khoei mosque and the Holland Park *Majma'*, and serves the *khormâ*, bread and cheese, fruit, etc. I have come across other women from similar backgrounds who work as domestic workers in Iranian homes in London.
58. From reading Betteridge's account of *sofrehs*, and speaking to different Iranian women before I attended the gathering, I was expecting the women to be more social and fashion con-scious. I wore a beige dress and colourful scarf. When I walked into the room, I wished I was wearing a black dress and scarf. Note that other *sofreh* gatherings held by Ms. Parvizi were less orthodox in manner. It depended on the participants.
59. It had not been decided whether or not non-Muslims were allowed to attend *sofrehs*. I was told of a discussion about whether or not a non-Muslim Western girl should be allowed to attend. During the *sofreh* I attended the women were very warm and welcoming. Many were curious as to why I wanted to learn about their religion. Understanding *târof* (Iranians' com-plex rules of etiquette) and trying to speak in Persian, I believe, were important reasons why I was invited back to many more *sofrehs*.
60. See A. Torab (2002), research on *jalesehs* for a discussion on how female preachers differen-tiate between themselves in Iran. A *jaleseh* is type of women-only religious gathering. Less emphasis is placed on the specific stories which call upon holy figures and correspond with votive food.

61. Z. Kamalkhani (1993), p. 91.
62. She also implied that I was Muslim or thinking about becoming Muslim. The women sitting next to me embraced me and all the women were saying *barikallâh* [well done]. Although I always said to the women that the reason I attended was because I was writing about their gatherings, many found my research project unimportant and insisted that God brought me to the meetings for a greater purpose. Many told me that I was a Muslim in my heart, but I hadn't realised it yet.
63. See L. Harbottle (2000), p. 98; M. Shaida (1992). According to B. Donaldson (1938), p. 193, *Ash* is also cooked to remove the influence of the evil eye from those named 'Bibi', which marks them as descendants of the Prophet. 'But no man may see this *ash*, nor should it be out under the sky, lest it turn to blood'.
64. I was told that it is customary that the *sofreh* Abu'l-Hassan-e Mujt'abâ is offered on the 28th day in the second month of the Iranian calendar, *Safar*.
65. L. Jamzadeh and M. Mills (1987), pp. 29–30.
66. B. Donaldson (1938), p. 124.
67. The amount of money given depends on the economic backgrounds of the women, whether or not they are loyal to other Shia institutions and how often they frequent *sofrehs*.
68. This woman, who occasionally visits the Thursday night gatherings, always walked in just in time to light candles, make wishes and eat. She tended to miss the reading of the Koran.
69. See M. Shaida (1992) and B. Donaldson (1938) for discussions concerning the symbolism of various Iranian dishes. *Shole zard* is traditionally prepared on the day of the death of Muhammad and his household. Donaldson mentions a porridge that is made of crushed wheat, meat, grease and spices, called *halim,* and *harisa*, which is cooked on the day of Fatima's death. I did not come across this dish at the *sofrehs* held for Fatima in London.
70. This is interesting because many accounts of *sofrehs* highlight the preparation of the food, saying, for example, that men can't be present.
71. I found out later that she is from a famous Iranian merchant family and endorses many of the Iranian events, particularly charity events, in London.
72. A. Torab (1998), p. 122.
73. I was told that this money was collected for the prayer leader. A lot of the donations were sealed in envelopes. Most donated ten or twenty pounds.
74. These two days were very helpful to me for understanding the various networks that stem from Parvizi's *sofrehs*. The Thursday night *sofrehs* and the calendar *sofrehs* consist of two main networks (on the one hand, the Kahrizak and Shahmaghsoudi Sufi network, and on the other hand the Holland Park *Majma'* network) which lead to diverse institutions, discourses, politics and social classes.
75. Grandmothers and mothers often attend *sofrehs*. The mothers will also go to the Shahmagh-soudi Sufi Order with their children. Many of the grandmothers I have spoken to are not interested in Sufism. They also complain about the length of the ritual (three hours, sitting on the floor).
76. It is worth noting that in 1997 the Labour government approved state funding for two Islamic schools.
77. There is a much larger number of Iranian girls than boys enrolled in the school.
78. I was told that age nine is significant because it is when girls used to start menstruation. According to Islamic law girls are considered legally responsible and can get married at age nine. Men are not made religiously responsible until they are fifteen. According to the women's magazine *Zan-e ruz*, the state televised the ritual when it was first performed at schools in 1981. See A. Torab (1998), pp. 160–66 and 416–23.
79. This certificate looked similar to a Western-style diploma or achievement award.
80. Similar to comments made by my contacts in London, Adelkhah noted a similarity between *jashn-e ebâdat* and the First Communion in the Catholic Church. In her analysis the cere-monies are illustrative of the wider movement towards the centralisation and institutionalisation of religion in Iran, while also being new space of individualisation, Adelkhah (1999), p. 120. Torab's research on religious socialisation and the new maturity rit-uals in Iran emphasised how the ceremony is reserved for girls. She writes: 'The ritual is

informed by the gender asymmetry that characterises dominant gender ideals. It follows that official encouragement of the ritual is an attempt to radically impose these ideals and to instil them abruptly at an early stage in a girl's life. The ritual, and its media coverage when held at schools, draws relatives, friends, school authorities and the wider public into the process with the effect of subjecting the conduct of girls to wider scrutiny and control.' Torab (1998), p. 162. Both Adelkhah and Torab discuss the different ways Iranian women question and negotiate the state's efforts to institutionalise the religious field. See F. Adelkhah, (2002), pp. 105–38; and A. Torab (1998), pp. 160–66.

81. See further discussions on the significance of the charity field in Iran after the revolution. F. Adelkhah (1999) argues that informal religious spaces lead to involvement in Islamic institutions or associations, especially in the charity field, and play a part in opening a public space for reflection and debate.

82. I found that more and more women started to attend the activities at the *Majma'*. This is a part of the wider movement of people redefining their relationship to the Iranian embassy and government.

83. I was told that it was an Arabic version of *shole zard*, and not as tasty as the Iranian version.

84. She would be considered a 'Kilburn woman'.

85. D. Kandiyoti (1996), p. 18.

86. Sura V. 4 of the Koran states, 'Forbidden to you [for food] are: dead meat, blood, the flesh of swine, and that on which hath been invoked. The name of other than God: That which hath been killed by strangling, or by a violent blow, or by a headlong fall, or by being gored to death: That which hath been [partly] eaten by a wild animal unless ye are able to slaughter it [in due form]. That which is sacrificed on stone [altars]: [forbidden] also is the division of meat by raffling with arrows: that is impiety.'

87. M.M.J. Fischer in L. Beck and N. Keddie (1978).

88. A. Betteridge (1989).

89. S. Zubaida (1993), pp. 106–7.

4

Iranian Sufi Orders in London

The tradition of Sufism has gained currency among some Iranians living out-side of Iran. Sufism [*tasavof*] is a term applied to the mystical tradition within Islam which emphasises the love of God and the grasp of divine realities. Generally speaking, it teaches that 'Sufis are God's friends, perpetually engaged in remembrance [*zekr*] of him. Sufism also constitutes a Path [*tariqat*], which begins with repentance and leads through a number of "stations", representing virtues such as absolute trust in God, to a higher series of ecstatic "states".'[1]

This chapter concentrates on the social significance of two London branches of the transnational Nimatullahi Sufi Order and the Maktab Tariqat Oveyssi Shahmaghsoudi (School of Islamic Sufism). The purpose is not to detail the various histories and lineages of these orders but to provide an overview of their trajectories which serve to illuminate contemporary developments. This examination sheds light on the processes whereby they simultaneously carve out a distinct Iranian place in London, and adapt to and make an impact on British society. It shows how Sufism, a culturally familiar Iranian tradition, provides a space for Iranians to shape and to express their Muslim identities, while staying clear of the politicised and culturally remote versions of Islam in both Iran and Britain.

Sufism, which was originally a Sunni phenomenon, became organised in the middle of the eleventh century in order to fill the vacuum left by the suppres-sion of Shiism by the Seljuqs.[2] The practice of Sufism, which had been limited to sessions between teachers and disciples, in private homes, spread into schools [*madresehs*], which indicates that Sufism was rapidly becoming part of the fabric of Muslim devotion. Sufi chapters, or *Khâneqâhs,* became highly cen-tralised and were headed by a spiritual leader from the twelfth to the thirteenth centuries.[3] According to Nasr, there are three distinguishable groups of mystics that can be found in the Shia world.[4] First, and most typically, there are those who are initiated into a Sufi Order that provides a highly centralised and hier-archical organisation, headed by a charismatic and spiritual leader who guides disciples on a spiritual path. The second group of mystics 'are those who also have had a definite spiritual Master and have received regular initiation but whose Master and those before him do not constitute an organised and "institutionalised" Sufi Order with an openly declared *selseleh* [chain of successive Masters] and established centre or *Khâneqâh*.[5] Finally, according to Nasr, there are those who have 'definitely received a Gnostic and mystical inspiration and have authentic visions [*moshâhedeh*] and experience spiritual states [*ahwâl*], but do not possess a human master'.[6]

The relationship between the different groups of mystics and the authority of the ulema throughout Muslim history has been examined and well documented. Sufi organisations, with their mystical and esoteric beliefs and practices, have been accepted by the orthodoxy since the eleventh century and have become a regular part of Muslim life. There have been a number of turbulent episodes between the Shia ulema and Sufi Orders across various moments in Iranian history. There are also points when the ulema involved themselves in the social and spiritual activities of the various Sufi associations.[7]

Groupings of mystics are highly diverse and need to be examined in relation to the given context. They have, for example, developed into several different kinds of associations: modes of social organisation, such as craft guilds and urban quarters;[8] lodges supported by the state as a mode of stable influence in the body politic;[9] powerful forces in religious and social reform;[10] a form of escapism from everyday life;[11] as a means of psychiatric treatment;[12] and as warriors in military bands,[13] to name just a few.

This chapter concentrates on the London branches of the Nimatullahi Sufi Order[14] and the Maktab Tariqat Oveyssi Shahmaghsoudi [School of Islamic Sufism].[15] It examines the social significance of these Sufi Orders as a base for some Iranians residing in Britain. This chapter argues that Sufi Orders in London are social associations participating in 'this-worldly' social action and bearing a variety of social meanings and functions. It will demonstrate how Sufi Orders and their religious tenets are designed and practised in a multitude of forms. It will discuss the structure of each Sufi Order and present their basic rules and tenets. An introduction to the profiles of some of the Sufi members and their broader religious and socio-economic networks, which extend outside of each Sufi Order, will follow. These networks will be examined in relation to the structure of each Order and in turn the socio-political conditions in Britain and Iran. Lastly, the expansion and hybridisation of the Sufi Orders will be considered in relation to the growth of new religious movements in Western Europe and America. First, a brief outline of the political and social conditions in nineteenth- and twentieth-century Iran will be presented in order to understand the development and dynamics of both the Nimatullahi Order and the Oveyssi Shahmaghsoudi Order.

Sufism in Iran

In the nineteenth century, Iran was being threatened both financially and militarily by the expanding European powers, Britain and Russia. The Qajar state (1794–1924), which was patrimonial, fragmented, weak and corrupt, did not carry out measures to oppose foreign influence, which led to the government accommodation of foreign companies and individuals in Iranian markets. Sections of the ulema enjoyed powerful positions in the fragmented Qajar government and controlled the education and judiciary systems and all social and charitable services. A number of religious and political reform movements emerged in response to the ulema's intellectual dominance and the immoderation of the Qajar's weak governing. Reform-minded Iranians, including those linked to indigenous messianic movements, some influenced by the West, and some members of the clergy, called for radical social and political change.[16] It is important to note that political involvement, often through royal patronage, existed between various Sufi Masters and the Qajar government.[17]

There were several expressions of religio-political debate within Shia Islam during this period that challenged the clerics' restricted definition of knowledge, including their positions regarding the rights and treatment of women. For example, a Shia splinter group called the Shaikhis, which was founded by Shaikh Ahmad Ahsai and developed in the 1810s, actively attempted to put forth socio-political and spiritual alternatives to the official Shia Islam. They believed that: 'God had given each generation a perfect Shia or *bab* [door] through whom the faithful could communicate with the Hidden 12th Imam.'[18] Unless people prepared the way, Mahdi's return would remain ambiguous. The Shaikhis movement denounced polygamy and apparently found men and women intellectually equal.[19] The Babi movement, which developed in the 1850s, continued the Shaikhis tradition in preparing the way for the impending return of the Mahdi. It also marked the beginning of the radicalisation of religious dissent.[20] According to Fischer:

> The Babi movement was a mixture of progressive ideas, and alternative and reactionary theocratic ones. On the one hand, there were the demands for equality of men and women, symbolised by the unveiling of *qorrat ol-'eyn at Badasht*; for the laicization of the clergy (abolishing their role in leading prayers, in making legal decisions, or in handling the finances of the community); and for more equitable distribution of land and wealth. On the other hand, there were notions of theosophically graded beings culminating in the 'point' or '*bab*', the supreme authority and access to divine wisdom: of a holy war intended to create a pure Babi land.[21]

New shades of Sufism also appeared in nineteenth-century Iran, offering different interpretations of Islam and questioning sections of the Shia clergy. More women were allowed to take part openly in many Sufi activities and some women reached a status of sainthood.[22] According to Bayat, 'late nineteenth century thinkers turned against the traditional sciences of theology and metaphysics … and against its corrupt, traditionally despotic Qajar government'.[23] Ideas associated with modernity, nationalism and feminism started to shape and be shaped by religious reform and nationalist movements. These currents were part of the climate which led to the Constitutional Revolution of 1906, which is considered the preliminary step in the formation of the modern Iranian state. Struggles and tensions in and between the clergy, successive Shahs and constitutionalist parties ensued until the take-over of Reza Khan and the Pahlavi dynasty in 1924.

Sufism was rarely publicly recognised by Reza Shah and the royal court. As part of the Shah's anti-religious policy he repressed the type of Sufis, typically from the *Khâksar* Order, who begged for food and money on the streets of Tehran.[24] Several sources suggest, however, that the royal court did not in fact defy all forms of Sufi mysticism, and there was an increased interest in the revision of Sufism during the early Pahlavi era of nation-state building.[25] According to Nasr: 'The *Khâneqâhs* flourished over the whole country during the Pahlavi period and continue to draw people to themselves.'[26] Within the Sufi Orders there was a need to find internal coherency between religious tenets and the succession of Masters, and the emergence of the Pahlavi state and their new policies of nationalistic modernisation. For example, the main line of Nimatullahi descent, which became the most widespread Sufi Order in the country, broke into several sub-orders: the Soltan Alishahi; the Safi Alishahi; and the Zor-Reyasateyn. The expansion of the *Khâneqâhs* during this time must also be explained by the internal schisms and newly formed branches of existing orders. Van des Bos writes, 'nationalism, nationalistic modernisation and the dismantling of traditional power bases that occurred in their name, were paralleled by Sufi struggles for spiritual authority. Sufi Masters and disciples took issue with self-explanatory, charismatic rule. What motivated them was never democracy, but rational – that is: reasoned – rule. What they asked for, if often implicitly, was relevance to the nation-state'.[27]

Between 1941 and 1979, the involvement of influential political and social figures of the Persian upper classes, in certain Sufi circles, continued to give credence to the Sufi tradition. This affiliation, however, must be explained in relationship to the political situation. One branch of the Nimatullahi, the Safi Alishahis, was popular for the Westernising tendencies of the politicised upper classes and was organised into a 'pseudo-Masonic' lodge.[28] Fischer presents two different uses of the Sufi idiom and its appeal to upper-class and Westernised Iranians. The first approach was developed by a small group of Persian and American intellectuals in Tehran in the 1970s, who wished to examine the socio-linguistic structuring of Persian behaviour and attitudes. This exercise explored the various ways in which the images of a 'Sufi' and 'dervish' are used in social interaction amongst Iranians. According to this group, known as the Culture and Personality Circle, the concept of a '*Dervish/ luti*' or 'Sufi' is defined as one who can always be pure, open and honest, and provides positive images within a corrupt world that forces one to lie and take nothing at face value.[29] Fischer also presents Seyyed Hussein Nasr's use of the Sufi idiom.[30] Nasr considered Sufism as the intellectual core of Islam and reserved for the intellectual elite. He was closely associated with the Pahlavi government and was head of Farah Diba's Office in the months leading up to the revolution.

Sufism and the Islamic Republic

After the revolution, the Islamic authorities invited the Iranian Sufi Orders to pledge their allegiance to Khomeini to ensure that there was no political or religious ambiguity between the government and their newly constructed brand of Islam, and the beliefs and practices of the various Sufi Orders. Many Sufi Orders declined the invitation extended by Khomeini and went into exile in order to preserve their freedom of expression. The headquarters of three Iranian Sufi Orders left Iran for Western countries at this time: Maktab Tariqat Oveyssi Shahmaghsoudi, Nimatullahi,[31] and the Zahabiya.[32]

After the revolution the situation for Sufi Orders depended a great deal on their reputations prior to the revolution. According to Van den Bos, the Safi Alishahis, who were known for their ties to the Pahlavi dynasty and freemasonry, had their lodge taken over by revolutionary guards and were closely monitored during the first years following the revolution. There are no documented records of Sufis being killed for their faith. In light of the Order's stained reputation, the Board of Trustees of the Safi Alishahi order, the mouthpiece for a number of internal rival groups, strategically reformulated its external reputation through organising a number of traditional religious ceremonies.[33] The Soltan Alishahi order was also monitored by the Iranian government. Their practices, which are more firmly rooted in Islamic law, made it easier for them to survive after the establishment of the Islamic Republic.[34] After Khomeini's death Sufi Orders in Iran continued to accommodate themselves externally to the socio-political and religious requirements of the state. This was further complicated by the Iranian government, which began to incorporate mystical notions, many of which were used and defined by Khomeini in his writings, into its political discourses.[35] Van den Bos's research demonstrates the increasing presence of Sufism in the public sphere, particularly when Khatami became president. He points out the various ways the language of Sufism is being used by the state, on the one hand, and by those who wish to steer clear of state religiosity, on the other.

I spoke to several Iranians who associated themselves with the different sections of the Nimatullahi Sufi Orders in Tehran, Kerman and Mahan (which is where Shah Nimatullah Wali is buried) during the summer of 1999. At the centre in Mahan, the Sufi music of Davoud Azad was playing over the loudspeaker – which is a small indicator of the more lenient setting for Sufism in Iran. Many said that they have continued their Sufi practices since the revolution, although that they have been sporadically repressed by the regime. Throughout the years they have received many warnings from the government to stop their activities. On some occasions the interior of their homes have been destroyed, and members have been arrested and tortured. They spoke openly about their distaste for Islamic politics and the current Iranian government. Safi-Ali-Shah's shrine in Tehran is recognised by the government as a historical site. Although they are sometimes monitored, men and women (sitting in separate rooms) meet together twice a week and perform the *zekr*. They invited me to attend a Sunday meeting. When I arrived, however, there were no women present and the Sheikh informed me the *zekr* was cancelled and that I had to leave the premises. Earlier that day they had received a warning from officials that they were mixing too closely with women, and that their hair and moustaches were growing too long.

Sufism in the West

The Oveyssi Shahmaghsoudi and the Nimatullahi, along with other Sufi Orders such as the Naqshbandi and the Shadhili, have enjoyed a growing popularity in Western countries among expatriates, some Muslims born and raised in the West, and Western converts. The growing market for Sufi-styled poetry, music and dance performances also indicates the increasing interest among broader Western audiences. This has led some writers to believe that the charismatic, esoteric nature of Sufism is the expression of Islam which will blur the boundaries between East and West. According to Ahmed: 'In its abjuration of materialism, Sufism provides a balance to the dominant values of Western civilisation … especially in the Sufistic message of *sohl-e kol* [total peace], Islam has a positive message of peace and brotherhood to preach.'[36] Other writers label the Sufism encountered in the West as 'pseudo-Sufism.'[37] For instance, Elwell-Sutton writes: 'Rejected in the East, and becoming aware of the mental and spiritual ferment in the West, with its uncritical search for some new teaching no matter where it is to be found, certain self styled Sufis have tried to emulate the fleeting success of the Yogis and the Zen Buddhists by setting up propaganda centres in Europe and America.'[38] Nasr, who believes that Sufism contains great value for both the West and the Islamic world, holds reservations that Sufism will be 'watered-down' in the West. He identified three styles of writings on Sufism in the West today: (1) scholarship or translations, some good and some bad, done by Orientalists;[39] (2) works by practitioners who claim an association with a current Sufi movement, all of which Nasr calls 'pseudo-spirituality inundating the West'; (3) 'authentic expositions' and 'genuine teachings'.[40]

This chapter continues to argue that internal and external dynamics and expressions of various Sufi Orders, whether in the East or the West, take on many forms and carry out a wide variety of practices. It is interesting to explore why Sufism gains and loses steam; and how it is practised and experienced across time and place. The next sections will examine two Iranian Sufi Orders, the Nimatullahi Order and the Shahmaghsoudi Order, and the ways in which they provide a contemplative framework for some middle- and upper-class Iranians in London. The Shahmaghsoudi and Nimatullahi Sufi Orders both accept that in order to undertake *tariqat* [spiritual path], one must first follow the Islamic law [*shari'a*]. At the end of *tariqat*, one arrives at the threshold of the 'The Ultimate Reality' [*haqiqat*]. Although both religious discourses share many concepts and ideas, their interpretations and practices produce organisations which vary enormously in character. It is important to note that I was able to gather much more material from the Oveyssi Shah-maghsoudi Order because, unlike the Nimatullahi Order, it has no formal initiation ceremony.

The Nimatullahi Order

The Nimatullahi Order has taken on many forms since it was founded by Shah Nimatullah in the fourteenth century. As Baldick points out, 'they accepted Shiism after the Safavid conquest; constituted the main Iranian brotherhood after the decline of the Safavid Sufis; in the seventeenth century their leaders lived in India; and were assigned to specific wards of Iranian cities, where they clashed with libertine dervishes'.[41] During the end of the seventeenth and the beginning of the eighteenth century the Order was reintroduced to Iran and was popularised by a charismatic leader named Ma'sum Ali Shah Dakkani (d.1799/1800). It was confronted, however, by the Shia ulema who were enforcing the Usuli doctrine which gave them supreme authority in all religious affairs.[42] Ma'sum Ali Shah and several of his followers were killed in 1797 by a *mujtahed* named Ali Behbahani, who strongly opposed Sufis. After Behbahani's death in 1801 the friction between the ulema and the Nimatullahi began to subside. The internal organisation of the Order and increasing local popularity brought the local rulers and the religious jurists to seek alliances with it. The Order continued to be persecuted, however, when the state felt threatened by its increasing prominence.

This led to the opportunity for the Nimatullahis to become established as a fixture of religious life in Iran during the nineteenth century. Good relations between the Qajar monarchs and the Nimatullahis developed, and Mohammad Shah himself became an initiate of the Order.[43] Van den Bos provides two configurations to explain the reorganisation of the Order during the Qajar period. First, the absence of centralised rule in the first half of the nineteenth century allowed space for the Order to compete with local rulers and religious jurists for power. Second, the rulers, in order to protect the reunified state during the second half of the nineteenth century, restricted and sidetracked the ulema whilst building political relationships with the Nimatullahi Order. Van den Bos writes, 'Nineteenth century Iran did not, therefore, see the disappearance of "traditional" Sufis through the ascent of jurist-led, "modern" religiosity, but, instead, Sufism's socio-political renaissance.'[44]

The expansion of the Nimatullahi Order was accompanied by many schisms and disagreements in regards to the succession of the Master. As discussed earlier, the fragmentation of the order, and the severing of its political ties to the late Qajar monarchy, must be considered in relation to the experiences surrounding the period of constitutional revolution and the emergence of Reza Shah's regime.[45] What is significant about such splits is that they established various influential organisations within Iranian society. Three orders, namely Safi Alishahi, Soltan Alishahi and the Zor-Reyasateyn, claimed to represent the Nimatullahi Order. It is important to note that each of the Sufi

Orders, and the relationship between master and disciple, have been reworked in the context of the nation-state. For example, a group from the Safi Alishahi Order founded the Society of Brotherhood [*anjuman-e ukhuwwat*], which became associated with Freemasonry networks. Its distinguished members reworked the organisation of the secret society along the same lines as an elected, hierarchical, freemason lodge. They were influential and involved in matters of the state.[46] One of the Sufis in Kermanshah produced a modernist magazine that targeted the Iranian nation as the readers, in addition to fellow-initiated Sufis. According to Nurbakhsh, they were largely responsible for broadening the influence of Sufism in the Persian upper classes.[47]

The Zor-Reyasateyn Nimatullahi Order is headed by Dr Javad Nurbakhsh, who became its *qotb* in 1953. He was a practising psychiatrist and a professor at Tehran University. He is the author of over ninety publications in Persian that have been printed at their own publishing house, *Khâneqâh*-e Nimatullahi Publications. He has established over one hundred Sufi chapters or *Khâneqâhs* throughout Iran.[48] According to Bozworth et al. 'he managed to recruit many members of Tehran high society at a time when the profession of a certain type of Sufism was becoming fashionable'.[49] Dr Nurbakhsh developed the first *Khâneqâh* in the United States in 1975 in order to cater to the Americans who became interested in the Order whilst living in Iran. Presumably he was also taking advantage of the increasing interest in Eastern spirituality in America and Western Europe.

Dr Nurbakhsh left Iran because of the Iranian revolution and the religious intolerance of the Iranian government. He lived in Los Angeles until 1983 and then moved to Britain. He currently lives in Banbury, a village outside Oxford, where he administers to a following of Iranian expatriates and Western converts from many cities in North America, Western Europe, Australia and Africa.[50] The Nimatullahi centres are connected via the Internet and share a common Web page, which consists of the teachings of Shah Nimatullahi, the spiritual principles and history of the Nimatullahi Order.

The Spiritual Path

According to the Master, in order for a *Salik* to undertake the *tariqat* [spiritual path] one must first follow the *shari'a* [the observance of Islamic Law]. One must feel spiritual need, have the desire for perfection [*faqr*], and maintain a continuous remembrance of God [*zekr*]. This is symbolised by the cloak of the dervish [*kherqeh*] which, 'is sewn with the needle of devotion and the thread of the selfless remembrance of God. He or she who wishes to be honoured by this cloak of poverty must, with devotion, become surrendered to a spiritual guide … this includes unquestioned obedience to one's spiritual guide'.[51] It is necessary for the master, who can be addressed in many ways,[52] to guide the Salik on the spiritual path towards 'eternal life through God' (*baqa bi'llah*). Dr Nurbakhsh states: 'There are many hazards, doubts, and mistakes made on this journey, so it needs to be made with the help of a master. One can only be liberated from the deceptions of the self by the grace of a perfect guide, who is truly a place of refuge'.[53] To be initiated into the 'World of Spiritual Poverty' [*faqr*], one must firstly observe certain rules and manners [*adab*] and ceremonies which are said to have been handed down by the Sheikhs. The rules and manners of initiation include the following acts of ablution or *ghosle*:[54]

1. *Tobeh*: repentance.
2. Islam: submission – all students, Muslim and non-Muslim, must surrender to Islam.
3. *Faqr*: initiation into spiritual poverty – one must be pure outwardly and inwardly.
4. *Ziyâaet*: pilgrimage.
5. *Qazâ-ye hajat*: fulfilment.

The acts of ablution are adhered to throughout the process of initiation into the Nimatullahi's Order. The preparations also include the gathering of five symbols of spiritual poverty.[55]

1. *Shalvâr*: the white cloth – indicates that the seeker surrenders oneself fully to God, one considers the Master's orders as God's orders and obeys.
2. *Joz*: whole nutmeg – represents the traveller's head, symbolises the consent to keep secrets between the Master and seeker.
3. *Angoshtar*: the ring is given to the Master upon entering the world of Spiritual Poverty. Signifies the band worn by slaves and one's devotion solely to God.
4. *Sekkeh*: coin – to represent material detachment from the material world.
5. *Nabât*: rock candy – the second birth of the seeker entering the spiritual world.

The initiated are also expected to observe five commitments.[56]

1. Obedience to the Holy Shari'at of Mohammad, the Seal of the Prophets.
2. Kindness towards God's creatures.
3. Preservation of the Secrets of the Path.
4. Service on the Path.
5. *Deeg-jush*: 'Upon entering the world of Spiritual Poverty, the Sufi declares inwardly, "I have come in order to sacrifice myself for the Friend". To demonstrate this, just as Abraham by God's command sacrificed a sheep instead of Ishmael, the Sufi should prepare a special meal made from a sheep in accordance with the *adab* and the traditions of Spiritual Poverty and distribute it among the dervishes'.[57]

Zekr *[Remembrance of God]*

The initiated dervishes are then permitted to take part in *zekr*. Through the inculcation of *zekr* the Salik is to learn how to be in continual remembrance of God in order to become liberated from selfish and egotistical qualities. According to Nurbakhsh: 'While the distractions of the senses can be over-come through observances of the shari'a, the distractions of the self [*nafs*] which darken and agitate the heart can be averted only by the devoted prac-tice of *zekr* – a practice based upon the negation of the thought of everything but God.'[58] It is required that the acts of ablutions and initiation, and the com-mitments listed above are observed by the Salik before performing the *zekr*. The Nimatullahi's literature also describes the correct positioning for kneel-ing, and for the hands to emphasise the negation of the Sufi sense of nothingness.[59] They must not lean against anything while sitting, must refrain from smoking, they should not speak with each other, and each Sufi should be seated according to his experience on the Path. *Zekr* is often used for *Samâ*, which is the musical and ecstatic aspect of Sufism. *Zekr* or poetry is usu-ally listened to during the gathering.

The Rules and Manners of a Nimatullahi Khâneqâh

The rules and manners of the *Khâneqâh* are listed in the text, *In the Tavern of Ruin: Seven Essays on Sufism*, which was written in Persian by Dr Nurbakhsh and translated into English.[60] A *Khâneqâh* is defined as, 'the private quarters and gathering-place of the Sufis. It is a place where those of spiritual states can assemble, the school of their inner journey toward Perfection'.[61] The text dis-cusses both the secular and spiritual advantages in going to the *Khâneqâh*, followed by descriptions of the various responsibilities in the *Khâneqâh* and their functions.[62] Titles are given to those who possess a deep understanding of Sufism and have experienced steps of the Path; the Sheikhs, the Counsellor [*pir-e dalil*], the Tea-master, the Dervishes of Service and the Stewards.[63] Also listed are the responsibilities that each Sufi has to the *Khâneqâh*. For example, a dervish should be neat in appearance and in a purified state when entering the *Khâneqâh*; if at all possible he should never come to the *Khâneqâh* empty handed; he should completely set aside all thoughts of the world; he should help preserve the welfare, prosperity and upkeep of its facilities; whenever possible, he should make a contribution to the treasury of the *Khâneqâh*; a Sufi must be present in the *Khâneqâh* on Sunday and Thursday nights. No dervish is permitted to be absent from the *Khâneqâh* without a reasonable excuse (pri-vate, travel or sickness). However, even if a dervish is excused from attending on a particular Thursday night, he must still be present in the *Khâneqâh* for at least a short period of time. When a Sufi who is fasting enters the *Khâneqâh*, he should inform the Pir-e dalil or Dudeh-dâr of his condition before sunset. It also states that the Sufi should concern himself with nothing but the remem-brance of God in the heart; the Sufi must neither speak, see, nor hear (that is to say, must not manifest the existence of his 'self') without the permission and order of the sheikh or the Pir-e dalil; the Sufi must unhesitatingly accept any food that is given, etc.[64] The duties of the Sufis to the Sheikh, the Counsellor or Pir-e dalil, the Tea-master or Dudeh-dâr, and to his fellow dervishes are then outlined in the text.

The Nimatullahi *Khâneqâh* in London

The gatherings are held every Thursday and Sunday, in a property owned by the Order, in the Notting Hill Gate area of London. When one enters the London chapter of the Nimatullahi Order one finds its members, both men and women, wearing casual clothes, sitting on Persian carpets and cushions, drinking tea, chatting and some smoking. There are usually around thirty to forty dervishes present at each gathering, approximately fifteen are non-Iranian. The members touch the ground and kiss their hand when walking through the doorway and are expected to take their shoes off. Those who are initiated then go to the upstairs of the *Khâneqâh* to listen to a lecture read in both Persian and English, and to perform the *zekr*. Due to the Nimatullahi initiation requirements, a researcher is not permitted to be present during the performance of the *zekr* and/or *samâ*. Those who do not wish to perform the *zekr* or those who are not initiated can, however, hear the music and lecture through loudspeakers. During my visits to the Order the dervishes were very welcoming, and happy to answer my questions and qualify my observations. The *zekr* is followed by tea and occasionally a meal, and conversations among the Saliks.

The Sufis

The members of the Nimatullahi Order consist of Iranian expatriates and Western converts who are educated, and mainly middle- and upper-class professionals. Many oppose the Islamic Republic. New initiates are usually introduced to the Order either through friends or by reading the Order's monthly magazine entitled *Sufi*. After visiting the *Khâneqâh* three or four times, those interested in pursuing the spiritual path are asked to bring in the five symbolic items (white sheet, whole nutmeg, ring, coin, and rock candy) for the initiation ritual. Once initiated the Nimatullahi Order is an organisational base for like-minded Iranians living in London. It provides a social and ethnic base for Iranians who do not wish to be dictated by rules of mainstream religion, but want a contemplative framework for their lives in London.

It should not be assumed that the written design of the Order is being enforced strictly by the Order and practised by the Sufis. I was repeatedly told that the different stages of the spiritual path are cognised and experienced differently by each Sufi. They stressed how each Sufi has a different kind of relationship and orientation to the Master, the Sheikhs and the programmes offered at the *Khâneqâh*. The varied adherence to the religious discourse of the Nimatullahi Order by the initiates can be explored by simplifying them into two categories. Firstly, 'regular' Sufis. These Iranians, who make up the majority of the Order, identify with the Nimatullahi Order, acknowledge the need to be guided by the Master on their pursuit to become a better person, and enjoy maintaining a connection with an Iranian organisation. For a regular Sufi the Nimatullahi Order is often decentred, being one of many social or professional organisations in which he or she is involved. Secondly, the 'devout' Sufi. This category represents those who place the Nimatullahi Order as central to their life. The events in a devout Sufi's life, such as marriage, travelling plans and career moves would be discussed with, or in some cases arranged by, the Nimatullahi Order. It is important to note that these categories are very loosely defined. One Sufi, for example, may become more or less devout over time. I was often told by 'regular' Sufis that although they don't regularly go to the *Khâneqâh* and adhere to the written rules, they consider themselves to be guided by the Master's strength and progressing through the different stages of the Sufi path.

The observance of the *shari'a*, or the duties and obligations, of Islam, are often reinterpreted or surpassed by Nimatullahi Order. Similarly, Fischer observes: 'For the ulema the law (Shari 'a) is a sine qua non; for the dervish or Sufi the law is a mere foundation to be transcended.'[65] For instance, the Muslim's duty to travel to Mecca [*hâj*], has been divided into two different kinds of pilgrimages by Dr Nurbakhsh: the ordinary pilgrimage of mainstream Islam and the elect pilgrimage of the purified Sufis. It is not necessary for a Sufi in the category of the elect to physically travel to Ka'ba. According to Dr Nurbakhsh: 'The ordinary pilgrimage requires physical maturity, mental stability, outward freedom and financial ability, while the fundamental conditions of the elect pilgrimage are spiritual attainment, freedom from the prison of the *nafs*, patience, the zeal of love and the capacity to see the beloved.'[66]

Another duty that the Sufis are expected to adhere to is the tradition of Ramadan, the annual fast during daylight hours lasting throughout the ninth month of the Muslim year. When I asked a 28-year-old man if he was currently fasting for Ramadan, he answered: 'I didn't even know that it was Ramadan. I am not concerned with Islamic rules ... I discipline myself through meditation. Ramadan hasn't been mentioned at the *Khâneqâh* either ... I'm not sure, but out of respect I doubt they would serve a meal.' A 'devout Sufi', under the master's supervision may fast while travelling on his or her spiritual path, but the fast is not necessary during the month of Ramadan. I also spoke to Saliks who regularly drink alcohol, which is a taboo in Islamic law. A woman in her forties stated: 'I am sure that there are many Nimatullahi Sufis who don't drink [alcohol] and eat pork, but I'm sure it has more to do with habit than believing it is wrong. The Order is lax regarding the superficial rules of Islam. People get so caught up in rules they lose sight to what is important'.

In addition to the *Shari'a*, the order's internal rules and guidelines are also not emphasised in practice. For example, the required attendance every Sunday and Thursday nights ('Even if a dervish is excused from attending on a particular Thursday night, he must still be present in the *Khâneqâh* for at least a short amount of time')[67] is not always observed. I was told that the more devout Sufis attend regularly at least one gathering a week. I also asked informants whether or not they perform the required ablution before entering the *Khâneqâh*. Many said that they make an effort to be clean and wear nice clothes, but they often arrive at the *Khâneqâh* straight from work and are not ritually cleansed. According to a 60-year-old woman, who occasionally attends the gatherings: 'As long as I am clean and my mind is clear, I am able to pray.'

The relationship between the Sufi and Islam is also an area that is unclear. The Nimatullahi Order states: 'The term 'Sufism' has meaning only in the context of Islam. That is to say, outside Islam, Sufism does not exist – for it is the fruit of the tree of Islam. Since a Sufi must be a Muslim, whoever claims to be a Sufi without being a Muslim, make a false claim.'[68] Yet I was often told by the Sufis that it is not necessary to become a Muslim, nor is it required to give up one's preceding faith in order to be initiated into the Order. One stated: 'I don't think of myself as a practising Muslim. The Nimatullahi Order welcomes people from all religious backgrounds. There are dervishes who are Christian and wear the crucifix to the gatherings. Thinking about different religious categories is irrelevant in a Sufi's path toward the "Truth"'. I asked a devout Sufi, who is a woman from a Catholic background, if she considered herself a Muslim. She hesitated and said that she accepts the two testimonies of Islam ('There is no god but God' and 'I testify that Mohammad is His Prophet'), but she doesn't think of herself as Muslim. What she likes about the Nimatullahi Order is that it is not limited to the teachings of one religion.

The rules surrounding the *zekr*, which were highlighted earlier, may serve as a guide for some dervishes, but are not strictly enforced by the Order. I was told that when the Sufis go upstairs for the *zekr*, they seat themselves in a darkened room and usually sit leaning against the walls. My contact said that he is not aware of any special seating arrangements and he doubts that they are facing Mecca. They listen to a lecture or poem by the Master or a past Sufi Master, followed by *zekr* with music lasting approximately thirty minutes. I was told that the *zekr* is a private link between the Sufi, the Master and ultimately God, and, therefore, it is difficult to be encased with uniform rules. Each of the Saliks, who are on different stages of the Spiritual Path, will 'forget themselves' and behave in different ways. For instance, one Sufi may sit properly (to emphasis the negation of the Sufi sense of nothingness) with his or her eyes shut, another may lean against the wall, another may clap their hands to the rhythmic beat, while another may become more ecstatic.

Social Organisation

The above account has touched on the interpretations of the external forms of Islamic practices such as fasting, prayers, pilgrimages, special events in the Islamic calendar and the lax attitudes towards the Nimatullahi Order's rules set out in various texts. The advancement on the Spiritual Path of Sufism does not depend upon adherence to rules, but on knowing God through love and remembrance and through the expression of mysticism in history, literature, poetry, music and philosophy. The Nimatullahi Order also encourages the dervishes to use the *Khâneqâh* as a social base. For instance, when I asked the Sheikh if talking among the dervishes was allowed in the *Khâneqâh*, he replied by saying that not only is gossiping allowed but it is an important element of a healthy community.

A devout Sufi tends to maintain a personal relationship with the Master and is actively involved with the happenings at the *Khâneqâh*. A devout Sufi would, for example, discuss personal, professional and spiritual events and decisions with other dervishes at the *Khâneqâh*. According to a devout Sufi, she was given the Master's blessing when she discussed her plans to marry a man outside the Order. The marriage was not successful and ended in a divorce. Some time later the Master arranged for her to marry a dervish in the Order, and the marriage ceremony was performed by the Master at his home in Banbury. Several dervishes have told me that the Master is very successful in arranging marriages. Other Sufis have described themselves as 'not as involved' or 'not as close to the Master'. They do not plan to have their marriage arranged by the Master or to be married in Banbury. Many 'regular' Sufis would also be reluctant to reveal their personal problems at the *Khâneqâh*. Instead they use it as a social base to discuss books and poetry, upcoming concerts and lectures, news in Iran, celebrate Iranian holidays, speak Persian and to seek answers to metaphysical and philosophical questions.

The Nimatullahi's uses of the media are also a part of the Order's greater design to reinforce its aims and objectives. For instance, a stylish glossy-covered magazine entitled *Sufi* is published quarterly (in both Persian and English) and is circulated by the Nimatullahi Order. Each issue contains material falling under the following headings: Discourse; Articles; Narratives; Poetry; Book reviews; and the Grapevine. A space is reserved for Dr Nurbakhsh to discuss various aspects of the Nimatullahi's religious discourse, including articles with such titles as, 'One Who Knows One's Self Knows One's Lord', 'A Selfless Master', 'The Family of Sufis', and 'Devotion'. The other articles are researched and written by academics and artists on a range of topics concerned with aspects of literature, psychology, philosophy, history and poetry. The first couple of pages of the magazine lists exhibitions, performances, new books and conferences currently being held in major cities throughout the world. For example, in the Autumn 2002 issue, a description of a number of exhibitions, concerts and books were highlighted: Silk Road Photographs by Kenro Izu; The Written Image: Japanese Calligraphy and Painting; The Legacy of Genghis Khan: Courtly Art and Culture in Western Asia, 1256–1453; Masters of Persian Music – Mohammad Reza Shajarian, Hussein Alizadeh, Kayhan Kalho and Homayoun Shajarian; The Voice of Unity Sufi Musical Traditions of Iran – Davoud Azad; Masters of Indian Music: Ali Akbar Khan with Zakir Hussein. The magazine also features a section entitled 'Cyberspace' where various religious web site pages are listed and discussed. For instance, the Spring 1998 listed the following: Julian of Norwich (http://www.luminarium.org/medlit/julianbio.htm) a page which focuses on the fourteenth-century English mystic who saw several visions of

Jesus and the Virgin Mary. The web page, The Kabbala (http://marlowe.win-sey.com), containing discussions on Jewish mysticism, and, the Mary Page (http://www.udayton.edu/mary).

The Nimatullahi's web site, which can be accessed in French, English, Persian, German, Italian, Russian, Swedish and Spanish, is designed to provide both general and introductory information regarding Sufism and the Nimatullahi Order, and up-to-date information regarding new publications and events for its initiates. It summarises, for example, the life history and teachings of Shah Nimatullah, the spiritual principles of the Order, the history of the present master, and lists the addresses of the Nimatullahi Sufi Orders in Western Europe, North America, Australia and Africa. It also discusses various aspects of the Spiritual Path, with headings such as 'Asceticism and Abstinence in Sufism', 'How is it possible to realize Perfection?', 'Purification and Stages' and '*Samâ*'. The web site provides a space that presents the sacred heritage of the Nimatullahi Order and reinforces the teachings of the *Khâneqâh*'s, while linking the twenty-one *Khâneqâhs* around the world.

The examination of the formation and continuity of the Nimatullahi Sufi organisation and its discourse set out to demonstrate the way in which it has been subject to numerous transformations in relation to particular conditions. In London, the Nimatullahi Order has provided some Iranians with a local social and ethnic base. It has also created a real and imagined connection with other Nimatullahi Sufi centres and initiates around the world. The religious practice of the Nimatullahi Order, which is varied in levels of adherence, tends to be meditative and ecstatic, often transcending the external forms of Islamic laws of *shari'a*.

The Oveyssi Spiritual Tradition

The Maktab Tariqat Oveyssi Shahmaghsoudi [Islamic School of Sufism] developed in Iran at the beginning of the twentieth century. Before discussing the contemporary modes of its discourse and the specific characteristics of this Order, it is necessary to highlight briefly the history of the Oveyssi tradition and point out the elements that the Maktab Tariqat Oveyssi Shahmaghsoudi has drawn upon. The word 'Oveyssi' refers to a Muslim mystic who looks for instruction from the spirit of the dead or physically absent person. Traditionally an Oveyssi is not initiated in an organised brotherhood with a human master.[69] It is derived from a legendary figure, Oveys Gharani, who is said to have lived in Yemen at the time of the Holy Prophet. Oveys Gharani, it is claimed, never physically met the Prophet but received the Prophet's teachings and communicated spiritually. There are a few references to Oveys Gharani and the Oveyssi spiritual tradition in Islamic literature. Baldick traced the instances in which the names 'Oveys' and 'Oveyssi' have appeared, and found the earliest accounts compiled by Ibn Sa'd (d. A.D. 845) from southern Iraq, and Ibn Hanbal (d. A.D. 855).[70] Other sources referring to the Oveyssi tradition are found mostly in Sufi biographies, which consist of varying anecdotes. Many refer to reaching a spiritual state (Baldick refers to this state as a 'method of telepathy') in order to seek guidance from Mohammad, the hidden Twelfth Imam of Shiism, and/or the spirits of the dead and hidden 'friends of God'. Having no need for a human elder or Master is also a theme in the biographies.

It is not necessary to outline the full accounts of the Sufi biographies for the purposes of this chapter, but it is important to note that these anecdotes demonstrate the multiple ways Sufi practices are shaped, perceived and expressed across time and place. For example, Baldick refers to a leading eleventh-century Oveys, who claimed to be a Sufi, and called upon the spirit of a ninth-century mystic for guidance. The attitudes towards this Sufi using the Oveyssi method of communication changed with the development of Sufi lodges which, from the eleventh century, became institutionalised. Baldick writes:

> Sufi Masters would condemn the practice of going to a tomb and shaving one's head there in order to become a disciple of the elder in the grave. They would insist on the necessity of a real hand clasp with a living elder...The brotherhoods have often been extremely powerful international organisations, well connected to Muslim rulers. Religious foundations have paid for the continuity of instruction at lodges and shrines, obviously putting Oveyssis at a disadvantage.[71]

Whereas in this situation the institutionalisation of the Sufi lodge marginalised the Oveyssi tradition, in other situations Oveyssis have taken advantage of their detached positions by avoiding the demands of a Sufi Master that may limit one's activities.

Even though initiation into a Sufi organisation is not a characteristic of the Oveyssi tradition there are accounts of Sufi Orders that have absorbed the Oveyssi method of telepathy into their brotherhood practices.[72] Baldick refers to an Oveyssi movement active in Central Asia during the sixteenth century. He writes: 'To turn this into a brotherhood of living people in day-to-day contact with one another might well seem contradictory, but during the rapid expansion of Islam in the sixteenth century in East Turkestan it made some sense. There was no particularly distinguished local Islamic past to which people could relate, apart from some long-dead royal martyrs.'[73] In an anonymous biography of the first master of this Oveyssi brotherhood, there is a story about how the ruler Abd'al-Rashid (reigned 1533–60) called upon the advice of the brotherhood's master, Mohammad Sharif.[74]

> Abd' al Rashid, wanting revenge, asked Mohammad Sharif whether the Kirghiz would be aware of his imminent counter-attack. The Sufi Elder replied that he would have to consult the 'friends', the 'good spirits'. They went together to the shrine of Yusuf Qadir Khan [reigned 1024–32] one of the country's greatest rulers. There they saw the prophet Khidr, Mohammad's friend Bilal, Uways, the famous preacher Hasan of Basra [d. 910], Satuq, and the great mystic Junayd of Baghdad, as well as the founder of the Kubrawi brotherhood, Kubra [d. 1221] of Khwarazm in what is now ex-Soviet Turkmenistan, and the founder of the Hamadani brotherhood, 'Ali of Hamadan in Western Iran [d.1385]. These gave their permission for the attack, and said that they would come along.[75]

The stories of the legendary Islamic figures were 'conveniently integrated into an imaginary history of the Uwaysi brotherhood and compiled by a certain Ahmad Uzgani'.[76] The newly constructed brotherhood, however, did not last long due to the rise of the local Naqshbandi Sufis. Interestingly the 'friends' or 'good spirits' referred to in the passage above have also been made significant in the Oveyssi Shahmaghsoudi Order and many are listed in the pedigree of Masters going back to Mohammad.

Maktab Tariqat Oveyssi Shahmaghsoudi [Islamic School of Sufism]

In the early part of this century a famous Oveyssi named Mir Qutb al-Din Mohammad 'Angha' attracted a circle of followers, who gradually developed into a regular *tariqat* named Maktab Tariqat Oveyssi Shahmaghsoudi [Islamic School of Sufism].[77] According to Gramlich, the community of dervishes in Tehran gathered at Mohammad Angha's home close to the Sipahselar Mosque. It is noted that members of the imperial court attended its meeting during Mohammad Reza Shah reign.[78] Gramlich also points out that Mohammad Angha's followers considered him as their master, although he never identified himself as the master of the Oveyssi community. Angha accepted the necessity of the role of the master but stressed that the relationship between the master and the student should be of an inner and emotional nature. This interpretation suggests that Man is essentially spiritual and invisible, and it is therefore not necessary for an Oveyssi to follow only deceased spiritual Masters, as the traditional teaching insists.[79]

The rise of the reformed Oveyssi movement was a reaction to the established brotherhoods and their Masters in Iran. It opposed the traditions normally practised by Sufi Orders, such as initiation ceremonies. According to Baldick: 'It has been characterised by attempts to improve Sufism by integrating modern Western findings in the natural sciences.'[80] Before discussing the way in which the Oveyssi movement combined its teachings with modern science and technology, I will show how the Order has drawn from the Oveyssi tradition of spirituality and was constructed into a regular Sufi Order.

The Maktab Tariqat Oveyssi Shahmaghsoudi's historical accounts begin with the legendary life of Oveys Gharani, which is based on the collection of Sufi biographies, entitled *Memorial of the Friends [Tadkhira al-awliya]* written by Sheikh Farideddin 'Attar (d. 1221). This version of Gharani's life says that he was born in Yemen, and was a very thin man of medium height. He was a camel herdsman who spent his life praying and caring for his blind mother. His duties to his mother meant that he could never visit the Prophet Mohammad; but he had accepted Mohammad's religion without ever seeing him. Mohammad is said to have faced Yemen at times, and to have said: 'A blessing blows in from Yemen.' People would ask him: 'Who lives in Yemen?' and the Prophet would reply, 'A man by the name of Oveys Gharani'. Just before his death, the Prophet called for Imam Ali and Omar (second Caliph), and said: 'Take my Robe to Yemen and give it to a man named Oveys. He is a man of moderate height, and is slender [*shaarani*]. There is a white mark on his side. When you see him, give him my blessing, and ask him to pray for my followers and to mediate for them, for many of my followers will be accepted by God through the mediation of this man.'[81]

Oveys Gharani, following the Prophet Mohammad and Imam Ali, is considered to be the third Master of the Oveyssi Shahmaghsoudi Sufi Order. They claim that he continued the 'chain' of authority by passing the cloak, and the method of receiving knowledge through the heart, to Hazrat Salman Farsi.[82] According to their accounts Salman Farsi, and the Masters that followed, stemmed from a group of pious individuals who met on the platform, or *suffe*, where Mohammad used to pray. These men are considered to be 'guided by the Laws of Islam, sought for the direct experience of the Divine … They were losing the limited self in His Divinity [*fanâ*], and remaining alive in that Reality'.[83] It is worth noting that Ali is described as, 'the greatest inspiration for many'. It has been narrated from the Prophet who said, 'I am the King of the believers; to the Sufis he is called *Vali*, the guide. He is the light of the way, without which the realisation of reality would be an impossible task.'[84] The Shahmaghsoudi reports that the unbroken chain of authority continues to the present master, Pir Molana Salaheddin Ali Nader Shah Angha, who was appointed as the forty-second Sufi master in 1970.

The Pirs

According to the Shahmaghsoudi's written accounts, Molana-al-Moazam Hazrat Jalaleddin Mir Abolfazl Angha (1865–1915) translated the knowledge of Sufism into scientific concepts. His son Molana-al-Moazam Mir Ghotbeddin Mohammad Angha (1887–1963) who, according to Nasr and Baldick, was an Oveys and the eventual founder of the Shahmaghsoudi Sufi Order, continued this method of integrating the knowledge of Sufism and modern science. During the period of reform in the early part of the twentieth century, the Oveyssi discourse developed in response to the 'backward' nature of Sufi brotherhoods. Its discourse aims to guide Iranians back to the 'reality' of religion, which is described as the essence of everything, including Western scientific notions. The Order's literature states: 'He [Molana-al-Moazam Mir Ghotbeddin Mohammad Angha] remarked on how Rumi described the particle as if he could have observed the conditions in the atom'. Speaking of scientists, he stated: 'But they do not know that sublime existence does not fit into the bounds of the inferior human brain, and heavenly identity cannot be weighted by a laboratory scale with electron and proton weights.'[85] He has written two books, published in Persian.

Angha's son, Molana-al-Moazam Hazrat Shah Maghsoud Sadegh Angha (1916–1980) studied law, philosophy, literature, mathematics, physics, chemistry, relativity theory, astrophysics, nuclear physics, physical chemistry and the science of Iranian alchemy.[86] He has written more than 150 books, dealing with a range of topics such as: 'Sufism as the reality of religions; Who is

an *âref*? Mental and physical well-being; Ecological harmony and the continuity of human society on this planet'.[87] Angha argued that a separation
between physics and metaphysics is unnecessary. He stated:

> I am a Moslem and a religious man, and whatever I do or have done is for indi-
> viduals all over the world, to make them acquainted with the real principles of
> *erfân*[88] and religion, and not for the unfounded traditions nor imaginary beliefs
> of one individual or group of people. This is because the smallest profit which
> an understanding between *erfân* and science can give humanity is the discovery
> of the truth of life.[89]

Molana-al-Moazam Hazrat Shah Maghsoud Sadegh Angha's oldest daughter,
Nahid Angha, is the author of several works dealing with Sufism, and is the
co-founder of the International Association of Sufism and the Sufi Women
Organization, established in 1983 and headquartered in Northern California.[90] She maintains that she was her father's first student and the first
woman allowed to teach in her father's Oveyssi tradition. In her publications
she does not acknowledge her brother who is the current Master of the
Oveyssi Shahmaghsoudi Order, and pledges her allegiance to Dr Shah Nazar
Seyed Ali Kianfar. According to the International Association of Sufism
literature, Dr Ali Kianfar is the spiritual son of Molana-al-Moazam Hazrat
Shah Maghsoud Sadegh Angha and became one of the followers who was
appointed by the Master as a teacher.[91] The associations mentioned above are
connected to Oveyssi Tariqat, which attracts mostly Americans. According to
Marcia Hermansen, they do not require the formal practice of Islam.[92]

Molana-al-Moazam Hazrat Shah Maghsoud Sadegh Angha's son, Molana
Salaheddin Ali Nader Shah Angha (b.1945) is the present Pir [Spiritual Mas-
ter] of the Oveyssi Shahmaghsoudi Sufi Order. He received the leadership of
the Order in 1970, when he was twenty-five years old. He studied and taught
mathematics and physics in the United States, and has written fifty books.
Sufi Orders in Iran were expected to follow Khomeini and the prevailing
interpretation of mainstream Shiism. Mohammad Angha, however, rejected
any domination by a leader and stated: 'it is that of the Oveyssi, for whom the
link to the master is purely spiritual and invisible'.[93] At the beginning of the
1980s the headquarters of the Order was established in San Rafael, California. It developed eighteen *Khâneqâhs* around the world and claimed to
have 400,000 members world-wide. Since 1995 over seventy more *Khâneqâhs*
have materialized, with thirty-nine located in Europe, forty-nine in the U.S.
and four in Africa and Asia.

The present Pir is often referred to by his Saliks as the link between
ancient and modern, East and West, and science and religion. In the introduction to the Pir's book, *The Fragrance of Sufism*, Nyang states:

> In a social universe where people are, in the language of William Shakespeare,
> cabined, cribbed and boxed in their little worlds of anonymity and private
> suffering, such a state of affairs has come about not because of the lack of spiri-
> tual means, but because of the absorbing and crippling nature of our
> increasingly secular world … Our author tells us that modern men and women

must develop the necessary self discipline to reach the inner resources of their being. Those who have developed these potentials in themselves are no longer slaves and servants of their material world. Rather their material world is reshaped in accordance with the spiritual demands of their lives.[94]

I have asked several Iranians in the Oveyssi Shahmaghsoudi Order in London about the pedigree of Masters going back to Mohammad. They all referred to Mohammad and Ali, and they were familiar with the legends of Oveys Gharani, and the life stories of the last four Masters. Some of my informants were familiar with Kubra (1145–1220), who is said to be the sixteenth Master of the Order. Kubra is significant to the Oveyssi Order because of his method of alchemy. According to Angha, through Kubra's method, 'eventually the mystic encounters his other self: one's heavenly "witness" [*shahid*], the elder of the invisible world, who appears in a luminous form'.[95] My contacts offered several reasons as to why they were not familiar with the other thirty-four Oveyssi Masters. The most frequent responses were: 'The Pirs are all the same … when you know one you know them all'. and, 'Hazrat-e Pir, through mental cognition, embodies the light and knowledge of all the Masters … there is no need to know the others'. I was also told about a legendary figure named *Khidr* who is significant to the Oveyssi Shahmaghsoudi Order. They described Khidr or *Khezr* as an invisible presence in the world and as the spiritual teacher who guides the Salik to union with God.

The idea of an 'absent' presence is a resonating theme which runs through many layers of Shiism. It stems from the Shias' special notion of the Imamate and the disappearance of the twelfth Imam, Al-Mahdi, and the ensuing wait and preparations for his reappearance. The organisation of the Oveyssi Shahmaghsoudi fosters this notion of an 'absent' presence. As we shall see, the Saliks are never told when the Master will be physically present at the gatherings. Although most weeks his chair sits empty, it is believed that his invisible presence guides the members through the various 'horizons of awareness' [*seyr-va-solouk*].

The Shahmaghsoudi Oveyssi Order in London

The Shahmaghsoudi Oveyssi headquarters are in San Rafael, California and Washington D.C. There are eight branches in Britain, located in London, Newcastle, Brighton, Oxford, Leeds, Cheltenham, Bolton and Manchester. Each centre promotes a number of activities, including weekly religious services; Koranic and *Hadith* studies; concentration and meditation classes; seminars for assertiveness training for women; stress management; Sufi poetry; Persian language courses; music lessons; courses on healing and sporting activities. The Order has its own research and publication centre, a museum located in Karaj, Iran, and a Memorial building designed by Hazrat Pir in honour of his father, which is located near Novato, California. The various branches are connected via sophisticated pages on the Internet, which are constantly updated using the latest technology, and can be read in nine languages: Persian, English, Arabic, Italian, French, Swedish, Spanish, Russian and German. The order has a thriving industry of manufactured goods including jewellery, t-shirts, picture frames, calendars, wall-hangings and many other goods, all of which are branded with their Sufi emblem and trademark.

The London branch of the Order was organised by several affluent Iranian families during the 1980s, and mainly consists of middle- and upper-class Iranians. The Iranian gatherings were held in one of their homes in north London until the chapter started to grow in size (at the end of the 1980s, thirty members; 1998, four hundred members; 2002, over one thousand members). The Sheikh, who is the Master's assistant, provides an English-speaking session in his house in north London every Thursday night. Around ten people, some English, some half-Iranian, sit and listen to a woman translate the Persian words of the Sheikh.[96] There are more than one thousand adherents to the teachings of the Oveyssi Shahmaghsoudi in London. I regularly attended the Friday night sessions in 1996 and 1997, and have periodically made visits since. When I started to get to know the members, I would make arrangements to meet with them outside *Khâneqâh.*

Most of the members are educated and come from the higher echelons of society. They include barristers, computer scientists, business men and women, students, engineers, teachers, physicists and restaurant owners who live mainly in central and north London. It is important to note that several men and women from the first generation have not been able to transfer their skills and qualifications to jobs in London and have experienced downward mobility. Many of those who own businesses are, in fact, educated and trained in a professional field. When I started my research many of the Sufis said they were supporters of the Shah and associated themselves with the monarchy. During the course of my research several of my informants warmed to Khatami and his reforms, and viewed him as opposition to the government. However, many have since become frustrated with the slow pace of change in Iran.

The majority of my informants were not practising Muslims or Sufis before becoming affiliated with the Order in London. The members I spoke to joined the Order through the informal agency of friends or relatives. For example, an Iranian woman heard about the Order through friends and decided she would attend, as long as her 30-year-old and 26-year-old daughters would accompany her. Once they arrived, they were surprised to find so many familiar faces.

When I was conducting the bulk of my research, the order met on Friday evenings, from 7:00 p.m. to 10:00 p.m. in a large rented church hall in Kensington. They have since bought a community centre in Highgate, north London. At the entrance of the hall there is a display of books and cassette tapes, written and produced by the current Master, his father, grandfather and other important members of the Order. I shall present the main points of one of the important publications written by the current Master, Salaheddin Ali Nader Shah Angha, entitled *The Fragrance of Sufism,* in order to convey an impression of the religious discourse and the ways in which members are encouraged to see their organisation and themselves.[97]

The Fragrance of Sufism consists of three texts: 'The Treasure on God's Path'; 'The Approaching Promise'; and 'The Secret Word'. These texts are central to the Order and are thought to relay the essence of Sufism in a manner suitable both as an introduction for beginners and as a guidebook for the more advanced student. 'The Treasure on God's Path' begins by discussing the need for some people to search for the cause and purpose of their existence, their present and future life, and ultimately their death. It is thought that these people, unlike those who are trapped in their material existence, will find the ultimate answer to these questions through the devotion and practice in the principles of *erfân*.[98] According to Pir Angha, before undertaking the principles of *erfân* it is necessary to be aware of the different levels of existence and one's relationship with the immediate environment. He categorises the states of man through four levels:

1. The mysterious inner level, which is the central point of stability of his true character and identity.
2. The development level, which is the locus for the development and interrelationship of the magnetic bodies, and for mental, sensory, and psychic powers.
3. The dependent, indigent and impressed cellular level which, in fact, is the mechanical level of man.
4. Nature, which is the locus for material manifestation and exchange – the examination and experience of man's aptitude, and the place to satisfy his needs.[99]

Angha discusses these levels of existence in relation to the contending philosophical schools of thought in modern times. He argues that the scientific advancement of empirical and theoretical sciences in the past few centuries, especially those dealing with the physical aspects of nature, demonstrates the stability of man's powers in the natural levels of existence. The conclusions of scientists, theologians, philosophers, mathematicians, naturalists, sociologists, psychologists and psychotherapists,

> are derived, and benefit from, the physical environment, their cellular level, and a minor aspect of their inner intellectual and developmental level and sensory powers. It is obvious, then, that this type of research and its resulting speculations and definitions is nothing but reasoning and deduction in words, because its practitioners do not have the access to man's central level of stability and identity.[100]

It is thought that due to the prominence of science and technology in today's world it is necessary for the Oveyssi Shahmaghsoudi School to use the language of science to demonstrate that 'truth' or 'oneness of existence' is constant. A student of Angha states:

Much of what we consider 'discovery' is a description. The stars named by astronomers have always been there. Electricity existed millions of years before Franklin put a key on a kite string in a thunderstorm. Einstein's Theory of Relativity describes what already exists. Gravity was present long before Newton described it after watching an apple fall ... nothing man has invented does not already have a basis somewhere in Nature.[101]

The Oveyssi Shahmaghsoudi School argues that the creative people in the world are not those who have rational minds and are well read in scientific knowledge. They are, instead, those who have been able to make a connection with God. They are mystics who have been able to tap into and understand the essence of 'reality'. The Oveyssi Shahmaghsoudi School wishes to serve as a medium to bridge the divide between the physical world, where man's natural powers, senses and other faculties are limited and inadequate in obtaining the 'truth', and the metaphysical world.

The Path

The remainder of Angha's text presents the guidelines needed in order to pursue the path to God. It discusses the role of the Pir, the various stages in which the Salik must be stabilised and balanced, and the codes of behaviour and self-discipline expected from the Saliks. It is important to point out that the methods developed by this Order were designed in opposition to the methods used by other Iranian Sufi Orders in the first half of the twentieth century. The reformers argued that Sufi Orders in Iran are blinded by tradition and rituals, and have been led astray from the 'reality of religion'.

This order locates itself at the heart of Islam. It claims to bypass 'religion' which is corrupted by tradition, politics and money. According to Angha: 'The Arif's method regarding cognition of truth is through self-discipline, purification, concentration and heart meditation. But only those inward discoveries which are approved and emphasised by religious laws are the true ones, otherwise he considers them as visual and auditory deviations, in other words, it is being misled by the senses.'[102]

It bases its methods on the spiritual relationship between Oveys Gharani and Mohammad, which is thought to demonstrate the possibility of a direct communication link to other spiritual beings. A student of Angha describes the communication link as follows: 'Professor Angha tells us that the human being is actually not a very material organization. It is not in the brain's biocomputer but in the electromagnetic fields and centres of our being, and in our receptive capacities that consciousness of reality lies. The electromagnetic elements and connections are those aspects of being traditionally perceived as spiritual.'[103] Many informants provided examples to describe this phenomenon: for instance, 'You know that feeling you get when someone is staring at you? Although no one touched you or spoke to you, someone can get your attention just by staring'. Another common example I came across was, 'Do you know that feeling you get when you know your friends or family have been talking about you behind your back? Although you have no evidence, you can feel their words.' The text continues with instructions to break the boundaries of time and space and reach the highest spiritual level.

The Role of the Master

Paradoxically it is thought that the Master plays a central role in guiding the Salik on their spiritual path. As mentioned earlier, this guidance, which seemingly contradicts the Oveyssi tradition of looking for instruction from the spirit of a dead or physically absent person, is justified by defining Man as merely spiritual and invisible. Angha makes it clear in 'The Treasure of God's Path' that the Salik needs to have constant guidance from the spiritual guide. He states: 'For the assurance of the heart, the Pir must be inwardly cognized in the heavens by the Salik, and his teaching shall be practised outwardly and inwardly, sincerely and faithfully ... In fact, cognition of the heavenly reality of the Pir and a burning love are both the way and the goal for the Salik.'[104]

To attain the intuitive bond with the Pir, the Salik is expected to continually forego sleep and illusions along with the obeying the following instructions.

1. *Zekr* [to remember]: remembering God at all times.
2. *Fekr* [to think, meditate]: persisting on the truth of meditation to attain the state of annihilation.
3. *Sahar* [to awaken]: awakening the soul and body through the teachings of the Pir.
4. *Jui'i* [to hunger]: anxiously eager to receive the truth, and keeping the heart and mind constantly ready for the disclosure of the secrets of the heart and revelations.
5. *Suamt* [to observe silence]: ceasing to think and talk about worthless things, purification of the heart from desires.
6. *Saum* [to fast]: fasting of body, mind and heart; refraining from involvement in exterior delusions and imagination; inwardly abstaining from desires, wishes, and duality.
7. *Khalvat* [to observe solitude]: praying in solitude, externally and internally, being free of all attachments and impurities.
8. *Khedmat* [to serve]: dissolving in the truth of the Pir and finally dissolving in the truth of Existence, God.[105]

These instructions are meant to guide the Salik along stages called *seyr-va-solouk* [The Horizons of Awareness] through which one must pass 'the state of natural strength and pleasure: Natural strength and pleasure refer to eating, drinking, sleeping, etc. The seeker must pass this stage, be content and moderate in his natural appetites, for he must separate his identity from those of animals and plants'.[106]

1. The state of self: through this stage the Salik should sever all dependence and start a quiet and solitary life. He must begin with the prayers, obey religious laws and, through repentance and endeavour, reach the point where he can step outside his illusive and imaginary world.
2. The state of heart: the word 'heart' is used here to highlight the firm level through which man is elevated from the inferior stages. The heart is the gateway to the hidden world of the truthful Salik.
3. The state of the soul: the heart is the connection between soul and self. The Salik in this state is free from earthly attachments and sentiments, and enters the realm of spirituality.
4. The state of the secret: here the Salik cognizes the truth and thenceforth everywhere he looks he sees nothing but God.
5. The state of hidden: the Salik will see and hear God only. He is dissolved (he will become lost) in God: the Salik and the sought are one. In this state there is no ignorance at all and the truth of life is revealed.
6. The state of more hidden: through this stage, where the Salik has ended the circle of eternity, he is no longer aware of annihilation. This is the stage for the Kingdom of the Supreme Being.[107]

The Saliks are expected to say their daily prayers and the Order has compiled a booklet written in both Persian and English entitled *Al-Salat: Namâz – The Manual of the Daily Prayers*. It begins with listing the components of ablution and stating the necessity of ablution prior to every prayer. It is important to add that by strategically locating itself at the heart of Islam the Order has constructed itself as a neutral and apolitical space, and has, therefore, not been dismissed by or isolated from some of the other Shia circles, including the Iranian Embassy, for being heretical.

The Sufi Gathering

Let us turn to the ritual and the methods used to execute the aims and objectives of the texts. The relationship between the Master and the Salik is meant to be one of authority, and the Friday night gatherings are designed to provide an environment for the construction of obedient wills. What struck me most about the gatherings was how silent the participants were before, during and after the session. Before the regular Friday night gathering began, attendants prepared the hall by covering the floor with Persian carpets and hanging verses from the Koran on the walls. The front of the hall was draped with white sheets which were used as a backdrop for the large portraits of the last two Pirs and for the present Pir's chair. His chair, the 'centre piece' in the hall, was a majestic purple colour marked with the Sufi emblem (a two-sided axe) and surrounded by fresh flowers. There were also several books placed on a shelf next to the Master's chair. Before each gathering, a video camera sits on a tripod focused on the Master's chair. The Saliks do not know if he is in London until they move the camera from the chair and focus on the Sheikh. Two video cameras, which mechanically move back and forth, are sometimes placed in the front of the auditorium facing the Saliks. A large-screen television is also placed at front of the room.

An increasing number of Iranians attended the gatherings during the course of my research. On average 350 Iranians (and five or so non-Iranians) arrive at the *Khâneqâh* dressed entirely in white. In complete silence they give their shoes to the attendants and sign their name and address on the attendance sheet.[108] It is at this time that the Sufis are expected to hand in any questions they have for the spiritual leaders, buy books and cassettes, and give money to the Order. I have asked several Sufis how much money they are expected to give to the Order. They said that the Sufi Order has never put a price on the Sufis' offerings. One 32-year-old male said he tries to give £100 every two or three weeks. Other informants said that the Order primarily depends on the contributions of wealthy families. Several women said that they give the Order money generated from vows or *nazrs*.

An attendant then individually seats each Sufi on the floor: women on one side of the room and men on the other. In keeping with *suamt* [to observe silence] socialising and conversation is forbidden. The attendants are responsible for keeping the *Khâneqâh* completely silent throughout the night. The silence continues after the gathering is finished, when the attendants roll up the carpets and the equipment is being disassembled. The rules prohibiting conversation made it difficult for me to get to know the Sufis and ask questions. After I had attended the gatherings regularly, many of the Sufis became familiar with my face. This made it easier for me to introduce myself after the gatherings, on the streets outside the *Khâneqâh* and at bus stops and tube stations.

During the gatherings, the Sheikh sits on the floor next to the Pir's chair facing the men's side of the room. If someone walks out of the *Khâneqâh* they are expected to walk backwards and never to turn their back to the spiritual leader or the Master. The gathering begins with either a reading from the Koran or a life history of one of the past Pirs; this is followed by a lecture given by the Sheikh. The topics of the lectures follow the events in the Islamic calendar and special occasions in the Order. The gathering is spoken entirely in Persian and interpreted through headsets for English speakers. It is important to point out that the Master is rarely present at these Sufi meetings. He lives and works in the U.S. His lectures are video-taped in California and then distributed to the *Khâneqâhs* around the world. The master is usually filmed (sitting in an identical chair to that which sits empty in London) at a *Khâneqâh* in California. The videos present, for example, the Sufis in California in a similar setting, all dressed in white and conducting the *zekr*.

The hall is darkened and the central ritual *zekr*, or the 'remembrance', of God begins. The Sufis, in a cycle of memorised chants, songs and prayers, repeat the names of Allah. The repetitious and rhythmic chants are expressed in different tones as the Sufis sit with their legs crossed and sway back and forth and clap their hands to their knees in increasing tempo, which builds up to a series of climaxes. The manner in which the Sufis sit is symbolic for 'nothingness' in that it forms an Arabic word '*La*' which means 'no' or 'not'.

I asked several informants why no music, dancing or drums are used during the *zekr*. Many said that once music and dancing are involved, *zekr* turns into selfish entertainment and is no longer a remembrance of God. As part of their training to become disciplined the Saliks are taught to stay in complete control of their bodies throughout *zekr*. The Sheikhs frown upon the women who often cry during the session. The Saliks then sit erect, on their knees with the legs folded under, and recite a creed which pledges allegiance to Mohammad, Ali, the Masters of the Order. The gathering is concluded with a glass of tea and Iranian sweets or an Iranian dinner is served, all in silence. The Sheikh is available after the gathering to answer individual questions. Those with questions are expected to sit quietly until the attendant seats them in front of the Sheikh. The Sheikhs move around the various *Khâneqâhs* around the world.

According to my informants, the Pir is in London approximately two or three times a year. I saw the Pir four times during the course of my research. Each time he gave a two-and-a-half hour lecture on science and God. I spoke to a number of people after one of the meetings who said they didn't understand a word he said – but most were very proud that their master is so intelligent. The master is strict: for example, at one event he scowled at the chanter and told him to stop singing. He would become frustrated when reading through letters written by various Saliks and hastily put them aside. On occasion he would rhetorically challenge individuals and make them feel inadequate. After the meetings I was told by various Saliks how they felt terrible for disappointing the master. They said that the master knew that they had been selfish and too caught up in their daily routines. They often compared themselves negatively to other Shahmaghsoudi *Khâneqâhs* around the world that are known to be very disciplined and advanced.

The various uses of the media, including the video-taped lectures of the master and having a camera focus on an empty chair, along with books and cassettes sold after each gathering, are all designed to transmit the knowledge and authority of the master. They are the media used to reach and construct an obedient Sufi. The cameras symbolise the absent presence of the master. I asked several Sufis why the cameras occasionally film the gatherings. The majority of my informants said they were mainly for security reasons. Many said the recordings are viewed by other Oveyssi Shahmaghsoudi *Khâneqâhs*, while others said they are being taped so that the Pir can review them in California. Several devout Sufis were disturbed when I asked if the Pir in California observed the Saliks in London. One informant said, 'You do not understand what this Order is all about. It makes no difference whether the master is here, Germany or California. We communicate with him spiritually not physically.'

The Oveyssi Shahmaghsoudi's Internet site is also a part of the Order's greater design to reinforce the aims and objectives of the organisation. The web site contains professionally designed pages containing information such as the genealogy of the Masters, the history of the Order which, they claim, stretches back to the Prophet Mohammad, and its principles and teachings. It unites the various *Khâneqâhs* around the world by listing the updated activities and events. The site is also space used by the master to give speeches. For example, in October 2002 the Master gave a live lecture that could be heard and seen by members around the world via their Internet site. It was possible also to listen to a live translation in German, English, and French. The web site also provides an on-line service for those wishing to purchase any books, tape cassettes and video cassettes (which are all produced in several languages) which are endorsed, trademarked and copyrighted by the Order.

The Sufis

Many of the Saliks are educated, coming from middle- and upper-class backgrounds, and are involved in many social and professional networks in London and Iran. Although many are comfortably placed in socio-economic terms, the realisation that London is a permanent home for their families has left many feeling without an overall framework for life, a certainty of their roots (especially for the second-generation Iranians) and a secure place in society. It was often said that the metaphysical, philosophical and spiritual pathway of Sufism transcends the hostile religion of the Islamic regime and serves as an ideal framework. My informants also stressed how, through Sufism, they were actively taking part in and learning about their sacred heritage while linking themselves to Iranians all over the world. They placed an emphasis on the figure of 400,000 members, the numerous active *Khâneqâhs* around the globe and how they are all united by the charismatic Pir Angha, whose lineage traces back to the Prophet. While these factors have created an imagined community, my interviewees also stressed how Sufism is individualistic, a private contemplative relationship between an individual and God, guided by the Pir. It stresses the need to be in good physical shape and guides individuals to overcome weakness and bad habits through mental training and disciplining of the body. Much emphasis is also placed on family life. Overall, the goal is to lead a healthy, involved and successful personal, family and professional life in British society as Iranian Muslims.

Unlike most Sufi Orders, the entire gathering is open to the public, and in accordance with the Oveyssi spiritual tradition they have no formal initiation.[109] I decided it was best at the early stages of my field research to get to know the Sufi members before posing questions to Sheikh and the Master. For the most part the Sheikhs welcomed me and my research questions. They would, however, ignore or sidestep my queries on the history and structure of the order and their relationship with the Iranian government, by saying how such matters are unimportant and blanket the true essence of reality.

The Sufis are supposed to know when they are initiated through a spiritual communication link with the Master. Once this connection is made, the Salik is not to reveal to anyone the secrets he or she is given. I asked several Saliks how a new member could make a spiritual link with the Master. 'Serious newcomers' would be expected to follow closely the Master's instructions listed in the publications. Directly after each gathering, they are asked to write a summary and a list of questions for the Sheikh. They are also expected to bring their worldly and spiritual problems to the Sheikh who will, if urgent, relay them to the Master in California. Through dedication and discipline, a Salik will be guided by the Master and the Sheikhs along *seyr-va-salouk*, (Horizons of Awareness). The Salik's progression along the stages is not something that is publicly recognised by the Order. It is meant to be a secret between Salik and the Master. The Sheikhs and other instructors who lead the *zekr*, read the Koran, and teach at other public sessions, play a central role in overseeing, supporting and maintaining the individual's momentum along the path.

When I asked a 40-year-old woman if she was initiated, she answered:

> It took a lot of concentration and discipline. Eventually I saw visions of the Master. Now I know I'm on the right path … imagine preparing *ghormeh sabzi* [meat stew] … you need the ingredients … herbs, limes, beans, lamb, cooking instructions, and so on. It is not until you taste *ghormeh sabzi* that you really know what it is. Now I know that *ghormeh sabzi* is different from *bâghâli polo* [beans and rice]. It is the same with the Master. One may have read all of the literature and know the history of Sufism, but until one cognises the teachings through the heart they will not be initiated on the path. I have 'tasted' the Master and I know that I'm initiated.

The importance placed on analysing and expressing oneself through dreams and visions can not be stressed enough. I found this to be the case not only with Iranians involved in Sufism, but also a pastime during women-only gatherings and programmes at the mosques. As we shall see in the next chapter, dreams are also a vital component of the Iranian Muslim conversion process to Christianity.

It should not be assumed, however, that the religious discourse outlined above and the design and goals of the programme have a direct and necessary effect on those who consume them. In order to understand the influence they have over their members, an examination of the Sufi members and their networks that extend outside the Sufi Order must be examined. Some members are enthralled by the Master and use his teachings as a complete framework for their lives. Some are involved in other religious institutions and like to compare and contrast the various Shia discourses on offer in London. Some come to perform *zekr*, while others attend to hear the Sheikh address the congregation. The attendance at the Friday gathering is certainly variable. In order to organise my research I have categorised the Sufi members into three groupings: the devout Saliks, the dilettantes, and the shoppers. It is essential to stress that these categories are by no means distinct. It is certainly possible, for instance, for one person to weave in and out of the different categories.

The Devout
Although the Order claims that no hierarchy exists amongst its members and that there are no formal procedures for reaching the different stages, one can

distinguish between the initiatic and associational elements of its membership from other lay members. According to Angha: 'When the Salik has fully adhered to the aforementioned he shall have reached his rank at the summit of devotion and servitude; his words and actions shall be strengthened by the Divine Light and he shall be blessed.'[110] Many of those who claim to communicate through 'heart to heart communication' with the Master have been assigned different tasks in order to further pursue the path to God. For example, some devout Saliks have gained permission from the Sheikh to discuss the teachings of the Master outside of the *Khâneqâh.* According to a devout Salik named Reza, 'a Salik is not allowed to talk about the teachings of the Master until they have reached a certain level of cognition. I was so happy when the school [the Order] let me know that I could talk about the teachings to my friends outside of the school. It let me know that I am making progress'. Ali, a 30-year-old devout Salik, has been given permission to do his doctoral research in psychology and is basing it on the Shahmaghsoudi's religious discourse. He said it took a lot of hard work to reach this level of cognition and be in the position to represent the Order.

A devoted Salik named Avideh Shashaani has written a book under the Oveyssi Shahmaghsoudi's name, entitled *Promised Paradise,* about her spiritual journey guided by the Master, whom she calls 'Agha [qâ] Jan'. The following passages of this emotive book should indicate the dedication she has for the Master:

> My story merely begins here; this was my first encounter. I went to each and every class [Sufi gathering] thereafter, many in number. Every discipline was covered. One day as I was leaving class, I thought, well where have I been all this time? ... Love's the law – the ruled and the ruler of the house. Every child with love obeyed the law, for they knew that wherever they'd be, they'd never be out of Âqâ Jan's sight. Their only care was to please, and to be loved by qâ Jan. So they studied hard, excelled in the sciences and arts, but above all, they kept their hearts intact for Âqâ Jan. Much I learned during this time. All children, young and old from all walks of life, counted their days one by one with the hope of Âqâ Jan's visit to enclose all their days into one. Âqâ Jan's visit was always a surprise! But was I to be Âqâ Jan's child?[111]

> Âqâ Jan, I worship and adore You. You are my sun. I love the ground upon which Your steps touch. When Your love oozes in my heart, my body feels but a speck of dust next to this expansion. Then I become forlorn, for I cannot be contained and the pain of separation brings me back to earth. I begin to wish, what can I be so I can be by you forever and ever. Once I wished to have the longest eyelashes in the world, then I would spread them wide underneath Your Feet, so when You take Your place on the Throne, they would cushion Your Feet from the cold marble floor. My lashes were like the peacock's tail, how magnificent they'd look underneath Your elegant Feet.[112]

While obtaining the permission to speak and write about the Oveyssi Shahmaghsoudi Order outside the *Khâneqâh* is considered to be an informal 'promotion', it is also a way in which the Order can control and monitor what is being said and written.

There are other signs that indicate a devout Salik is excelling on the Spiritual Path and has reached greater levels of devotion. For example, a Salik may be assigned to stand at the front doors of the *Khâneqâh*, serve tea, seat the members, teach at the Saturday children's school, prepare food on special occasions and recite the Koran. The devout Sufis also wear to the gatherings a special white outfit [*lebâs-e tan*] and a badge marked with the Shahmagh-soudi logo. Many also wear a special ring, often on the wedding ring finger. It is possible, through service and self-discipline, to move between the various *Khâneqâhs* located around the world and ultimately to reach positions in California with the Master.

One experience in particular taught me a little about how the chain of command works. I wrote a letter to the Pir asking him to read and make comments on this chapter before publication. I brought a letter to the *Khâneqâh* and asked a girl in her twenties, who was in charge of greeting and seating women, to give the letter to the Master. Prior to my arrival the Master, who happened to be in London at the time, instructed all helpers not to accept any more incoming letters. When I explained that I was researcher and the letter was about a forthcoming publication she became flustered and said apologetically that she could not disobey her orders. I asked to speak to the next in the chain of command, who was a man in his thirties who has a high profile within the order. Although he, too, was not allowed to take the letter, he agreed to ask his superior for instructions. He asked me to stay behind after the *zekr* session. Keep in mind that throughout these exchanges the Master was sitting at the front of the room, but it would have been completely out of order had I handed the letter to him. As I waited after the session I watched the select Saliks silently and efficiently disassemble the props used during the gathering. Finally I was approached by the young man, who handed me an address in San Rafael, California, and said that I should post the letter.

Devout Saliks reported that they ask the Master and the Sheikhs for advice regarding their physical and spiritual problems, in dealing with death, marital choices, professional life and family problems. A 36-year-old man named Bahram said that through discipline and meditation he became so close to the Master that he desired little sleep, food or sex. Prior the relationship, Bahram said he was able to see visions of the Master and communicate with him spiritually. His obedience was interrupted, however, when he fell in love. The spiritual guide (and the Master through meditation) made it clear to Bahram that this woman was not good for him and he should not pursue the relationship. He ignored their wishes. Although Bahram continued to attend the Friday night gatherings, he said that he had 'fallen' from the spiritual path he was once on. The relationship ended bitterly after a year, and Bahram was upset and full of regret that he had not listened to the Master.

The devout Sufis were often critical of other Shia religious associations and practices, including other Sufi Orders, mosque-related activities (such as passion plays) and *sofrehs*. The women I spoke to about *sofrehs* argued that most are gossipy social hours. One woman said, '*sofreh* circles in London have lost the true meaning behind *sofreh* … they gather in the name of God to show off jewels and Chanel outfits'. I asked several women of the Order whether or not they attended *sofrehs*. They responded that they do hold *sofrehs* once in a while, but they hold them in the 'correct' manner.[113] When they make a vow [nazr] and their wish is granted, the money or service promised in return is given to the Oveyssi Shahmaghsoudi Order. I also asked why several people who attend the Sufi gatherings also visit religious events and *sofrehs* outside of the Sufi Order. I was told that they may pay lip service to the Master and the Order but they don't understand the 'reality' of religion nor the teachings of the Master.

Another example is the Iranian New Year, *Noruz*, which is a national holiday that falls on or around 21 March. There are numerous celebrations held by the various Iranian networks in London that count down the minutes to the start of the New Year. The Oveyssi Shahmaghsoudi Order schedules their gathering so that it is held at the start of *Noruz*. Each year during my research, it was telling to observe the Sufis who chose to attend the Sufi gathering at the start of the New Year instead of attending one of the other celebrations. The devout Sufis partake in the extracurricular activities highlighted earlier, such as Sufi meditation classes [*tamarkoz*], sporting activities and send their children to the Persian-speaking classes provided by the Order. Many of the devout Sufis associated themselves with the Pahlavi regime.

The Dilettantes

Those who frequent the Friday night gatherings but are not strictly devoted to the Master and his teachings can be loosely categorised into two groups, the 'dilettantes' and the 'shoppers'. The dilettantes lead busy professional and social lives and describe the Sufi Order as a base, familiar in its Persian language and décor, that enables them to think about improving themselves and contemplate their existence. The Sufi Order, for the most part, is the only Iranian and Muslim religious association in London they would choose to participate in (although some of the women occasionally attend a *sofreh*, but not regularly). While having a drink at a nightclub with a 32-year old woman informant, I asked her why she started to attend the Friday night Sufi gatherings:

> My mom wanted me to go with her. I don't go every Friday ... I don't need to go every week. The people who are completely into the Order have personal problems and need support. I like to go occasionally to listen to the lecture. I also like to see who's there. I don't like to follow the rules ... I like my gin and tonics.

A 46-year-old male informant told me everything in his life is 'crazy'. He has a full-time job in London and is dealing with court cases concerning his property in Iran. His family, living in London, California and Iran, need him to be strong. He has never liked going to mosques, but he likes to attend the Sufi gatherings because they are so quiet and orderly. Some dilettantes want to have some sort of religious guidance in their lives but are not interested in mainstream Islam. Many noted that they prefer to be labelled 'Sufi' rather than 'Muslim'. They noted that they felt comfortable talking about Sufism to non-Iranian friends and sometimes even brought them along to the gatherings, because they too were interested in Eastern spirituality. Many informants said that they feel a sense of loyalty to the Order, but have not developed a spiritual bond with the Master.

The Shoppers

The second group of people who frequent the Friday night gathering, but are not immersed in the teachings of the Master, are those who attend several Shia institutions in London (and Iran). By frequenting the various Iranian Shia institutions in London, they learn, compare and contrast different interpretations and practices. For example, Narges' weekly schedule would start on Wednesday night with prayers and a lecture at the Islamic Unity Centre, on Thursday at 4:30 p.m. she attends a *sofreh*, followed by the 'Supplication of Kumayl' at the Holland Park *Majma*'. She spends Friday night at the Shahmaghsoudi Sufi Order and often attends a programme at the Khoei Centre. She is attracted to the Sufi Order not only because they observe the five pillars of Islam, and the men and women are seated separately, but especially because the women, unlike at the mosques or *Majma*', are required to remain silent, which enables her to listen to the lectures. Several women commented on the orderly atmosphere of the Sufi Order compared with the noisy, messy and overcrowded women's and children's section at the *Majma*' and the mosque.

Unlike the devout and dilettante Sufis, many of the Iranians who are accustomed to mosque-related activities are critical of the Master and prefer to attend the gatherings when he is not present. They are particularly displeased with the Master's view that women should not wear veils. I heard several discussions among practising Shias (both women and men) regarding this issue. Reza, for example, a practising Shia in his fifties, said he does not allow his wife or daughter to attend Sufi gatherings for a number of reasons. First, he argued that in order to properly say their prayers, women must be covered. Second, even if his wife and daughter were covered at the gathering they would be supporting the uncovered women praying. He felt that his wife and a daughter would be belittling themselves by praying in the presence of men. He was also worried that the meat served at the gathering is not halal. The women said that the Sufi Order expects women to say their *namâz* at home, covered. I have also heard the Master's private life criticised. They wonder why a Sufi Master, someone so close to God, would need to go through two (some say three) marriages.

A 56-year-old businessman, who attends the Holland Park *Majma*'-related activities and *dorehs*, told me he is very concerned about his children's religious upbringing in London. He, and therefore his children, are born with the status of being *seyeds* or descendants of the Prophet. He is worried that his children, who have no interest in going to the mosque, will lose interest in Islam while living in London, and in turn dishonour their status of being *seyeds*. He heard about the Oveyssi Shahmaghsoudi Order from a friend and decided to attend a couple of the gatherings. Although he was initially hesitant because of its apparent link to the ex-Pahlavi government, he found that it is, first and foremost, a religious association. He said that his teenage children, without complaining, attend the Friday night gathering weekly. I asked the children what they liked about the Sufi Order and they both answered, 'the *zekr*'. They said the clapping and chanting feels similar to moving to the beat at a nightclub.

It is interesting that the Oveyssi Shahmaghsoudi Sufi Order, which consists of Iranian families who were tied (often indirectly) to the ex-Pahlavi government, and those who oppose a version of Islam that prioritises and politicises institutional rules and beliefs, would attract some scriptural and orthodox Iranian Muslims. Although they were not politically active, I did come across Sufi members who were employed by the Iranian government. As discussed in Chapters 2 and 3, since Khatami has been president there have been changing attitudes towards the Iranian government. I was told by a number of members of the Order that due to several factors, such as the improvement of foreign relations towards Iran, the loosening of Iranian visa control, relaxing censorship, prospects for reform, the opening up of some cultural restrictions of the revolutionary regime, some of the opposition towards the Iranian government has subsided. Although the division between the royalists and the Islamic government has become shaded by business and religion, many Iranians complain increasingly about the slow enactment of the promised reforms.

The Oveyssi Shahmaghsoudi Sufi Order and New Religious Movements

This chapter has put forth a number of reasons to explain the Order's increasing popularity for some Iranians living outside Iran. It discussed how Iranians who wish to preserve and assert aspects of their Iranian and/or Muslim identities are attracted by many things: its sacred history rooted in Islam; the invisible and visible presence of the Master, whose lineage is thought to trace back to the Prophet; the socially-relevant lectures given in Persian by the local sheikhs, and the *Khâneqâh* draped in Iranian cultural forms. The analysis continues by relating the Oveyssi Shahmaghsoudi Sufi Order to the wider growth of American-style, new, religious movements influenced by 'Eastern spirituality'.

In the last thirty years, while the number of people attending mainstream churches in Western Europe has diminished, there has been an expanding interest in 'Oriental' wisdom and new religious movements.[114] At the end of the 1960s, more Europeans and Americans took an interest in religions based on 'Eastern spirituality', such as Zen Buddhism, transcendental meditation, the Meher Baba Movement, the Divine Light Mission, Krishna consciousness, and the Healthy-Happy-Holy movement of Yogi Bhajan. Various types of psychotherapies such as Werner Erhard's Seminar Training or est, Arica, bioenergetics, Silva mind control, and insight have also become more popular.[115] Although evidence suggests that very few people in Britain have actually joined such religious movements there has been a proliferation of publications, music, poetry, dance, relaxation programmes and techniques, and many other commodities that are marketed and inspired by Eastern forms of spirituality.[116]

Those searching for a spiritual experience may be attracted to a number of characteristics associated with 'new' religious movements. For example, the novel way in which a hybrid form of an immigrant faith melds with the organisational styles borrowed from the host country; the like-minded middle- and upper-class participants; and the guided, but individual, pursuit of self-fulfilment and perfection. According to Turner:

> Within the cultural marketplace, choices are not politically constrained and the selection of cultural life-styles is, in principle, limitless. One can opt for Buddhism on Monday, Zen on Tuesday, Sufism on Wednesday and have the rest of the week off. In advanced democratic societies, there are no effective constraints on these personal options, provided they do not impinge on the day-to-day operations of the state's regulative bureaucracy.[117]

Marcia Hermansen, writing about American interest in Sufi Orders, stresses how taking part in some sort of Sufi organisation provides a support system for like-minded spiritual seekers. The mushrooming of Sufism on the Internet has also made information about it much more accessible.

Several Iranians said that they have tried (and many continue trying) several religions, or variations of the same religion, while living in London. One Iranian family, for example, attended Yoga classes throughout the 1980s until they heard about the Sufi Order. Several Sufi members are involved in practices such as astrology, I Ching and tarot, whereas others frequent many different Shia institutions. I have also interviewed Iranians who were members of the Oveyssi Shahmaghsoudi Sufi Order at the beginning of the 1990s and have recently converted to evangelical Christianity.

Similar to Turner's and Bruce's research on 'new' religions, the Oveyssi Shahmaghsoudi Sufi Order appeals mainly to those who are materially satisfied. It is important to note that although there is no sense of a withdrawal from social or material life among the members, many Sufis consider themselves to be ascetic.[118] For example, I scheduled interviews with a younger group of Sufis, all aged around thirty years old. I was picked up in a Mercedes 600, and taken to a smart restaurant in central London, which was followed by exclusive clubs. When I asked them if they felt any sense of contradiction between Sufism and a privileged lifestyle or the acquisition of wealth, they replied by saying that wealth and the Western lifestyle is not 'reality'. In order to see 'reality' one must look at the inner layers of things, not the shell. One informant said, 'I will be a millionaire, I will be successful, but it really means nothing.' This is similar to Gilsenan's work on the Sufism of the elite in Egypt, which states:

For them the 'true' Sufism is not the religion of the streets (from which they are totally cut off). It is rather a journey on a path to illumination that requires that one see behind the mere appearances and forms of religion – where they consider the *turuq* to be hopelessly trapped ... wealth, business affairs, or all the appurtenances of Western values and lifestyles are surface matters and the reality exists beneath. In that dimension of reality he, too, is an ascetic.[119]

The Oveyssi Shahmaghsoudi Order provides the methods for those searching for self-realisation and personal fulfilment, while also serving as an ethnic and spiritual base for middle- and upper-class Iranians living in secular countries outside Iran. I regularly heard comments, such as 'everything in my life is good, but I lack energy'; 'I've spent my first 10 years in this country trying to be "British", now I just want to try being myself'; 'I'm tired of thinking and hearing about "identity crises"; it is possible to be an Iranian and Muslim in this country'; 'Sufism allows me to live the way I want to, and enriches it at the same time'. According to Turner: 'The new religious movements can be seen as contemporary versions of the old inspirational American literature which promised personal success and material reward as a consequence of religious adherence.'[120] The following section examines the psychologised elements of the Order and the way in which it claims to help its members improve themselves mentally and physically.

It is important to add that although Sufi practices are still marginalised in Iran, publications on Sufism, mysticism, positive thinking techniques and other self-help manuals are certainly in vogue and are selling extremely well.[121] Should the socio-political setting in Iran continue to relax, it would not be surprising to see the Oveyssi Shahmaghsoudi style of Sufism attracting large numbers from the burgeoning middle class.

Personal therapy and self-help programmes are central themes that run through the discourses of many new religious movements. In order to demonstrate the Oveyssi Shahmaghsoudi Order's 'scientific methods' in pursuit of health, happiness and perfection, I will illustrate some of the main points taken from a book endorsed by the Order, which was written by Dr Lynn Wilcox, entitled *Sufism and Psychology*. Wilcox, who is a psychologist at California State University, Sacramento and a practising counsellor and psychotherapist, was personally accepted as a Salik by Angha in 1984. Interestingly, Wilcox is also the West Coast director for Wayfinders, Inc., a wellness programme which is recognised as part of the Oveyssi Shahmaghsoudi's greater design. Dr Wilcox promotes the order by conducting Sufi meditation workshops [Tamarkoz] around the world. In March 2002 an English-speaking session was held at the University of Westminster and attracted around fifty non-Iranian participants. The following passages, which are taken from the official Oveyssi Shahmaghsoudi's Internet web pages, demonstrate how the Sufi Order endorses corporate-style motivating programmes.[122]

Wellness programmes for organisations and the community are offered through Wayfinders, which offers classes on Nutrition and Fitness Awareness and Life-Style and Stress Management. Wellness and meditation retreats are also offered.

Healthy employees create sound companies, and healthy companies create healthy communities.

1. It ill-becomes a man to lower himself before anybody but his God ... the sight of humiliation of one man before another never pleases me. It is the worst form of tyranny that can be practised'. (Amir al-Mo'manin Ali)
2. 'Words do not convey the meaning'. (Molana Shah Maghsoud Sadegh Angha).[123]

The following exposition of Dr Wilcox's book, which is popular among the Sufis in London, further illustrates how American-styled self-help therapy has been integrated into the Oveyssi Shahmaghsoudi's religious discourse. She critically examines the goals and methods of Western psychology and psychotherapy by comparing them to the therapeutic goals of the Oveyssi Shahmaghsoudi Sufi Order, which sets out to 'develop the perfect human being, and to develop the perfect society'.[124] She states:

> Psychology has existed in its present form only during the last century, while Sufism is as old as humanity, and is more than 1,400 years old in its pure form ... While psychotherapy is concerned about mental health, Sufism is concerned with healing the soul, with achieving union with the Beloved. Psychotherapy uses conversation as the primary method of improving one's troubled life. Sufism uses inner, heart cognition guided by the spiritual master, the Pir. The changes resulting from psychotherapy are usually minor and involved appearances and 'adjustment'. The Way of Sufism is a deep, permanent transformative experience. In psychology and psychotherapy, the primary focus is on man. In Sufism, the focus is on God.[125]

Wilcox's book attempts to demonstrate the incomplete nature of modern psychology and psychotherapy by examining their descriptions of 'personality', including 'memory', 'creativity', 'intelligence', 'self-actualisation', 'the central nervous system', 'language' etc., and reconceptualising the notions based on the Oveyssi Shahmaghsoudi's religious discourse and the instructions a Salik must follow in order to attain the intuitive bond with the Pir. She argues that modern research techniques are used in the Salik's path towards the cognition of truth. Western science, however, ignores the role of God in each individual and the concentration and meditation needed in order to cognise the truth. Wilcox quotes the Master:

> Focusing – meaning concentration – is gathering all the energy of the sources ... That is, if there is a certain illness or weakness in a certain organ of the individual, that source for some reason is not functioning well either it has been disconnected from outside energies, or it has been misused by the individual, who then is not able to direct the energies toward that organ. The main source is the source of life, which is sitting in the heart.[126]

In order to attain cognition a Salik must completely be cleansed from negative energies that have created or continue to create physical, mental and spiritual maladies. By controlling sleep and diet, managing stress, and by transcending the senses through meditation, by tuning into the electromagnetic spectrum, it is thought that the Master will lead a Salik to perfection.

Wilcox discusses other similar therapies used for healing, such as psychoneuroimmunology, which focuses on the mind, the nervous system and the immune system, relaxation, visualisation, biofeedback, prayer, and meditation. She states: 'The methods now being utilised in Psychoneuroimmunology have been used effectively by Sufism for centuries, and are today, under the supervision of Hazrat Pir and in conjunction with other techniques and a spiritual foundation, helping AIDS patients stay healthy. Sufism recognises and utilises another system of the human body, the electromagnetic system or field.' [127]

Several contacts described the various ways in which the Master's teachings have directly and indirectly healed aspects of their lives. The teaching and meditation urges the Sufis to clean their homes, sort through paperwork, pay off all outstanding bills, exercise and diet, settle arguments, and so on. If a Sufi is leading a healthy physical and spiritual life, it is unlikely that the Sufi will suffer an illness. I have been told by devout Saliks, that when illnesses, such as colds, influenza, insomnia and arthritis do occur, they have been known to be healed telepathically by the Master through intense meditation. The following passage, written by a Salik named Avideh Shashaani, describes her experience with the Master's healing powers:

> Âqâ Jan, You know I've always asked God for God only. But after that statement You made how could I ask You for trivial things. One day I gathered enough courage to ask you for a remedy for a sudden eruption of acne that our sophisticated medicine wasn't able to remedy. Well, that night when I went to sleep I felt like as if [sic] bees were nesting on my skin. When I looked in the mirror the next morning not a trace of it was to be seen. Thank you, Âqâ Jan … I remember the time I came to ask You permission to have my gall bladder taken out, because the doctor said there were just too many stones, You looked me straight in the eyes for a while. Then You said, go for another check-up. I did. The results to my doctor's complete surprise, were negative. Not a trace of the stones.[128]

The Oveyssi Shahmaghsoudi Order, like other new religious movements, provides a social milieu for individuals to learn to manage stress and illness, and find inspiration and self-worth. The religious discourse, which is discussed in scientific terms such as, 'vital centres', 'energy power', 'superconductivity', 'electromagnetic centres', ' brain cells' 'atoms', 'molecules' and the 'basic phenomena of quantum mechanics', appeals to some Iranians who are materially satisfied, seeking self-fulfilment, and taught by fellow Iranians in the Persian language.

Conclusions

This analysis has demonstrated that neither 'Islam' nor 'Sufism' can be taken as given, denoting a set of common defining characteristics. Sufism has been subject to multiple transformations in relation to particular conditions and discourses. In order to understand the dynamics of Sufism it was necessary to understand how a particular Sufi Order creates or interprets the meanings of their doctrines and to examine how the religion interacts with other cultural, economical and political forces. The increase of educated and professional Iranians attending Iranian Sufi Orders coincided with the overall growth of Iranian socio-cultural institutions and events in London (see Chapter 2).

The summary of the long history of the Nimatullahi Sufi Order showed how it was developed and redeveloped into many different kinds of associations. In Iran (and some places in America) during the period between 1953 and the revolution, the present master of the Nimatullahi Order, Dr Nurbakhsh, was successful in drawing members from the universities and intellectual circles. The organisation attracted those who wanted a spiritual experience, but not in the form that was practised by mainstream society. This trend proliferated when the Master, due to the revolution, moved the Order outside Iran and developed several *Khâneqâhs* in cities throughout North America, Europe, Australia and Africa. I presented the continuity of the clearly-defined rules and ceremonies designated by the Order, including the steps to initiation, the *zekr*, and the responsibilities of the Sufis. I then showed the varied adherence to the religious discourse practised by the initiates. I found that the Nimatullahi centre in London serves as a contemplative and familiar social, religious and cultural base for Iranian intellectuals and professionals, many of whom object to elements of the Islamic government and their anti-secular policies. The flexibility and relaxed attitudes towards the Shari'a [Islamic laws] has also enabled the Nimatullahi Sufi Order to attract a number of non-Muslim and non-Iranian members.

The shorter history of the Oveyssi Shahmaghsoudi Sufi Order traces back to the early part of the twentieth century, to the Oveys, Mir Qotb al-Din Mohammad 'Angha' and his sons. The development of this hereditary-based Sufi Order was particularly interesting to outline because it evolved from the Oveyssi tradition which rejects organised brotherhoods with living Masters. The Oveyssi tradition, which is based on the spiritual link between Oveys Gharani and Mohammad, refers to a Muslim mystic who seeks for instruction from the spirit of the dead or a physically absent master. The rise of the new Oveyssi movement was a reaction to the established brotherhoods in Iran, and it opposed the traditions normally practised by Sufi Orders, such as the initiation ceremony. I introduced their interpretation of the Oveyssi tradition, which holds that if a living Master is pure and without fault he is essentially spiritual and invisible, making it unnecessary for an Oveys to follow only deceased or physically absent spiritual Masters. The new movement, which attracted members of the imperial court, set out to improve Sufism by integrating modern Western findings in the natural sciences.

I demonstrated the ways in which the Oveyssi Shahmaghsoudi Order, since the revolution, has incorporated aspects from its past into its new design. The way the Order uses the physical absence but spiritual presence of the Master as a strengthening tool at the gatherings echoes the Messianic hope that is generated in the Shia belief of the absent twelfth Imam and his pending reappearance. To draw another parallel, the way the Order is structured also allows Iranians to maintain a spiritual connection to their home-land in spite of their physical absence.

Its religious discourse uses scientific terms to provide explanations that the 'oneness of existence' is constant. By controlling sleep and diet, and surpass-ing the physical world through meditation by tuning into the electromagnetic spectrum, it is thought that the Master will lead a Salik to perfection. I argued that their discourse reads like other therapy-based, new religious movements, which are aimed mainly at professionals in pursuit of self-fulfilment. My dis-cussions with the Sufis outside the meetings, which were described in the loose categories of the devout, the dilettantes and the shoppers, revealed many different levels of commitment to the Pir and his teachings. It also showed how the members stem from a wide range of political, social and religious backgrounds, which I found, in many cases, were in a state of flux due to the changing political situation in Iran. The remarkable growth of this Order is also indicative of its broad appeal. When I started researching this Order in 1996 there were eighteen *Khâneqâhs* around the world. Presently, there are over seventy.

Despite the popularity of Eastern spirituality and positive thinking tech-niques, the Oveyssi Shahmaghsoudi Sufi Order has not been popular among non-Iranians or non-Muslims in London. I gave a number of reasons why this Order tends only to attract Iranians. Along with the interpretations based on science, their all-encompassing religious discourse emphasises the obser-vance of the five pillars of Islam. The orthodox underpinnings of this Sufi Order, however, do not seem to attract non-Muslims, who tend to be attracted to 'Oriental' faiths with more ecstatic styles. I also argued that the Iranian characteristics of the gatherings, which are conducted in the Persian language and decorated with Iranian cultural forms, have been specifically designed for Iranians living outside Iran, and therefore do not appeal to those who are not Iranian.

Many described the spiritual pathways of Sufism as rooted in the 'reality' of the pure and authentic Islamic tradition, clearly surpassing the contami-nated religion promoted by elements of the Islamic regime and other political groups around the world. Although the discourses of the Nimatullahi Order and the Oveyssi Shahmaghsoudi Order contain similar vocabularies and forms, the implementation and observance of the *shari'a* [Islamic law] and *tariqat* [The Spiritual Path] greatly varied between the two organisations, and were defined in relation to political, social and economic processes. This analysis demonstrated that Sufism does not designate or signify a fixed set of features and practices. It showed how the religious frameworks of the Sufi organisations are defined differently by the two Orders. Whereas the Nimat-ullahi Order, with its more euphoric and meditative style, transcends many of the duties and obligations of the *shari'a,* the Shahmaghsoudi Order, with its more strict and sober style, expects the observance of the five pillars of Islam and all of the significant dates and events on the Islamic calendar.

This chapter argued that many of the emerging Iranian popular cultural forms have been constructed in the Iranian past, to revitalise either the pre-

Islamic time or the pre-revolution period. Both the Nimatullahi Sufi Order and the Shahmaghsoudi Sufi Order fit well in this trend by creating both a 'local community' and 'imaginary community' of members united by a Pir, whose lineage is believed to trace back to the Prophet Mohammad, while at the same time transcending the religion of the Islamic regime. The organisation of these transnational 'communities' are reinforced and strengthened by interesting uses of technology and pages on the Internet.

The significance of Sufism in Western societies can not be analysed as a totality, but instead involve a sociology of how religion interacts with other forces in relation to the given situation. Each with their own life histories, social positions, and social and political networks, a Sufi Order serves as one of many bases for some Iranians living in London. Sufism has become a component of associational life with a degree of social normative and ritual order. This research has indicated that finding a distinct Iranian place in London, and adaptation in the British society, are processes both at work.

Notes

1. J. Baldick (1989), p. 3.
2. M. Momen (1985), p. 208.
3. Many of the guidelines for the Sufi Orders developed from one of the most important doctrines of Sufism, written by Ibn Arabi (1164–1240), the Andalusian-born Arab mystic. The doctrine stated that union with God is not an eventual reaching or meeting, but rather becoming aware of a relationship that has always existed. It went on to say that there is always a man [*qotb*] on the earth who is the perfect channel of grace from God to man. See B. Mangol (1992), p. 11.
4. H. Nasr (1988), p. 107.
5. Ibid.
6. Ibid.
7. S. Zubaida (1995), pp. 164–66.
8. Ibid., p. 165.
9. See M.M.J. Fischer (1980), p. 140.
10. See A. Ahmadi and F. Ahmadi (1998), p. 44–54; M. Gilsenan (1973).
11. See A.J. Arberry (1979).
12. V. Crapanzano (1973).
13. See P. Van der Veer (1994), p. 33–43.
14. Three orders, namely Safi Alishahi, Soltan Alishahi and the Zor-Reyasateyn, claim to represent the Nimatullahi Order. What follows focuses on the Zor-Reyasateyn Order, which has been reshaped by Javad Nurbakhsh. For research on the other two orders see M. Van den Bos (2002).
15. Referred to as 'Oveyssi Shahmaghsoudi' Order for the remainder of this chapter.
16. A. Rahnema (1998), p. 7; M. Amanat (1993), p. 5.
17. M. Van den Bos (2002), p. 76.
18. M.R Ghods (1989), p. 25.
19. P. Paidar (1996), p. 36.
20. See M. Bayat (1982b).
21. M.M.J. Fischer (1991), p. 230.
22. P. Paidar (1995), p. 34.
23. M. Bayat (1982b), p. 52.
24. See M. Van des Bos (2002), p. 74.
25. Ibid., pp. 73–75.

26. H. Nasr (1980), p. 108.
27. M. Van den Bos (2002), p. 109.
28. Ibid.
29. M.M.J. Fischer (1980), p. 142.
30. Nasr claims discipleship under Allam Tabatabai, in Qom. Nasr was associated with Rene Guenon, Titus Burkhardt, Martin Lings and Henry Corbin.
31. For the remainder of the chapter 'Nimatullahi' refers only to the Zor-Reyasateyn.
32. The Zahabiya's headquarters are located in Southampton. The present leader, Dr Ganjaviyan, left Iran after the revolution and has lived in Britain ever since. According to Van den Bos, the Zahabiya are one of Iran's largest Sufi Orders. He writes: 'Although their main centres in Shiraz and Tehran remain unimpaired, the Zahabiya retain a secluded existence. Not only do they refrain from proselytising, they are also reluctant to allow non-affiliates around ...' Van den Bos (2002) 'Sufi Authority in Khatami's Iran, Some Fieldwork notes' forthcoming in state source – p. 7.
33. Ibid. p. 169.
34. C. Bozworth et. al. (1997), p. 47.
35. See M. Van den Bos (2002), pp. 171–204.
36. A. Ahmed (1994), p. 118.
37. See L.P. Elwell-Sutton, quoted M. Galin (1997), pp. 35–37. Nasr also fears that some Sufi Orders in the West are 'pseudo-spiritual'.
38. Ibid. pp. 35–37.
39. According to Nasr the 'good' ones include the works of L. Massignon, H. Corbin, E. Dermenghem, L. Garde, C. Rice, F. Meier, P. Filipanni-Nonconi, R.A. de Sacy, and A.J. Arberry.
40. R. Guenon, M.Lings, J.L. Michon, L. Schaya, F.Schuon, T. Burckhardt, W. Stoddart, V. Danner, J.Conteins, and M. Chodkiewicz.
41. J. Baldick (1989), p. 197.
42. C. Bozworth et al. (1997), p. 46.
43. Ibid.
44. M. Van den Bos (2002), p. 69.
45. Ibid.
46. Ibid.
47. J. Nurbakhsh (1991), p. 156.
48. J. Nurbakhsh quoted H. Nasr (1991), p. 203.
49. C. Bozworth et al. (1997), p. 46.
50. The Nimatullahi Sufi Order has developed centres in the following locations: New York, Washington D.C., Boston, San Francisco, Los Angeles, Santa Cruz, Seattle, Chicago, Sante Fe, U.S.; Lyon and Paris, France; London and Manchester, England; Koln, Germany; Madrid, Spain; Sydney, Australia; Ivory Coast and Benin, Africa; Montreal and Toronto, Canada; and Sweden.
51. J. Nurbakhsh, (1978), p. 6.
52. Such as, *Shaikh*, Pishva, Morshed, Hadi, Baleq. The Perfect Man, Mirror which reflects the Universe, Goblet which reveals the world, the great cure, the sublime elixir, Jesus, Enoch, Solomon, Noah, Pir, Master of the winehouse, Master of the holy fire, Master of the tavern of ruin, Axis of the universe. See J. Nurbakhsh (1978), p. 6.
53. The texts list both the Master's nineteen responsibilities to the disciple and the disciple's twenty-four responsibilities to the Master. See ibid., p. 122.
54. J. Nurbakhsh (1989), pp. 119–21.
55. The devout saliks often wear the ring on their wedding ring finger. The five symbols of spiritual poverty are listed in J. Nurbakhsh (1989), pp. 121–22.
56. The five commitments are listed in J. Nurbakhsh (1989), pp. 121–25.
57. Ibid.
58. Ibid., p. 39.
59. It describes three different positions, all of which form the Arabic word '*la*' which means 'no' or 'not', which stresses the Sufi's nothingness. The positions of meditation are illustrated in ibid., p. 79.

60. J. Nurbakhsh, (1978), p. 65.
61. Ibid.
62. It carries on with the secular advantages of the Sufi Order, such as 'learning the ethics of humanity, resolving material and worldly problems with fellow dervishe'; it prevents one from attending other gatherings 'coloured by the attachments of the world of multiplicity', provides a counsel in one's difficulties. See J. Nurbakhsh (1978), p. 68.
63. The Stewards of the *Khâneqâh* must have twelve years' experience in Sufism. 'The *Shaikh* appoints three, five, or seven stewards or *Khâneqâh*; the duties of the stewards of the *Khâneqâh* are as follows: 1) The stewards secure the financial needs of the *Khâneqâh* from the Sufis, who are individually responsible to determine the sum they wish to give ... 2) The expenses entailed in holding the Thursday and Sunday night meetings in the *Khâneqâh* are under the supervision of the stewards ... 3) The Stewards prepare and organise the mourning ceremonies and festivals in the *Khâneqâh* while supervised by the Pir-e dalil. 4) The stewards take care of the *Khâneqâh*'s building, its repairs, and all its daily expenses according to the Pir-e dalil. 5) They organise the financial accounts of the *Khâneqâh* and the upkeep of its facilities. 6) the stewards help out in the building of any new *Khâneqâhs* and volunteer to aid to those already built.' J. Nurbakhsh (1978), p. 85.
64. Ibid., pp. 77–78.
65. M.M.J. Fischer, p. 147.
66. J. Nurbakhsh (1997), p. 40.
67. J. Nurbakhsh (1978), p. 77.
68. Ibid., p. 107.
69. J. Baldick (1993), p. 6.
70. According to these stories, Oveys lived in Western Iraq, in c.A.D. 640. He was poor and suffered from leprosy, but gained respect by being honoured by the conqueror and ruler Omar, who reigned from 633 to 644. Baldick describes the legend as follows: 'Umar had been ordered by Mohammad to ask Uways to pray to God to forgive Omar's sins ... He was killed at the famous battle of Siffin in 657, taking the side of Mohammad's cousin and son-in-law Ali against his fellow Muslims. Muhammad was supposed to have said of Oveys that he was his bosom friend [khalil] in the Islamic community of believers, and that he would be the best of the generation of "Followers". Ibid., pp. 16–17.
71. Ibid. p. 7.
72. For example, the Naqshbandi Order during the fourteenth century in Bukhara. 'The founder, apart from having an ordinary Sufi elder and "chain", claimed to have been taught by a mystic who had died centuries earlier ... his successors would also favour the Oveyssi technique.' Ibid., p. 7.
73. Ibid. pp. 130–31.
74. Baldick suspects that the author is Ahmad Uzgani, who is also the author of book, *History of the Uwaysis*, c.1600, and presented an imaginary brotherhood from the seventh to the fourteenth century.
75. J. Baldick (1993), p. 36.
76. Ibid.
77. S. Nasr (1991), p. 124.
78. J. Baldick (1993), p. 28.
79. R. Gramlich (1981), pp. 235–36.
80. J. Baldick (1993), p. 28.
81. M. Angha (1996), p.xiii.
82. Salman Farsi is considered to be one of the earliest representatives of Islamic esoterism. Baldick states: 'Salman the Persian, a convert from Christianity, alleged in an early Christian source to have had a hand in the composition of the Koran.' In J. Baldick (1989), p. 28.
83. N. Angha (1991), p. 4.
84. Ibid., p. 9.
85. L. Wilcox (1995), p.14.
86. A. Shashaani quoted in S. Angha (1996), pp. xiii–xiv.
87. Ibid.

88. Angha defines *erfan* as, 'the *gnostic* cognition of the all-pervasiveness of God, the highest attainment of the Sufi experience'.
89. A. Shashaani, in S. Angha, pp. xv.
90. See, N. Angha (1991).
91. Ibid. More research needs to be carried out on these associations. I've been told that a schism occurred due to disagreements about the role of women in Sufism. The web site can be accessed at: http://www.uwaiysi.org/index.html
92. M. Hermansen (2000), p. 12.
93. R. Gramlich quoted in Y. Richards (1995), p. 55.
94. S. Nyang (1995), p. xviii.
95. M. Angha (1996), p. 9.
96. I attended both the Thursday night and Friday night sessions. I was able to ask the *Shaikh* questions during the Thursday night gatherings.
97. M. Angha (1996).
98. Ibid., p. 33.
99. Ibid., p. 7.
100. Ibid., pp. 10–11.
101. L. Wilcox (1995), p. 93.
102. M. Angha (1996), p. 16.
103. L. Wilcox (1995), p. 168.
104. M. Angha (1996), p. 25.
105. Ibid., pp. 27–30.
106. Ibid., pp. 27–30.
107. Ibid.
108. They would then be placed on the mailing list for the monthly newsletter.
109. Most Sufi Orders do not allow someone not initiated to take part in their rituals.
110. M. Angha in L. Wilcox (1995), p. 34.
111. A. Shashaani (1993), pp. 4–5.
112. Ibid., p. 94.
113. When I asked them to tell me about the 'correct' way to organise *sofreh*, they described the same procedures and types of *sofrehs* discussed in Chapter 3. They stressed that poor people should benefit from *sofrehs*.
114. B.S. Turner (1994b), S. Bruce (1996).
115. S. Bruce (1996), p. 170.
116. According to Bruce, relatively few people in Britain have joined new religious movements. He states: 'At the start of the century around 25% of the British adult population was in membership of the mainstream Christian churches. Now it is around 10%. That leaves somewhere around 36 million adults outside the churches. In the 1980s alone more than five million adults were lost to the mainstream churches but the total membership of new religious movements in Britain was less that five or six thousand. If it was six thousand, then only one in every six thousand available British adults joined a new religious movement.' Bruce (1996), p. 188.
117. B.S. Turner (1994).
118. S. Bruce (1996).
119. M. Gilsenan (1992).
120. B.S. Turner, p. 200.
121. See F. Adelkhah (1999), pp. 149–150; and M. Van den Bos (2002).
122. See http://mto.shahmaghsoudi.org/wellness.html.
123. Ibid.
124. L. Wilcox (1995), p. 23.
125. Ibid., p. 207.
126. M. Angha in L. Wilcox (1995), p. 33.
127. L. Wilcox (1995), p. 41.
128. A. Shashaani (1993), p. 45.

5

The Iranian Christian Fellowship and Elam Ministries

This chapter focuses on Iranians from Muslim backgrounds who have converted to Pentecostal Christianity. Since the revolution Christian missionaries have been successful for the first time in converting some Iranian Muslims to Christianity both inside and outside Iran. Conservative Christian missionary groupings have shown a greater interest in evangelising Christianity to Muslims. According to the Center for the Study of Global Christianity at Gordon-Conwell Theological Seminary in Massachusetts, the number of missionaries to Islamic countries grew from 15,000 to 27,000 between the years 1982 and 2001 – and around 1 out of every 3 is Evangelical. The following research is mainly based on the experiences of those who are involved in the Iranian Christian Fellowship (ICF) and Elam Ministries. Both were developed in the London area in 1986. The Iranian Christian Fellowship provides a Persian language Bible study and a Persian and English language church service every Sunday. Reverend Yeghnazar is also the main organiser of Elam Ministries located west of London, which is the first residential Iranian Bible College that trains Persian speakers from Muslim backgrounds to become Christian pastors. It also claims to be the first college in Christian history to have many of its courses taught via computer links from the International Correspondence Institute (ICI) in the U.S.[1] All of the courses are taught in Persian.

The primary mission of Elam Ministry and the Iranian Christian Fellowship is to establish and maintain the Church of Jesus Christ in Central Asia and the Persian-speaking world. They list the following groups as possible candidates for conversion: Persians, Azerbaijanis, Armenians, Baluchis, Gilakis, Hazaras, Kazaks, Kurds, Pathans, Tatars, Tajiks, Turkman, Uzbeks and over fifty others.[2] Their mission is inspired by a passage in the Old Testament, in the book of Jeremiah, which states:

> The word of the Lord that came to the prophet Jeremiah concerning Elam, at the beginning of the reign of King Zedekiah of Judah. Thus says the Lord of hosts: I am going to break the bow of Elam, the mainstay of their might; and I

will bring upon Elam the four winds from the four corners of heaven; and I will scatter them to all these winds, and there shall be no nation to which the exiles from Elam shall not come. I will terrify Elam before their enemies, and before those who seek their life; I will bring disaster upon them, my fierce anger, says the Lord. I will send the sword after them, until I have consumed them, and I will set my throne in Elam, and destroy their king and officials, says the Lord. *But in the latter days I will restore the fortunes of Elam, says the Lord.*[3]

I asked several informants to explain the significance of the passage cited above. The most frequent response was that millions of Persian speakers will respond to God's Gospel and restore the fortunes of the Elamites. Many adherents noted that Islam is the darkness that has spread across Elam, and the Lord is using the dispersion of Iranian exiles to build his church and convert Muslims to Christians. A pamphlet distributed by Elam Ministries explains the passage as follows:

> Long before the birth of Christ the ancient kingdom of Elam in the South-West of the Iranian plateau had risen and fallen. But as the Bible records, the people of Elam kept their identity and exerted a strong influence over the region. Most important of all, God has specifically promised to restore the fortunes of the Elamites, who today are the people of the Farsi speaking world. Elam Ministries exist because God's promise will not fail. Millions of people in Central Asia and [the] Persian speaking world will hear and respond to God's Gospel of restoration.[4]

Invoking the pre-Islamic history of Elam, which is thought to have been a pure, powerful and authentic culture before being contaminated by Islam, is an ideal that some Iranians have used to create a positive vision of the future while dealing with problems in the present. This process of reworking aspects of history is similar to Iranian Sufi Orders striving to transcend the religion of the Islamic regime in Iran, by focusing on sacred histories rooted in the 'reality' of Islam, and Masters whose lineage traces back to the Prophet. The interpretation of the above passage links together more than fifty independent Iranian evangelical churches that have developed around the world since the Iranian revolution. It is significant to note that one of the six elders of ICF said that the quote should not be overemphasised. It has been taken out of context and used to suit the present circumstances. He finds the Bible passage in Acts (2: 9), which discusses the presence of Elamites on the day of Pentecost, a much more accurate and powerful passage concerning Iranians.

This chapter will examine the processes involved in Iranian Muslims converting to Pentecostal Christianity. This entails a brief look at the history of the American Pentecostal movement, its basic tenets and the theories put forth to explain the growth in the membership of Pentecostal churches.

The Pentecostal Movement

Pentecostalism first developed in Kansas in 1904 and appeared soon after in Europe. There are currently more than 150 Pentecostal denominations and sects (and many independent Pentecostal churches) and an estimated fifty-one million Pentecostal adherents in the world.[5] The growth of Pentecostalism has been most evident in United States, Latin America, large areas of East and Southeast Asia, the South Pacific and sub-Saharan Africa.[6] Bryan Wilson describes the Pentecostal movement as 'a generic designation for a very large number of sects which differ on many details of theology and ecclesiology, and, more incidentally, in style, sophistication, and social composition, but all of which share doctrinal commitment to the continuing operation in the present age of those "gifts of the spirit" described in the New Testament, and in particular to the significance of "speaking in tongues".'[7] The development of Pentecostalism has been examined within the wider tradition of Protestant revivalism. Writers such as David Martin and Steve Bruce divide Anglo-Saxon Protestant religiosity into three main waves, namely: Puritanism, Methodism and Pentecostalism. The following section illustrates the way in which the evolution of Protestant movements has provided and continues to provide a 'space' for people dealing with social change and cultural transition. It does so by focusing on the rise of Methodism as a sect, its gradual transition into various denominations, and the subsequent emergence of the Pentecostal movement.

Methodism developed in the 1730s. It was led by John Wesley, a cleric in the Church of England, who was inspired to revive the Church's waning condition. Methodism, which developed when England was shifting to a modern industrial society, called on men and women to take active control of their lives. It also provided opportunities for self-improvement. John Wesley's style of preaching called for individuals to become moral and ethical in their behaviour, and promised 'salvation for the saved and the evils of hell for the sinners'.[8] Methodism mainly attracted the new working class and independent small farmers. Bruce offers an explanation of why people from these backgrounds were in the market for a new religion:

> The Methodist church for the first time gave the upper working class and the lower middle-classes positions of authority and responsibility. Here was something which they were not excluded from by virtue of birth. Personal merits and aptitude were enough to allow a good man to rise in the movement, and, until the movement shifted to denominational respectability, it gave women similar opportunities ... Further, their social and economic positions were highly precarious. Newly acquired, they could be lost easily, and there was a persistent dread of sliding back down into the not respectable working class, the lumpen proletariat which crawled around the slums of the cities. Their good living and religious conversion were immensely important to the Methodists because they created a clear barrier between themselves and the undeserving poor below. And they had the additional virtue of justifying criticism of the upper classes.[9]

There have been many discussions concerning the side-effects of Methodism in relation to the socio-economic and political situation in Britain. For example, Methodists claimed that in order to solve the increasing social problems that accompanied industrialisation and urbanisation, individuals needed to become more moral and ethical. Social change, therefore, depended on individual reform rather than being a task for the community.[10]

A well-known argument discussing the unintended consequences of Methodism maintains that the moral discipline and self-improvement encouraged in Methodism was, in fact, a process that produced hard-working individuals well suited to the industrial age. For E.P. Thompson, for example, the Methodist's emphasis on the discipline of the body brought about a hard-working and reliable labour force.[11] He writes: 'First, it produced disciplined labour by demonstrating that irrational behaviour (gambling, alcoholism and laziness) blocked the achievement of salvation. Secondly, Methodism made labouring bodies docile by offering compensation for the deprivations of urban conditions and for the routines of factory life in emotional conversions, collective rituals and chapel fellowship.'[12] Methodism gave individuals religious, social and economic security while latently providing a self-disciplined and hard-working labour force for the industrial democracy.

Methodism, due to factors such as cultural pluralism, increasing religious toleration, individualism and the decline of enthusiasm in the following generations gradually evolved from a radical sect into a mainstream denomination. H.R. Niebuhr discussed the pattern of waning radical sects and their transition to acceptable and more liberal denominations.[13] Three generations after Wesley's death, Methodism gradually became more tolerant, conventional and upwardly mobile in mainstream society. There are those, according to Niebuhr, who sought to revive the waning condition of the church and chose to break away from Methodism in order to create new radical sects. Bruce points out: 'In the English-speaking world one sees the phases like sedimentary layers of rock: Anglicanism gave way to Methodism and a rejuvenated Baptist movement. That wave was followed by the Salvation Army and the Holiness Movement. That wave was in turn followed by Pentecostalism.'[14] It is important to note that the dynamics of this pattern must also be considered in relation to structural transformations of society at large.

The Pentecostal movement was developed by unsettled ministers of the 'Holiness Movement', who were discontented with Methodism growing closer to the liberal theology of mainstream Protestant Christianity.[15] Pentecostalism grew in America during the Great Depression and was mainly attractive to those experiencing economic hardship. Pentecostalism also provided a framework for people who clung on to rural values and lifestyles, which were threatened by industrialisation and urbanisation.

Basic Tenets

Although the various Pentecostal associations within the movement have no common theology, the tenets set out below are usually recognised by most Pentecostal churches. The main objective is to become 'Born Again', which means to receive an insight that one must serve God and be baptised in the Holy Spirit. In order to become Born Again, and to be saved from damnation, it is necessary for an individual to carry out the following instructions, which stem directly from various passages cited in the New Testament of the Bible. First, an individual is expected to make an admission of sins and profess his or her belief in Jesus Christ.[16] Second, repentance: after professing the commitment to be a follower of Christ an individual must turn away from sin. Third, an individual must be baptised with the Holy Spirit, and is expected to give a public testimony declaring their belief in Jesus Christ.[17] Fourth, once an individual is Born Again, or receives the Holy Spirit, the Spirit will enable one to 'speak in other tongues' or glossolalia, which is either indecipherable or apparently echoing existing languages not consciously known to the speaker.[18] This phenomenon stems from the event described in Acts 2, when around fifty days after the death and resurrection of Jesus Christ, the Holy Spirit was said to have come upon his apostles in Jerusalem, enabling them to 'speak in other tongues'.[19]

> When the day of Pentecost came, they were all together in one place when suddenly a sound like the blowing of a violent wind came from heaven and filled the whole house where they were sitting. They saw what seemed to be tongues of fire that separated and came to rest on each of them. All of them were filled with the Spirit and began to speak in other tongues and the Spirit enabled them.[20]

In addition to the power to speak in tongues the Pentecostalists have faith in healing powers and prophecy. It is worth adding that many Pentecostalists were pre-millennialists, believing that the Second Coming of the Lord was meant to come at the millennium.

Pentecostalism in America

There has been a notable growth of Pentecostal associations (and other conservative religious organisations) in the past thirty years.[21] In order to understand the growth of evangelical Protestantism it is necessary to discuss briefly the process of secularisation and the overall decline of the Christian tradition. According to Turner, 'the dominant Christian tradition, inherited from the pre-industrial period has experienced a major shrinkage in institutional significance and social impact. In this sense, institutionalised Christianity has been secularised in terms of a decline in membership, adherence, wealth and prestige'.[22] The decline in institutional Christianity, however, has been much more apparent in Europe than in America, where at first sight church involvement has shown little or no decline.[23]

In order to explain the seeming disparity between secularisation and religious practice in America, I will present the argument put forward by Steve Bruce in the chapter entitled 'America and God' in his book, *Religion in the Modern World*.[24] Bruce argues that the maintenance of a strong religious culture in America until the 1950s, was due to the ethnic and immigrant nature of American churches. He then introduces material that indicates various changes in Americans' commitment to religion since the 1950s and contends that mainstream Christians are shifting from the essential 'one true faith' position found in churches and sects, to more liberal denominational positions. He writes:

> Americans attend church less often than they used to; the pattern of twice Sabbath attendance and midweek prayer or Bible Study meetings has declined except among the smaller and more fundamental bodies.[25]

> A smaller proportion of all reading material is religious ... Religious titles were on average 7.4 per cent of books published in the early 1955 and 1959 but only 5.2 per cent of books published in the early 1970s.[26]

> Considering the very high claimed rates of church attendance, knowledge of elementary facets of Christianity is poor. In 1978 only 42 per cent of Americans could name five of the Ten Commandments. Only 46 per cent could name the four gospels.[27]

> Americans give as much to the churches as they did fifty years ago, but what they spend on everything else has more than doubled.[28]

> ... in 1984 Gallup reported that the percentage of those asked who believed that the Bible is 'literally true' had fallen from 65 per cent in 1964 to just 37 per cent.[29]

> Consider the attitude of most American Catholics to contraception. By the late 1970s Catholic birth-rates, family size, and contraceptive practices were indistinguishable from the US norms and that despite the Church's very clear policy.[30]

Bruce argues that the religious distinctiveness and content of mainstream American religion has diminished and has been replaced both by attitudes that are more tolerant to other religions, and by positive thinking methods that set out to assist individuals in overcoming obstacles in order to live a happy life. The liberal Presbyterian minister, Norman Vincent Peale, characterises the shift in the interpretation of mainstream Christianity in his first book, *Power of Positive Thinking*, where he portrayed the Christian message as the individual pursuit of personal satisfaction.

Instead of focusing on abstract notions of good and evil that are external to us, Peale preached that good and evil are within us. Those who think positively and conform to the middle-class norms of the 1950s are 'good' people, as opposed to those who are 'evil', who lack self-confidence and are unhappy. Bruce points out that, 'religion as relationship to the supernatural was replaced by religion as personal therapy. It was no longer about glorifying God by obeying his command but about personal growth.'[31] The liberalisation of mainstream Protestantism and the quest for personal satisfaction can be seen as a part of wider socio-economic and political changes that spread across America, which made people richer and the country more powerful. As a result of these social changes, ascetic lifestyles gave way to more material lifestyles with increasingly liberal moral and ethical standards.[32]

The conservative Protestants (especially the Pentecostalists) in America resisted liberal and secularizing influences longer than mainstream Christians. Following Bruce, one of the reasons why the conservative Protestants continued to read the Bible literally and practise ascetic lifestyles (which prohibited divorce, dancing, alcohol, sexual promiscuity, movies, and so on), was because the socio-economic and political changes that spread across America took longer to reach the regions most populated by the conservative Protestants (the southern part of America and the rural areas of the west and mid-west). Throughout the 1950s and the beginning of the 1960s, the Evangelicals and Pentecostalists rejected divorce and the break-up of families, Peale's style of positive thinking, televisions, smart clothes, and so on. These prohibitions, however, eventually loosened as the prosperity of industrial America reached the conservative Protestant communities.[33]

This is not to say that the conservative Protestants in the U.S. have not done their best to sustain homogeneous subcultures. As Bruce points out, they have been able to create their own worlds in the U.S., due to such factors as the relative freedom that ethnic and religious groups in the U.S. enjoy; it is not difficult for the groups to isolate themselves demographically; and it is possible to set up independent schools, political parties and develop communication networks (including private television stations).[34] Sectarian subcultures, according to Bruce, have enabled parents successfully to pass on their faith to the next generation. This is not true for mainstream Protestants, whose children are exposed to many ways of life and often become indifferent to their parents' faith. Although conservative Protestantism has been successfully passed on from generation to generation, it has not been able to cut itself off from liberal influences. Bruce states:

> As the conservatives have grown relative to the rest and become more affluent, they have also lost a great deal of what made them distinctive. As we have seen, the psychologised gospel of 'positive thinking' that was anathema to conservatives in the 1950s and 1960s is now well established in Fundamentalists and Pentecostal circles, and much of the behavioural distinctiveness that marked those groups off has also gone.[35]

The summary of Bruce's analysis on 'America and God' throws some interesting light on the dynamics of religion in the U.S. in relation to complexities surrounding the processes of secularisation. The changes in Protestantism that are particularly relevant to themes found later in this chapter are the shift from orthodox belief and practices in the supernatural to the 'psychologised gospel of positive thinking',[36] and how it is providing techniques for self-realisation and personal fulfilment. What follows is a discussion on the spread of North American Pentecostalism around the world. We shall then turn to the growth of Pentecostalism in Iran.

The Expansion of Pentecostalism

Building on the groundwork laid by British and American Protestant missionaries of the nineteenth century, Evangelical groups in the twentieth century set out to develop the main Protestant denominations into worldwide bodies. Pentecostal missions, especially in the past thirty years, have been successful in proselytising individuals and villages in Latin America, Africa and parts of Asia.[37] There have been many theories put forth to explain the growth of conversions to Pentecostal Christianity. It is often argued that Pentecostalism provides an enclave of meaning and support for those trying to come to terms with a transitional period such as migration or those dealing with rapid social and economic transformations. Bruce, for instance, writes: 'Into a gap created by rapid social change and the collapse of the old world has flowed a Pentecostal version of evangelical Protestantism which stresses the role of the Holy Spirit in providing such gifts as prophecy, healing and speaking in the tongues of men and angels.'[38]

'Conversion', which etymologically means 'turning' or 'turning around'[39] has mainly been explored in psychological accounts and what are known as 'intellectualist' accounts.[40] According to Hefner: 'Intellectualist accounts explain conversion as a change in religious belief, where beliefs are viewed as instruments of explanation and control of actual time-space events. In line with this view individuals are assumed to change their beliefs as a result of social developments that promote comparison of the relative coherence of one set of beliefs with that of another.'[41] Hefner agrees with the intellectualist accounts in that individuals should be thought of as 'active agents who are at times capable of critically evaluating their cultural heritage', but Hefner also argues that social, political and moral influences are often more powerful than the intellectual explanation in the process of conversion.[42] Drawing from his study of Christian conversion in Muslim Java, he writes:

> Issues of community and identity were glaringly apparent in the three moments of Javanese conversion discussed here. In the nineteenth century, Christian conversion advanced but then stalled because of its identification with European colonialism. In the 1920s, Javanists in the Tengger highlands balked at converting to Christianity because it was still too closely linked to European life-worlds. By the 1970s that linkage had weakened, and the mountain Javanese described here, like Javanists in many parts of Java, could more comfortably contemplate the possibility of converting to the Christian faith. Converts in the Tengger highlands were drawn to the faith not so much by its explanations of space-time events in the world, as an intellectualist model would assume, as by its answers to problems of self-identification in a shattered social world.[43]

Taking a similar approach, David Martin examines the processes in which people in various structural and cultural milieus become susceptible to a religious conversion. He argues that the structural relationship of the development of Methodism in English society is an instructive model for looking at the relationship of Pentecostalism in Latin America. Martin explains, 'Methodism and Pentecostalism can both be analysed as anticipations of liberty, initially realised in the religious sphere and stored there until a shift in cultural underpinnings actually undermined the structural barriers, or protest moved from a cultural expression.'[44]

Martin examined the power struggles of various rival groups in relation to Protestant conversion following the 1944 revolution in the El Peten district of Guatemala. He demonstrated how Protestant organisations came forward and created a 'free space' in which groups could join.[45] Martin writes: 'What we do need to probe are the complicated feedbacks whereby people perceive the possibility of change and so grasp and are grasped by religious ideas which can accelerate that change and/or help them to cope with it'.[46]

Martin convincingly describes how people need to be economically independent and/or detached from communal and familial support systems before conversion becomes an option. Research on Christian converts in Africa (the number of which has increased to over 160 million, in little more than 100 years) has focused on different types of situations in which conversions have become widespread and socially acceptable.[47] For example, in some areas, such as Uganda, entire populations accepted the new faith quickly, and in some areas of Southern Africa, the chiefs were the first to be converted.[48] Many writers have attempted to link the phenomenon of Christian conversion in Africa in with a period of rapid socio-cultural change, colonialism, industrialism and modernisation. According to Ifeka-Moller, massive conversions in regions of Nigeria in 1953 were due to frustrations among the inhabitants, who were under the impression that the rapid social change would bring economic prosperity. They turned to Christianity because it promised a new kind of power and the means to success in the modern world. This is in accordance with Martin, who makes the point that the attractiveness of Pentecostalism is due to its institutional ability to 'conform and transform'.[49] He states, '[Pentecostalism] finds out the morphology and shape of the local society and participates in the life of people. At the same time it provides new networks of participation and offers lines of organisation and communication along which signals of modernity and symbols of equality may travel.'[50]

This section has shown that the rise of Pentecostalism in the U.S. and the growth of Pentecostal churches in Africa, South America and parts of Asia should be placed within the wider tradition of Protestant revivalism and must be examined in relation to particular social and political configurations. Pentecostalism, which is highly adaptive to the contingencies of particular situations, provides a flexible framework for an individual (who for various reasons is independent and/or detached from established socio-economic and familial institutions) or for entire villages coming to terms with rapid social change. Pentecostalism offers an ethical code and techniques of self-realisation, which concentrates on self-improvement and personal therapy.

Protestant Christianity in Iran

There are many different historical accounts that seek to explain the beginnings of Christianity in Iran. For example, there is a legend based on commentaries of Matthew's Gospel,[51] which claims that the three kings who came to worship the birth of Jesus Christ were Persians. The beginning of Christianity in Iran has also been connected to Luke's account in Acts (2:9), which describes the day of Pentecost when Parthians, Medes, Elamites and inhabitants of Mesopotamia were all present in Jerusalem. The Eastern Christian religious minorities groups, the Assyrians and Armenians, have been present in Iran dating back to pre-Islamic times and maintain their own historical accounts explaining the beginnings of Christianity in Iran.[52]

Along with the Zoroastrians, Jews and Sabeans, who are considered as the *Ahl al-Ketab* or 'People of the Book', Christians have traditionally been tolerated in Iran and represent 1 percent of the population (of sixty-five million people).[53] Up until new legal codes concerning the religious minorities were introduced by Reza Khan Pahlavi (1924–41), they were governed by a system of social organisation which granted them the status of *Ahl al-Dhimma* ('The Protected People').[54] This unevenly implemented system allowed the religious leaders and elders of the recognised religious groups a measure of internal self-government in matters of personal status and community affairs. It also institutionalised the status of religious minorities by legally recognising them as inferior and subjecting them to a number of disadvantages, including being subject to a special tax called *Jazieh*.[55] It created a manoeuvrable space in which the relationship between the religious minorities and mainstream society would change according to the socio-economic and political situations. Although it is not within the scope of this chapter to survey the changing shape of the Eastern Christian communal boundaries in relation to various historical periods in Iran, it is relevant to bring to light the social and political standing of the Eastern Christians during the Qajar dynasty (1794–1924), the period in which Christian missionaries first arrived in Iran.

Eastern Christians during the Qajar Dynasty

In the nineteenth century Iran experienced an increasing financial and military presence from British and Russian imperial powers. According to Algar:

> Among the non-Muslim minorities in Iran, the Christians, both Armenians and Assyrians, were able to attain a new position of prominence in government and commerce during the Qajar period. They acted as intermediaries between Muslim Iran and the Christian West, functioning as interpreters, agents of European

commercial enterprises and even furnishing some of the first Iranian envoys to be posted to Europe. For the Armenians, this was a continuation of the analogous role they had played in the Safavid period.[56]

As summarised in Chapter 4, the relationship between the Qajars and the European powers gradually exposed the weakness and corruption of the Qajar government, who did not take measures to oppose the foreign influence. In response to the Qajar's weak government, a number of religious and political reform movements emerged, and demanded a rule of law and a protection of Iran's national interests from the growing role and influence of imperial powers. Armenians are recognised for their political involvement during the Constitutional Revolution.[57]

Protestant Christian Missionaries in the Qajar Era

Protestant churches entered their greatest period of expansion in the nineteenth century, largely due to the impact of the rise of industry and religious revival in parts of Europe and the United States. The Church Missionary Society (CMS) was developed in England in 1799, and the interdenominational American Board of Commissioners for Foreign Missions was founded in 1810.[58] The American missionary activity began in Iran in 1892.[59] Note that French Roman Catholic missionaries also embarked on missionary work in Iran during the nineteenth century.[60] The CMS was established in Iran in 1869.[61] Missionary work, which was carried out both by men and women, was divided between the American Presbyterian mission, which was based in the northern half of the country, and the Anglican Christian Missionary Society, which was based in the southern half of the country.[62] The American Presbyterian mission concentrated on the following areas: Urmiah, Mashad, Rasht, Kermanshah, Tehran, Hamadan and Tabriz. The Anglican Christian Missionary Society concentrated on Isfahan, Shiraz, Yazd, Julfa and Kerman.

The Christian missionaries, who were not allowed to openly proselytise Muslims, settled in areas in Iran that were populated with Armenian and Assyrian Christians. The ultimate goal of the foreign missions was to make a successful transition from a mission to an indigenous church, which was accompanied by the establishment of hospitals, schools, universities and orphanages. The foreign missionaries also set out to gather information regarding the living conditions of Muslims living in Iran, and to disperse Western notions and ideas.[63] It is through these types of channels that Iranians in the nineteenth century heard stories about the standard of living and social and political reforms in Europe and America. For example, many Iranian women were inspired by news of women's lifestyles in Europe. Paidar writes: 'The family in Europe, portrayed in an idealised fashion by Christian missionaries, presented images of romantic love, happiness, stability, mutual support and absence of divorces. This contrasted in the eyes of the Iranian intelligentsia with the image of family in Iran based on arranged marriage, polygamy, suppression and exploitation of women, incompatibility between spouses, and easy divorce.'[64] Whereas their proselytising activities amongst the Muslims were for the most part unsuccessful, a number of converts were gained from the Assyrian and Armenian populations, and several 'native' churches were established.[65]

Throughout the nineteenth century, 'mainly through Russia, Britain and France, Europe was exposed to the eyes and ears of Iranians as the magic model of power, prosperity and progress',[66] while at the same time being seen as a political, social, economic and a territorial threat. These mixed perceptions towards Europe would often be projected onto Christian missions which, on the one hand, were given much credit for introducing modern medicines, medical technology and systems of education while, on the other, were resented and seen as a threat by spreading Western (Christian) propaganda. The Christian missionaries received help and protection from the Western Consulates (especially the British Consul).[67] The Armenians and Assyrians, who were in direct contact with the proselytising activities of the missionaries, had varied reactions towards the missions. For example, in 1835 in north-western Iran (Urmia), the Nestorians were in need of aid and protection, and therefore welcomed the missionaries' financial, medical and educational assistance.[68] Other Armenian, Assyrian and Muslim religious leaders showed more resistance to the Protestant missionary activities. According to Dehqani-Tafti:

> In the early days resistance was shown to these missionary establishments by the religious leaders, particularly to the schools. Parents were forbidden to send their children to Christian schools; often students would climb over the walls because the doors were watched, knowing that they risked being caught and beaten. But as time went on the missionary institutions became accepted and increasingly used by the people. Even religious leaders would call in missionary doctors for medical treatment. Occasionally Ayatollahs, and more often lesser religious dignitaries, would attend hospitals for surgery. Gradually even sons and daughters of religious leaders went to missionary schools and colleges for study.[69]

Members of the Qajar government, who were increasingly known throughout the nineteenth century for accommodating foreign interests in Iran, welcomed the missionary stations that were established throughout the country.[70] According to Joseph, there are several reasons why the Persian government did not oppose the activities of the foreign missions:

> A number of Persian top government officials such as Malkom Khan, Abbas Mirza, and Kazem Mirza (the uncle of Mohammed Shah) favoured reform in Persia and welcomed missionary secular educational activities among their subjects. Undoubtedly, the royal family in Tehran and other provincial towns was eager to maintain good relations with the imperial powers by offering protection to the 'English Mullahs' as Kazem Mirza put it. The royal family also intended to learn the modern ways from the missionaries. Perkins' journal is full of narratives that indicate the extent to which royal princes were emulating the West: attempting to learn English, establishing schools to spread the Western education, adopting Western customs, wearing European clothes, and serving tea '*a la Farangi*'.[71]

Various religious and national reform movements that campaigned against the arbitrariness of the Qajar government and its accommodation of foreign influence, spoke out against the Protestant missions. According to Joseph, at the end of the nineteenth century, 'Communist propaganda, along with that of the nationalists, attacked the foreign missionaries as agents of imperialism who are using Christianity to enslave people. In Iran Communists recently printed the Beatitudes in full and explained how Christian evangelists, representatives of foreign nations, were trying to make Iranians "poor", "weak" and "long suffering" in order to take away their country from them.'[72]

The accounts of both the Anglican Christian missionary society and the American Presbyterian missions stated that in spite of the widespread unrest and growing anti-foreign feeling during the latter half of the nineteenth century, the missions were able to carry out their work with relatively little interference. There are reports that indicate a growth of mission schools and hospitals, and give accounts of a few Iranian Muslim converts to Protestant Christianity. For example,

> By 1876 there were enough converts to warrant the founding of a church, whose services were sometimes attended by Muslims. In 1880 a government order forbade Muslims to attend at services and the chapel was closed. But services were resumed in 1882 and, from then on, all that wished were free to attend. By then Bassett (a British missionary) reported that the church had twenty-nine members and that recent converts included four Muslims, one Jew and three Armenians.[73]

In 1871, Robert Bruce, an Anglican missionary, reported that nine Muslims he evangelised in Isfahan asked for a baptism.[74] The Presbyterians claimed to have converted a few Muslims, including the son of a mullah, named Saeed Khan, who became known as one of Iran's most qualified doctors.[75] In 1886 Dr and Mrs Jordan arrived from America and developed Alborz College. According to Waterfield, 'by 1901 it had all the classes necessary for a complete high school. In 1913 a new site was purchased outside the city. During the war, two residences and a boarding department were built. In 1924 the main buildings were added, so that by 1933 the campus occupied some forty-four acres'.[76]

The foreign missionaries were also able to set up committees that encouraged non-Muslims to settle their disputes before the government instead of among themselves.[77] The Protestant community, by 1880, was allowed to elect a representative to deal with its cases before the government.[78] Joseph writes, for example, that in the late nineteenth century the committee and the British Consul met with the Persian Minister of Foreign Affairs in order to discuss the following laws: '(1) According to the Persian law which then prevailed, if a member of a Christian family turned Muslim, he or she became entitled to all the property of the family, and "family" was defined not only as the parents but as its collateral branches as well; (2) The testimony of a Christian against that of a Muslim was not accepted in a court of Justice'.[79] In 1881 these laws were modified by the British Minister in Tehran, and 'respecting the question of testimony, the authorities were instructed that suits between Christians and Muslims would thenceforth be tried, not by religious but by the civil courts, and Christians would be placed on a footing of equality with the Muslims in the giving of evidence.'[80]

Protestant Missions in the Pahlavi Era

The relatively unrestricted activities of the Protestant missions throughout Iran during the nineteenth century were either interrupted or shut down due to the political and social unrest of the Constitutional Revolution and the outbreak of the First World War.[81] According to Fischer: 'At the turn of the century protests against financial indebtedness to the British and Russians and against economic concessions to foreigners often took the form of riots against religious minorities who were seen as clients and agents of European powers.'[82] Fischer notes that Jews, Armenians, European missions and especially the Baha'is were all targeted. The discrimination against religious groups was legalised in the 1905 constitution by provisions such as Article 8, which stated that *non-Ja'fari* Shia could not become cabinet ministers or judges.[83] In 1914 the CMS missionaries in the south of Iran were ordered by the British Consulate to evacuate their mission stations and travel to Ahwaz for safety.[84] The American Presbyterian mission was forced to close down in Urmia in 1934.

Due to the growing nationalist resistance around the world, the Protestant missionary associations in the 1920s and 1930s were forced to re-examine the missionary situation in Asia. It is important to emphasise that the small grouping of missionaries largely believed that the best way to lessen deprivation in Iran was by converting Iranians to Christian ideals. Francis-Dehqani states: 'As deliverers of the Christian message, missionaries were convinced they possessed the necessary solution to ensure a positive future for Iranians. Their motivation was genuine, as was the desire to alleviate suffering. However, the figurative generalizations to which they clung in order to express their ideas, together with deeply embedded assumptions of superiority, meant a patronizing tone remained inevitable'[85] The World Mission Conference, held in Jerusalem in 1928, focused on abandoning the assumptions of Western superiority and declared that Christians should 'look forward to the continued co-existence of other religions with Christianity, each stimulating the other in growth toward the ultimate goal – unity in the completest religious truth',[86] and: 'To seek with people of other lands and work what we have learned through Jesus Christ, and endeavouring to give effect to his spirit in the life of the world'.[87]

The Constitutional Revolution of 1906 to1911 was followed by the takeover of Reza Khan and the Pahlavi dynasty. According to Fischer: 'Under Reza Shah in the 1930s, the old Qajar economy was reorganised into a self-reliant and nationalistic system; thus the direct connection between foreign domination and local minorities was lost, and the form of protests no longer used the minorities as hostages.'[88] The CMS missions reported that: 'There were many signs in the early 1920s of the mission moving out confidently into new fields and, if converts were still few, the number of baptisms was significantly larger than those of any other CMS mission in Muslim lands.'[89] By 1925 there were signs of a growing Anglican Church in Iran, with new Persian clergy, over twenty thousand copies of the scriptures being sold a year and over four hundred members in the Anglican Church.[90] The American Presbyterian mission reported that their schools 'were at the peak of their influence and efficiency'.[91]

Reza Shah's programme of modernisation and building of a national identity, however, proved to be damaging for hospitals, schools and orphanages owned by the foreign missions. From the late 1920s the Pahlavi government began to pass legislation that put pressure on the Protestant institutions. For example, in 1927 the Department of Education issued a new regulation requiring the teaching of the Koran and Islamic law (the *Shari'a*) as the condition for government recognition of a school, and banned the teaching of Christianity in the curriculum.[92] In 1930 a regulation prohibited the use of Christian hymns in school prayers.[93] This was followed by legislation established in 1932 that restricted all Iranian nationals from attending primary schools under the control of foreigners. The remaining Protestant mission schools received a notice in 1939 that all foreign-owned schools, or schools that received funds from abroad, must close and be turned over to the government.[94] These new regulations forced six CMS schools to close down and the Presbyterian mission to be sold off. According to Waterfield, 'after months of negotiations, all the properties except the Girls' Middle School in Tehran were sold to the government for $1,200,000 and over a century's educational work was at an end.'[95]

As discussed in Chapter 1, during the1940s, political activity was being organised against the Pahlavi government by a coalition of secular reformers called the National Front. It is important to note the different strategies that the American Presbyterian and the Anglican CMS missions used in dealing with the legislative pressures of the Pahlavi government and the period of political unrest, during which Dr Musaddiq was brought to and from power. According to Dehqani-Tafti, in the early 1950s,

> So far as the church was concerned, foreign missionaries who were outside the country at the time were not allowed back. The Anglican Bishop of the time, the Right Reverend W.J. Thompson, who was a British citizen, was expelled. The Christian hospital in Isfahan was given six months' notice to close down. We had no option but to comply. Then Dr. Musaddiq fell and the Shah, who had gone into exile, came back. The next day we were told by the Department of Health to begin accepting patients again.[96]

Due to both political and economic reasons, the Presbyterian mission decided that it was best that their seven hospitals in the north, and other institutions, should be handed over or sold in order to become national institutions.[97]

The Anglican Church decided to continue owning and managing the hospitals and other institutions despite the political and socio-economic situation. It was also decided by both the missionaries and nationals that the Anglican Church in Iran was in need of indigenous leadership. In 1960 Hassan Dehqani-Tafti, who had come from a Muslim background and was raised in a poor family in a village near Yazd, was appointed as the first Iranian Anglican Bishop.[98] He continued to develop educational and medical programmes and tried to establish amiable Christian–Muslim relations in Iran through his sermons, writings and contacts. The Anglican institutions were able to develop and run in the 1960s during the implementation of the Pahlavi's social reforms, known as the White Revolution. The heads of the religious minorities were formally invited to attend the government's celebration of the 2,500th anniversary of the monarchy in Iran.[99] Throughout the 1970s, however, the Pahlavi government became more dictatorial and repressive and the Anglican Church was increasingly under surveillance by the government's secret police (SAVAK) and different Muslim groups.[100] The church members were being threatened and prevented from entering the church. Church property was being vandalised and its publications were not allowed to be printed.[101]

The Development of Pentecostal Churches in Iran

Pentecostal Churches started to appear in Iran in the late 1950s, which corresponds with the development of Pentecostalism in Latin America, Africa and parts of Asia.[102] The first Pentecostal church (Assemblies of God) was established in Tehran in 1955, after Mohammed Reza Shah's government was able to regain stability. The founder of this church, who is the father of the present pastor of the Iranian Christian Fellowship (ICF) in London, was born in 1908, and comes from an Armenian background. He said that he became a Born-Again Christian during the 1930s and it has been his duty ever since to establish an Evangelical church in Iran. He said that the church is currently associated with a Pentecostal organisation in Springfield, Missouri, but that it was independent at its inception. According to an elder of the ICF, who worked as a Presbyterian missionary in Iran, there were four main Persian-speaking Evangelical churches that developed in Tehran during the 1960s and 1970s: the Assemblies of God; a church located in south Tehran which is associated with the Bible Society; a Presbyterian church in north Tehran, which was known to have Jewish converts; and the Brethren church, which mainly consisted of Kurds. He also noted that the vast majority of those who became Born-Again Christians were from Armenian and Assyrian backgrounds, with a small minority of Muslim converts. While it is hard to obtain accurate figures, the Iranian Christian International (ICI)[103] reports that approximately two- to three-hundred Muslim converts lived in Iran before the revolution in 1979.[104]

The Protestant Churches and Khomeini

According to Fischer, all the religious minorities supported the social and political goals of the revolution, but they became concerned when the goals were being expressed in Islamic and not secular terms.[105] Khomeini's general attitude towards religious minorities followed conventional Shia Iranian traditions, based on the system of *dhimma*, which holds that non-Muslim communities can function as separate but unequal, as long as they pay special taxes and respect the conditions of the Muslim state.

Article 13 of the Constitution of the Islamic Republic of Iran guarantees religious freedom for Christians. This law, however, does not protect those who converted to Christianity from Islam, who can be charged with 'apostasy'.[106] At first, the 'People of the Book' – the Jews, Christians and Zoroastrians – were promised protection by Khomeini. According to Dehqani-Tafti, 'though the tone was definitely Islamic, the religious minorities were not forgotten. At Christmas time (1978) a printed bulletin from Imam Khomeini and addressed to Christians was pushed through our door, reminding Christians of their long-standing close ties with Islam, and asking them to rise against oppression. So we felt reassured that under an Islamic Regime our rights would be preserved.'[107] In response to Khomeini's bulletin the Bishop sent a letter to Khomeini in February 1979 declaring the Anglican dioceses' 'co-operation with the aims of the Revolution, and praying to God for the establishment of freedom and justice in our country'.[108]

According to a British missionary (who left Iran during the course of the revolution) the Presbyterian and Pentecostal churches were able to continue their church services without uniform persecution for the first ten years of the Islamic regime. The Anglican Church, however, was targeted, starting in February 1979 when many of its members began being tormented, and its institutions were forcibly shut down. It is important to emphasise that the early attacks were carried out by local groups such as the Islamic Propagation Society.[109] The following series of incidences have been listed by Bishop Dehqani-Tafti:

19 February 1979
The murder of the Pastor (Arastoo Syah – from Muslim background) in charge of Churches in the Fars Province, in his office in Shiraz.

11 June 1979
Confiscation of the Christian hospital in Isfahan after over a century of service.

12 July 1979
Confiscation of the Christian hospital in Shiraz and intrusion on church property.

12 August 1979
Raiding the Bishop's House and Diocesan offices in Isfahan, and the looting and burning of documents and personal effects.

3 October 1979
Illegal confiscation of the farm for the training of the blind in Isfahan, belonging to the church.

8 October 1979
Disregarding the sanctity of the church, and my pointless and humiliating arrest in Isfahan.

26 October 1979
Attacking the Bishop's House in Isfahan, an attempt on my life and the wounding of my wife, in our bedroom.

1 May 1980
Savage attack on Miss Jean Waddell, the fifty-eight year old secretary to the Diocese, and severely wounding her in Tehran.

6 May 1980
The assassination of my only son, twenty-four year old Bahram Dehqani-Tafti, on the way back from his college to his mother in Tehran.

5 August 1980
The arrest of Dimitri Bellos, the Diocesan Administrator, in Tehran.

9 August 1980
The expelling of three women in Iran, who had been responsible for blind work in Isfahan.

10 August 1980
The arrest of Dr. and Mrs. Coleman in Tehran.

17 August 1980
The arrest of the pastor in charge of St. Luke's church in Isfahan.

20 August 1980
The arrest of the pastor in charge of St. Andrew's church in Kerman.[110]

The attacks were justified through allegations made by the 'Revolutionary Committees'. Tehran radio, television and the Revolutionary Press made reports that the Anglican Church was cooperating with spies who were involved in anti-revolutionary activities.[111] Both Dehqani-Tafti and an elder at the ICF believe that the reasons why the Anglican institutions were targeted by the Islamic regime came down to the fact that they, unlike the Presbyterian and Pentecostal institutions, had not been nationalised and were still partly owned with foreign money. According to Dehqani-Tafti, by the time of the revolution the Anglican diocese was responsible for the following:

> Churches established in six main towns; Eight clergy: five Iranians and three expatriates; Two hospitals in two main towns and both expatriate and national staff; Two clinics one in a small village outside Isfahan and one in the town of Yazd; The Christoffel Centre for the Blind; The Nur Ayin Institute for the Blind; The Cyrus the Great training for the Blind; Schools and hostels for boys

and girls. Altogether there were thirty to forty expatriates working in these institutions. The total membership of the church was about 4,000, of whom half were expatriates from English-speaking countries including workers in the oil-fields. During a hundred years the Anglican Church had baptised altogether about 3,000 men, women, and children.[112]

Khomeini claimed that false notions of Islam were spread through Western institutions such as schools, universities and publishing houses.[113] The suspicion that Anglican Christians were allying themselves with foreigners was complicated by the fact that many of the Anglican Church members, including the Bishop, were from Muslim backgrounds and were considered to be apostates. The regime's campaign against the Anglican Church left no Anglican priests in Iran, and church activities were either cancelled or organised secretly.

The treatment received by the Anglican Christians reflects the attitudes towards non-Muslims and apostates held by Khomeini and his adherents in the years leading up to the revolution and the first couple of years after the Islamic regime came to power. Khomeini, in accordance to Shia doctrine, categorised non-Muslims, along with urine, stool, dead bodies, etc., as one of the eleven things that are *najes* or ritually unclean.[114] During the first four years of the newly established Islamic regime, Khomeini adopted a more radical rhetoric which he added to the conservative attitude towards religious minorities. He often referred to religious minorities as 'traitors', 'economic plunderers' and the 'enemies of Islam, the clergy, and Muslim intellectuals'.[115] Khomeini's popular rhetoric targeted at religious minorities, which provoked a great amount of anger and violence from the public against religious minorities, started to soften in 1982.[116] Abrahamian demonstrates the ways in which Khomeini's rhetoric towards religious minorities was toned down:

> He thanked the minorities, including the Jews, for producing 'martyrs' in the struggle against the shah. He distinguished Judaism, an 'honourable religion that had arisen among the common folk,' from Zionism, a 'political "ism" that opposed religion and supported the exploiters'. He argued that Imam Ali had treated all as equal and had not distinguished between the Muslim and Jew. As a gesture of goodwill toward the Christians, the Islamic Republic issued a postage stamp bearing Jesus' silhouette and a Koranic verse in Armenian.[117]

Khomeini's gestures did not include Muslim converts to Christianity or members of the Baha'i faith who are not recognised in the constitution, and therefore fall into the category of 'unprotected infidels'.[118] It is under this law that apostates have no rights and are subject to capital punishment.

Iranian Converts and the Persecution of Evangelical Churches

With the Iran–Iraq war, rapid population growth and the weak economy, the 1980s resulted in a decline in per capita income and a fall in living standards for the average Iranian household.[119] People were increasingly becoming disillusioned with what the Islamic Revolution had brought them. My contacts (those who converted to Christianity in Iran and are now members of the Iranian church in London) said they felt both trapped by the Islamic rules that were being forcibly implemented by the police and defenceless, with no space to mobilise against the state's policies. Many said that before the revolution they identified themselves as Muslims and participated in some religious traditions, but they did not regularly say their prayers everyday or follow all the dietary laws. Many stated that they became increasingly disillusioned with Islam when the Islamic regime started to force people to practise its faith. It was then that many of my contacts formed the opinion that Islam is a harsh religion, with a degenerative effect on society.

The disillusion with the revolution, exacerbation by the Iran–Iraq war and economic instability, accompanied by new restrictions forcibly introduced in the name of Islam, created an unstable environment that allowed my contacts a 'space' to question the 'common sense' of the Iranian society, and in turn made them susceptible to change. This has resulted in Christian missionaries in Iran being successful, for the first time, in converting several Iranians from Muslim backgrounds to Pentecostal Christianity. As Martin points out: 'Evangelical religion represents an advanced form of social differentiation and can operate best where hitherto monopolistic systems are disintegrating. Once the monopolies begin to crack and to lose contact with the core structures of society, evangelical Christianity can emerge to compete within the sphere of culture.'[120] According to several sources such as the ICI, Open Doors, Elam Ministries and my Iranian informants who converted to Christianity in Iran and currently live in London, despite the increased pressure on Evangelical Christians throughout the 1980s, more Iranians then ever before became receptive to Christianity.[121] It is difficult to obtain an accurate number of converts. According to Open Doors, at the end of 1990 there were approximately 15,000 Protestants in Iran.[122] Iranian Christians International estimate there to be 25,000 Iranian converts around the world in 1999. The Assemblies of God church, which has been the most active in the evangelical movement in Iran, claims to have 8,000 church members there.

From the 1980s to the present, Christian churches (especially Protestant) were questioned and often monitored by the Ministry of Information and Islamic Guidance, the Ministry of Religious Affairs and Endowments, and the Ministry of the Interior and State Police.[123] They are not a recognised religious minority and fall into the category of 'unprotected infidels'. Under Shari'a law apostasy is a crime which is punishable by death. It is also important to point out that there might be civil punishment for the family and relatives of a convert. For example, marriages could be dissolved and children could be separated from their parents.

Due to the number of Muslim converts to Christianity a campaign against the Assemblies of God churches developed throughout the 1980s and culminated in the first half of the 1990s. Similar to the government's campaign against the Anglican Church in the early 1980s, the Pentecostal churches faced the assassination of Christian leaders, the official closing of churches, the closing of the Bible Society and the confiscation of Bibles and Christian literature. All foreign missionaries were forced to leave Iran, and in 1988 the following Christian churches were closed by the government: Mashad Church (1988); Sari Church (1988); Kerman Church (Spring 1992); Shiraz Church (1992); Gorgan Church (October 1993); Ahwaz Church (1993) and Kermanshah Church (date unknown).[124] The Iranian Christians were threatened either to be sentenced to imprisonment or to be killed if they were caught evangelising. Reverend Hossein Soodman, who was a Muslim convert to Christianity and a pastor of the Assemblies of God church in Mashad, was asked several times by Mullahs to stop preaching and revert to Islam. In December 1990 he was tortured and then hanged for apostasy. His body was not allowed to be seen by his friends or family.

In 1993 the Islamic regime adopted 'a policy of gradual eradication of existing churches under legal pretences', and the Assemblies of God churches were ordered to comply with the following directives:

> No church service must be conducted in the Persian language. All members must be issued with membership cards and their admittance to the services would be on production of the appropriate card. Photocopies of these cards and appropriate membership lists with their addresses to be given to competent authorities. Sunday meetings were to be for members only. No meeting to be held on any other day, in particular Friday. No new members to be admitted without informing the appropriate department of the Ministry of Information and Islamic Guidance.[125]

Bishop Haik Hovsepian-Mehr, who was the Superintendent of Assemblies of God churches in Iran and was chairman of the Council of the Protestant Ministers, did not accept the conditions and said that, 'never would he or his ministers bow down and comply with such inhumane and unjust demands' and that 'our churches are open to all who want to come in'.[126] He also refused to sign a letter stating that Christians are allowed full constitutional rights in Iran.[127] Bishop Hovsepian-Mehr, who was from an Armenian background, actively campaigned for religious freedom in Iran and was committed to the international campaign for the release of Reverend Mehdi Dibaj, a Muslim convert to Christianity who was in imprisoned in Sari for nearly nine years. Dibaj was imprisoned by the Shari'a court in Sari for the following three charges: 'First, that he had insulted Islam, the prophet Mohammed and Ayatollah Khomeini in a letter; Secondly, that he was acting as a spy for the West; Thirdly, that he was an apostate.'[128] According to Jubilee Campaign, 'Iran's Supreme Court on two occasions dismissed the first charge on grounds that the letter was not proved to be in Hossein's handwriting and the second charge as unfounded. He continued to remain in prison solely on grounds of apostasy.'[129] Bishop Haik's international campaign for the release of Mehdi Dibaj, and his public appeal to the United Nations and other international organisations to investigate the abuses of human rights against Christians in Iran, pressured the Iranian government to release Dibaj on 16 January 1995.[130] Three days later Bishop Haik disappeared, and he was found dead on 20 January. A family member was quoted by Agence France Presse, declaring that

Mr. Hovsepian felt endangered following his actions in January to draw the attention to the international community to the case of the Iranian priest Mehdi Dibaj who was also a member of the 'Assemblies of God' ... He had no enemies. The only problem was that he led the 'Assemblies of God'. Our church is very active in promulgating the Bible. The government has asked us to stop our proselytization.[131]

Six months after the murder of Bishop Hosvepian-Mehr, Mehdi Dibaj disappeared, on 24 June 1994, and his body was found murdered in a park in western Iran on 5 July.[132] This was followed by the murder of Reverend Tateos Michaelian on the 1 July 1994, who was the former General Secretary of the Iranian Bible Society and had taken over Bishop Hovsepian-Mehr's position as Chairman of the Protestant Council of Ministers. The Iranian government arrested three women who were members of the political opposition group, the Mujahedin, for the murders of Dibaj and Michaelian, and for planting a bomb at the shrine of Imam Reza in Mashad which killed twenty-six people.[133] The Christian community, various Human Rights groups and the Mujahedin questioned the authenticity of the charges placed against the three women, because of the circumstances surrounding the murders and the unconvincing evidence. The Iranian government's accusations involving the Mujahedin in the murders of the Protestant pastors was also discredited by a United Nations Special Rapporteur who listened to the testimony of the three women.

According to information received, the Iranian Government had apparently decided to execute those Protestant leaders in order not only to bring the Mujahedin organisation into disrepute abroad by declaring it responsible for those crimes, but also, at the domestic level, partly to decapitate the Protestant community and force it to discontinue the conversion of Muslims, which was regarded as apostasy and was therefore prohibited according to the government's interpretation of Islam. It was apparently felt that those conversions weakened Islam and, hence, the Islamic Republic of Iran; that could explain the restrictions imposed in the religious field, as well the executions of the leaders of the Protestant community.[134]

The latest Pentecostal pastor murdered in Iran was the Iranian Assemblies of God pastor Mohammed Bagher Yusefi, who was found dead, hanging in a tree in a forest near his home city of Sari, the capital of the north-western Iranian province Mazandaran.[135] Yusefi was thirty-four years old and was born in a Muslim family but became a Christian at the age of twenty-four. He attended Bible school and became a pastor of the Assemblies of God churches in Sari, Gorgan and Shahr, in the province of Mazandaran. He and his wife (who was also from a Muslim background) have two children and had also raised the two sons of the Reverend Mehdi Dibaj, discussed earlier. It is thought that he was killed because his church in Gorgan had been growing in size.

It is important to emphasise that the converts report that the authorities are mainly concerned with pastors and converts who actively proselytise. Many said that although they attend church and socialise with fellow converts they are afraid to openly practise Christianity because of the likelihood of some form of persecution. They often said that their fear is based on the uncertainty of the Iranian officials' actions and the uneven application of the apostate laws.

The Iranian Diaspora and Pentecostalism

According to Iranian Christian International (ICI), which developed in America in 1980, there are approximately 20,000 Evangelical Iranian Christians living outside Iran.[136] The lack of studies on this aspect of the Iranian diaspora makes such estimates difficult to verify. The world-wide directory of Iranian/Persian Christian churches (this listing only includes Pentecostal and Evangelical churches) lists forty-five (above ground) Iranian churches that have developed around the world since the 1979 revolution. These records indicate that evangelical churches can be found at the following locations: Arizona, Arkansas, California, Georgia, Illinois, Kansas, New Jersey, New York, North Carolina, Oklahoma, Texas, Pennsylvania, Washington, Washington D.C. in the U.S. and Canada, England, Germany, Sweden, Turkey, Australia and Iran. Many of the churches have their own web sites which often outline (in both English and Persian) their doctrinal commitment, an updated listing of their local activities and events, a posting of their church members' public testimonies, offers of Bibles, Christian videos and books on sale by mail order, and the lyrics of songs and prayers.

Although the churches are affiliated with different types of Evangelical organisations, and therefore have different doctrinal understandings of the Bible, they are linked together on the Internet by the shared interpretation of the passage in the Book of Jeremiah, which states: 'In the last days... I shall restore the fortunes of Elam, declares the Lord.'[137] Most Iranian Christian web sites have this passage written on top of their homepage with the following explanation:

> Elam is the name of an ancient kingdom in the South-West of Iran. In the Bible we learn that though the Elamites were to be judged, God made a special promise 'I will restore the fortunes of Elam', God has a wonderful plan for all the descendants of the Elamites in the Iranian plateau. These are the people we are reaching out to.[138]

This construction of a common vision that motivates and underpins their Christian identities is greatly strengthened by various letters, poetry, songs and newspaper articles written by and dedicated to the recent Christian martyrs and their family members. The following section will focus on the Iranian Christian Fellowship in London, which was officially established in 1986 and is a part of this wider movement.

The Iranian Christian Fellowship in London and Elam Ministries

A group of fifteen to twenty Iranian, Armenian, Born-Again Christians in the 1980s formed a prayer group that met in a rented hall in Ealing once a week. The Armenian language was spoken during the group sessions until a couple of Iranians from Muslim backgrounds joined the prayer sessions and they switched to the Persian language. The leader of this prayer group, who has been described to me as a charismatic, 'Jesus loving' man, decided to return to Iran. In the meantime, the current Pastor of ICF, moved to London with his family in order to continue his work with the Bible Society. He had trained to become a minister in India and then worked with the United Bible Societies in Asia, the Middle East, and Europe.[139] He eventually resigned from his post at the Bible Society and became the pastor of the Armenian prayer group in Ealing. He set the goal of pastoring an Iranian Church in London with two thousand members by the year 2000. According to his wife, they knew he had made the right decision to resign from the Bible Society when he received a telephone call, on his first day of being unemployed, from the British Pentecostal Association with information about a run-down church for sale in Chiswick. The pastor's wife believed this was a 'sign' from Jesus; it reassured them that they were meant to build an Iranian Christian church in London. The next step was to raise the money needed to rent and eventually buy the property in Chiswick. The founding members of the church are mostly university educated and employed in professional jobs. Although it was not easy, the pastor's wife said it was possible to raise enough money to buy the property because of the help from the church members who are accountants, bankers, solicitors and businessmen.

The Constitution of the Iranian Christian Fellowship

The Iranian Christian Fellowship is an independent Pentecostal association. The teachings are made applicable to the Iranians' cultural needs, while also claiming to be faithful to the religious tenets of the major Pentecostal associations, such as Assemblies of God and the ICI University in America. One of the reasons the founders of the ICF decided to exist independently from the major Pentecostal associations was in order to have distance from the doctrinal debates within Pentecostalism, which could be confusing for the newly converted Iranians. It is important to note that although they refer to their religious organisation in English as the 'Iranian Christian Fellowship', I was reminded by an elder of ICF that it is a 'church', not a 'fellowship'. The difference between a church and a fellowship, according to the elder, is that a 'church' meets on Sundays and has an ordained pastor who gives out communion and perform water baptisms. A Fellowship, on the other hand, does not meet on Sundays, serve communion or perform water baptisms. Fellowships are usually organised by people who belong to the same church and decide to meet together and pray outside of the church. For example, the Kensington Temple, which is the largest Pentecostal church in London, has a number of fellowships that satellite the church, which are based on the different language and ethnic groups. There is an Iranian Christian Fellowship in Croydon that was organised by a graduate of the Iranian Bible College in Shackleford. Iranian Christians (from Muslim backgrounds) meet every Friday night in Croydon, because the location of the church in Chiswick is inconvenient or because they work on Sundays. They take communion two or three times a month at ICF and the new members are baptised in the church.

The Constitution of the Iranian Christian Fellowship is written in both Persian and English and is separated into six parts, namely: The Constitution; The Purpose; The Statement of Faith; The Membership; The Leadership; and The Administration. According to one of the elders, they based their constitution on other Pentecostal associations such as the Open Brethren and Assemblies of God. The mission declaration of the ICF is:

> The Iranian Christian Fellowship is a community of God's people, mostly of Iranian origin. The purpose of being an Iranian fellowship is for worship, fellowship and discipleship of people of Iranian background and is open to people of other nationalities that spiritually relate to and become a genuine part of the ICF. We are committed to the Great Commission of Mt. 28:19, 20,[140] in evangelistic outreach to, and discipling of Iranians and others, firstly in the UK, and then Europe and elsewhere in cooperation with others of like vision.

I have asked several church members different questions regarding the mission or purpose of the Iranian Christian Fellowship and questions concerning the ICF's basic doctrinal position on a variety of issues, such as predestination, the second coming of Christ, and the ordination of women. I found that the majority of the members could not answer my questions and suggested that I ask one of the elders. One of the elders, who was not at all surprised that members of the congregation were not familiar with basic Christian tenets, said that the Church does not want to confuse the potential Christians and newly converted Iranians with complex theological debates within Christianity. They are more concerned with building a community of Iranian believers who repent and become baptised of the Holy Spirit, and joyfully and optimistically worship Jesus Christ. According to the elder, the Iranian Christian Fellowships falls more within the Arminian (followers of Jacobus Arminius) tradition than the Calvinist tradition, in that it places more weight on preaching, and reaching the hearts of the church members, rather than engaging in turgid sermons that analyse theological issues. What is interesting is that the founders of the ICF have not only remained vague in their teachings about theological issues in their Sunday sermons, they have also purposely remained vague concerning various theological issues in their Statement of Faith, written in their constitution.[141]

Whereas several asseverations in the ICF's Statement of Faith – the virgin birth, the Trinity, the deity of Christ, the universal sinfulness and the guilt of the fallen man, the baptism of the Holy Spirit and the water baptism – are clearly stated, other issues, such as the notion of predestination and the second coming of Christ, are uncertain.[142] One of the founders of the ICF said they have not explicitly stated their positioning on every issue because they do not want to limit themselves, and as the church grows they want theological issues to be discovered and debated by the church members. They try not to confuse the new Iranian converts with Christian doctrinal questions. It has been interesting to observe the different aspects of Christianity that the elders have carefully chosen to introduce to the congregation and integrate into the service. For example, the pastor started to teach the congregation the 'Lord's Prayer', for the first time, in 1998. He had it translated into Persian and he spent the entire sermon discussing the meaning of each verse.

Unlike the Statement of Faith in the ICF's Constitution, which is not explicitly transmitted by the elders or understood by many of the church members, the following points on the membership requirements are addressed.

The Membership

Members joining the Church shall be such as through the operation of the Holy Spirit profess repentance before God and faith in the Lord Jesus Christ, whose lives bear evidence of their Christian profession and who obey the Lord in the ordinance of Baptism by the immersion in water. Exceptional circumstances will be considered by the Elders. They shall acknowledge agreement with the Church Constitution, Purpose and Statement of Faith.

Entry into Church Membership shall follow interview and acceptance by the Elders. Unless prevented by some reason they can consciously lay before the Lord Jesus Christ, Church Members should be faithful in their attendance and support of Church gatherings, both central and local, for: worship, teaching, fellowship, communion, prayer, business and evangelism. They shall maintain a spirit of love, unity and peace and shall uphold the work of the Church in prayer, and personal support. Church Members are expected to give to the Lord's work in direct proportion to their resources according to the Scripture. The fellowship in turn will set example in tithing its funds. (1Cor. 9: 6–8).

Church Members shall respond to the discipline of the Elders, and in instances of private offence between Church Members, open backsliding or doctrinal error shall act in accordance with the scriptures upon the advice of the Elders. (Matthew 18:15–17; 2 Thes. 3:6,14,15; Tit.: 3:10,11, 1., Cor 5:2–5). [143]

I asked an elder if they had ever punished or acted on 'instances of private offence between church members, open backsliding or doctrinal error'. He said that ICF will not water baptise a person who is not living according to Jesus' plan. For example, the ICF refused an Iranian Muslim couple from converting to Christianity because they were living together out of wedlock, and they refused to live apart. The church is also very careful about baptising people who are not truly believers. They monitor the pledge and commitment to Christian beliefs and church activities in order to determine whether or not the conversion is legitimate and not being used as a strategy to stay in Britain to gain religious asylum.

It is important to add that the ICF teaches that male and female have an equal standing before God and were created by God to complement one another. While maintaining that men and women have an equal standing before God as sinners in need for salvation, they claim that the Bible assigns different functions to men and women, lending the leadership and authoritative role to men and a supportive role to women. The Iranian Christian church acknowledges the following four titles: Brother, Sister, Pastor and Elder. The position of power and authority of the pastor and elder, which deals mainly with important decisions concerning the scripture and finances, is reserved for the male members of the congregation. The ICF (and several conservative Protestant Churches and the Roman Catholic Church) argue that even though there were many women who were filled with the Holy Spirit, Jesus never appointed a woman as an apostle.

Both male and female informants said that women's ordination should not be confused with the Holy Spirit, who calls and empowers women with gifts for ministry. The ICF claims that in working within the biblical structure, women are called to pray, prophesise, speak in tongues, preach, evangelise, sing and pray in the church, and engage in some forms of teaching. Women, however, must realise that they are 'forbidden to teach or have authority over men',[144] and in exercising their leadership gifts they must be willing to do so under the authority and leadership of men who are responsible for the official teachings of the church.

The Sunday Service

The ICF hall can hold approximately three hundred people and is situated in a quiet, middle-class, residential area in south-west London. The service takes place in a simply designed building, with the front used for the Sunday service, and the back containing a kitchen and a large room used for the children's Sunday school, socialising after the service and selling religious books and cassette tapes. The place of worship contains rows of chairs for the congregation, an area for the song leaders and their instruments, a raised rostrum for the pastor and to place a stand for the Bible. The rostrum also covers a large pool of water used for baptisms.

Every Sunday there is a Bible study in Persian and English, followed by a Persian-speaking service. An English-speaking service is held as well. As the congregation arrives they greet each other and socialise until the service begins. There are no seating arrangements as both the men and women are free to sit or stand where they please. Both the adults and children are expected to attend the first hour of the service, which is dedicated to singing and rejoicing. Singing is an extremely important element in the worship at the Iranian Christian Fellowship. During one session the song leader described the biblical importance of singing and rejoicing through a discussion of biblical expressions of praise and worship.

Song leaders lead the congregation in both Persian and English. The musicians, usually playing tambourines, electric guitars, a full set of drums, a flute and a piano would start playing softly as the song leaders would say, for example, in both Persian and English: 'Are you ready to rejoice and reach out to Jesus? Are you ready to clap your hands and sing praise?' The congregation usually responds by clapping their hands and yelling yes or *baleh*. The song leaders ask questions such as 'Why do you need Jesus?' The members of the congregation yell out in Persian and English, 'to forgive our sins', 'for hope', 'for love'. As the musicians proceed the congregation rise to their feet and sing. The melodies of the choruses are emotive, uplifting and charismatic. The words usually stress either the need for the world to be 'saved' by Jesus or celebrate the joy of already being saved. The lyrics of the songs, written in Persian (both in script and phonetically in Roman script) and in English, are put on an overhead projector. Some of the songs were written by Iranian Christians in Iran (for example, many were written by the late Bishop Hovsepian-Mehr) and are stylistically and melodically Persian in style. Other songs were written by American and English evangelicals and are translated into Persian.

As the congregation sings, many will reach out their arms and hands to the ceiling, sway back and forth and clap their hands, and people will periodically yell out, '*Isâ*', or 'alleluia'. Periodically, in between the songs, various members of the congregation take turns declaring their love of Christ. An example of a weekly testimony is as follows (the testimony, depending on the speaker, is translated into either English or Persian by the song leaders): 'Lord, I was so weak before I didn't know you, continue to give me the strength to walk with you…'. The person giving a testimony is comforted and supported by other members of the congregation. Music is played softly throughout the testimonies which are followed by an uplifting song.

After an hour of singing and testifying, an organiser of the ICF will inform the congregation about future church events, such as 'Ladies' fellowship', 'Men's breakfast', 'Fellowship and prayer in Persian', and special prayer events in association with other Evangelical ministries. The details surrounding the annual Elam ministries' conference is an important event for discussion, and greatly anticipated by the congregation. Money is then collected from the congregation. I was told by members that, if they can afford it, they are expected to give the ICF 10 percent of their earnings.

As the congregation is seated, and the children leave the hall to attend the Sunday school class, the pastor and interpreter stand at the lectern to give the sermon. The pastor usually begins with a personal gesture by wishing someone a happy birthday, welcoming a visiting guest, or announcing a birth or marriage ('Brother John is joining us from America' or 'today is sister Mary's birthday', – they refer to each other as brother, sister or elder). The sermon consists of a combination of the pastor's own words and Bible quotations, and is usually based loosely around themes such as love, obedience, purity, patience, self-control and the advantages of being a Christian. One sermon, for example, discussed the dangers of organised religions. The Reverend described the 'walls', that have been created by man, that stand between different organised religious and ethnic groups, such as Jews and gentiles,

Arabs and Jews, Scottish and English and Christians and Muslims. He argued that people do not 'see' God because the walls exist not only between different organised religious groups, but also between God and the organised religious groups. Organised religion, he argued, needs to be terminated in order for individuals to be genuinely closer to God. I was told that they do not practise a 'religion'. One informant stated: 'Organised religion is caught up with politics and evil ... just look at what happened in Iran. We are in a direct conversation with Jesus ... with nothing in between us'. Another informant stated: 'I don't believe that true Christianity is a religion but a revelation of God through his son Jesus to man. The unity with God of course, isn't this convincing enough? Where there is no condemnation, no punishment but forgiveness and eternal life. And you also have to follow God's rules and decrees.'

Members of the congregation often follow along with their Bibles, the majority of which are printed in Persian, and many take notes throughout the sermon. The style of the sermon, which is meant to be charismatic and delivered rigorously, does lose its rhythm while constantly being translated between English and Persian. Several members of the congregation who speak both Persian and English fluently find the translation necessary but tiring.

After the sermon the pastor leads the congregation in an uplifting song and then invites people to pray with him around the rostrum. He says, for example: 'If you want Jesus Christ in your life, or if you want to strengthen the bond between you and Jesus Christ, stand and declare your belief in Jesus Christ ... turn away from a destructive lifestyle and live a new life with Jesus.' This is an important part of the service for several reasons. Up until this point the individuals collectively partake in the service and remain anonymous. The first time individuals walk to the front of the hall and profess their love for Jesus or ask for Jesus' help or forgiveness, he or she places the spotlight on his/herself. This indicates to the congregation that he or she is taking the first step towards being 'saved'. Several of my informants described the first time they answered the call to prayer. For example, a 47-year-old Iranian woman, who used to be Muslim, stated: 'I went to the church many times, and just listened to the music. One Sunday I don't know what came over me ... I found myself walking to the front of the church ... it was so good, people were praying for me and hugging me. All I could do is cry.'

As many members of the congregation move out of the pews and crowd around the rostrum and the centre aisle, those who are 'saved' will gather around those who are not 'saved' and place one hand on an individual's back and the other on the side of the neck, and pray. Some people begin speaking in tongues, which is often accompanied by crying. Many informants described speaking in tongues as a 'spiritual gift'[145] which transpires when they are so overwhelmed by the power of the Holy Spirit that they lose control of their own capacity to speak, and babble uncontrollably. Being the receiver of the 'spiritual gifts' is considered to be proof that a person is invoked by the Holy Spirit.

On some Sundays 'divine healing', which is also considered to be a 'spiritual gift', takes place when a member of the congregation is ill, struck with a disease, or undergoing a surgery. For example, the Reverend asked a young Iranian boy, who was struggling with cystic fibrosis and was to be admitted in to hospital the following day, to stand before the congregation to be spiritually healed. The congregation reached out their hands to the boy and the Reverend placed his hand on the boy's shoulder as they all prayed for his recovery. I asked a member of the congregation if the prayers healed the boy and he answered: 'Every bit counts. It may not have healed him completely but it may have taken away some of his suffering.' Several members of the ICF told me about a visiting pastor from America who miraculously healed members of the congregation with his healing powers. An Iranian Muslim woman in her sixties, who started to attend the church service because she wanted to try to understand why her son converted to Christianity, was no longer wary of Christianity after she witnessed the American pastor heal sick members of the congregation. She claims that her health, including her sore knee, greatly improved due to his healing powers.

After the sermon and prayers the congregation are told that they can continue to pray together or socialise in the back of the building, where coffee, and occasionally an Iranian lunch, is served and religious books, cassettes and videos in both Persian and English are sold. Socialising after the service is looked forward to and the majority of the people stay for at least another hour. The time is used to celebrate birthdays, anniversaries and other special occasions. I used this time to converse with the members of the congregation.

On my first visit to the Iranian Christian Fellowship in 1996, I asked a visiting pastor from Iran, a man in his late sixties, if he could tell me the history of the Iranian church in Iran. He answered, 'Is Jesus Christ in your life?' When I told him I was raised a Catholic, he asked me: 'But, has your tongue been on fire with the Lord?' He then asked me to find an English-language Bible and read the Acts of the Apostles 2 out loud to him. He explained: 'The Holy Spirit can touch you; it makes no difference where a person is from, what religion they were born into, or what language they speak.' I then asked when he encountered Jesus Christ for the first time. He said that he was raised in a Muslim family in the north of Iran, and he became a medical doctor. When he was a practising Muslim he would ask Allah, during his prayers, why Iran is in a state of turmoil. He said that he was introduced to Christianity by a book written by Billy Graham, which was available in Persian in the 1970s.

The Iranian Christian Fellowship Hosting Other Pentecostal Churches

Representatives from Elam Ministries and the Iranian Christian Church frequently meet with missionary societies and churches throughout the United Kingdom and around the world, in order to generate awareness and support for Elam Ministries and the Pentecostal Christian churches in Iran. They have also tried to create exchange programmes with other Pentecostal churches. For example, representatives from Elam Ministries and the Iranian Christian Church travelled to Pentecostal churches in Reclife, Brazil in 1996 and, in turn, a group of twenty-five to thirty representatives from Brazil were guests of the ICF and took part in a Sunday service in 1998.

The first hour of the service consisted of the congregation singing American evangelical hymns. This was followed by a Brazilian pastor speaking in Portuguese, which was then translated into English and Persian. Even with the layers of translations he attempted to give an emotional and charismatic speech. He spoke about how Brazilians have been praying for the last two years for Jesus Christ to touch the millions of distraught Muslims in Iran. He said that ever since Elam Ministries came to Brazil and described the ways in which the Iranian Christian martyrs sacrificed their lives for Jesus, they have been praying day and night for Iranian Christians and for the families of the martyrs. He then pointed to the son of Bishop Haik Hovsepian-Mehr, and led a prayer in the Bishop's honour who was killed in 1994 in Iran. I asked a number of the Brazilians where they learned about the Iranian Christian martyrs, and they said that they heard about them from Elam Ministries and many Christian sites on the Internet.

The Brazilian guests were then asked to stand and pray with the Iranian church members as music was being played passionately in the background. Some of the Brazilians approached individual Iranians and placed their hands either on the Iranians' foreheads, side of the neck and/or back, while other Brazilians would gather a group of four or five Iranians and huddle together with their arms around each other. As the Brazilian guests were touching the Iranians they prayed in Portuguese, which eventually led to a crescendo of crying and speaking of tongues. The Brazilians' style was far more intense and impassioned than the practices that normally take place at the ICF. Although many Iranian Christians have invited me in the past to take part in the 'fellowshipping', I made it clear that I was a researcher learning about Born-Again Christianity and other Iranian religious practices in London. The Brazilian guests, however, didn't know my situation and treated me as a fellow 'sister'. When the Pastor called the Brazilian guest to pray with the congregation, I had several women and men approach me and place their hands on my forehead, neck and back and fervently pray and cry in Portuguese, and speak in tongues.

During the course of the day I spoke to several Iranian church members about their impressions of the Brazilians and their style of praying. While some found the Brazilians 'strange' or 'weird', others were very excited about the cultural exchange. Several said, for example: 'Did you feel the power of Jesus?', 'We don't speak Portuguese and they don't speak English or Persian, yet through the power of prayer we can break every boundary'. The Brazilian visit was significant in that it demonstrated the powerful combination of three factors. First, it showed how Iranian Christian martyrs were a source of great strength for the Brazilian guests. This was heightened by the presence of the son of one of the martyrs. Second, the acknowledged and accepted method of touching each other when Pentecostalists pray. This breaks down boundaries of personal space between the church members and creates spaces of intimacy and vulnerability. Third, the way in which simple and popular Evangelical tunes are used to forge a sense of familiarity between the members of the church and members of other Pentecostal churches. The music certainly stirred emotions throughout the church service.

Elam Ministries and Ex-Muslims Training to Become Christian Pastors

The Iranian Christian Fellowship is directly associated to Elam Ministries, and many members of the congregation are either employed by them or in training to become pastors at their headquarters, which is located near Shackleford, Sussex. There are usually around twenty students, with an equal number of men and women, who are mainly from Iran and a few from Central Asia. They reside at the headquarters of Elam Ministries while studying for an Associate Arts Degree in Bible and Theology. Elam Ministries provides a full scholarship for each student, which includes transport, tuition, board, food and stipend. The majority of the students come from Muslim backgrounds and have converted to Pentecostal Christianity in Assemblies of God and Evangelical churches in Tehran, Isfahan, Rasht and Mashad. One student decided to become a Christian pastor while living in Los Angeles, whereas another was proselytised by the Persian-speaking church in Germany when living in a refugee camp. The daughter of Reverend Mehdi Dibaj (murdered in Iran in 1994) and the son and the niece of Bishop Haik Hovsepian-Mehr (also murdered in Iran in 1994) were trained at Elam Ministries.[146]

In order to qualify for the Associate of Arts Degree in Bible and Theology at the Iranian Bible Training Centre (IBTC) it is required that students take at least sixteen courses per year; take part in 'Ministry', which includes mission trips, preaching, worship leading, Sunday school teaching, singing, visitation and evangelism; and are involved in a work programme of housekeeping, maintenance and gardening. The students are also involved in translating and publishing material into the Persian language. For example, the Michaelian Project (named after the Reverend Tateos Michaelian, who was an Iranian church leader and translator of over sixty Christian books into the Persian language and was killed in 1994) aims to translate the previous edition of the Bible, which was written in Persian in 1895, into modern standard Persian. Other projects include translating the crusades, led by popular evangelists like Billy Graham and John Stott, into Persian and make them available on video; publishing a bi-monthly Persian magazine named *Kalameh*; and publishing a series in Persian which deals with theological issues and an assessment of modern thinkers, such as C.S. Lewis, Rousseau and Tolstoy.[147]

The ministers in training are expected to share their conversion experience and their strong faith in Jesus Christ, in churches and homes, at street corners, in trains, whilst standing in queues – everywhere. Elam Ministries organise weekend conferences for Iranian converts, and potential converts living outside Iran. They travel to churches around Britain in order to give talks, teach and lead the services in the Persian language. For example, the assistant minister at the Cornerstone evangelical church in Nottingham said, during a conversation in October 2002, that Elam Ministries have played an important role in catering to the cultural, language and religious needs of the increasing numbers of Iranians in their congregation. Elam's Persian translations of the Bible and other Christian writings have been important sources for Iranian Christians around the world.

They are sent on missions with the task to evangelise Persian speakers in Britain and other countries, such as Turkey, India, Pakistan, Tajikistan, Iran, Armenia, Azerbaijan, Sweden, Norway and Germany. According to the Elam students, although it is not easy to convince Persian speakers from Muslim backgrounds to accept Christianity, they have faith in their missionary work and 'have seen the Lord work in miraculous ways'. Their missionary work and aid programmes usually focus on Persian speakers who have been badly affected by various socio-economic and political situations, and have migrated, usually to impoverished urban settlements, and are in need of both financial and social support. A student named Fatima stated: 'The Iranians who will listen to us talk about Jesus Christ are, for the most part, going through very difficult points of their lives. Most come from backgrounds where religion played an important role but they have become disillusioned with Islam for various reasons.' The following quotes, which are excerpts taken from various Elam Ministries newsletters, refer to the trainee pastors' first experiences in proselytising other Iranians. They also serve as an introduction to the following section, which focuses on Iranians who converted to Christianity in transit to Britain.

The winter 1996 Elam newsletter states:

> Turkey is a country that is crying out for trained Iranian Christian workers. There are about a quarter of a million Iranians living there, many as refugees, and another quarter of a million come in the summer as tourists as they don't need visas. The vast majority of Iranians in Turkey come to Istanbul where for the last ten years there has been very fruitful Christian outreach. Though there is danger, there is relative freedom to share the gospel, and many of the Iranians, especially the refugees, are very open. Their lives are in turmoil and they are longing for a message that will help them make sense of it all. Many are separated from their families, others have marriage problems, and all of them struggle to cope with a foreign culture in often appalling living conditions with hardly any money. At least 150 have come to faith in the last few years, but there is no full time Farsi speaking pastor to look after these believers.

A student went to Istanbul twice in order to speak to Iranian refugees about Jesus Christ. His journey has been described as follows:

> Firouz spent time with a large family of Iranian refugees who are living in one room. He talked to them all privately about Christ and two responded however one man was well known for his hostility to religion and his love for drink. During his second visit something amazing happened. In the morning this man's

son made a commitment to Christ, and then in the afternoon, the father asked Christ into his heart – 'for at least one hour, with tears and loud sobs, he repented and surrendered his life to Christ'. People of course were sceptical, especially the family, but after a few days his daughter came to Ali and said 'Brother Firouz, my father has been changed'. This was a moment Firouz will never forget.

The following quotes are taken from Elam students describing the various missions taken in February 1998:

> Most Kurds in Armenia are Satan worshippers. I was worried about how they would treat me as I'd heard they'd try to kill Christians. So I went with fear, but found these people were ordinary, hard-working people. Their beliefs were more traditional than active.

> This trip strengthened my faith. My mind would say 'no' to many things, but the Lord's ways are different. The story of how the Kurdish church started in Armenia proves this. Should a believer walk 80 kilometres to witness to three women? The mind says 'no', but it happened and it was from these three that 1,200 Kurds became Christians in Armenia.

> I have seen Afghanis in Iran, but I never thought I'd share Jesus with them. In fact they frightened me. In Islamabad I got rid of my fear and saw their faith in Jesus as being strong and pure. We saw a whole Muslim family on the verge of breaking up, come to the Lord. We felt Jesus' love for them so strongly.

Focus Prayer Day on Iran and Central Asia

Elam Ministries, in association with the Evangelical Alliance and the Evangelical Missionary Alliance, organised a focus prayer day on Iran and Central Asia in memory of the Iranian pastors who were killed in Iran. The speakers, representing various associations, such as Youth with a Mission, World in Need, Operation Mobilisation and the Church Missionary Society, focused on missionary work, the safety of the missionaries and the safety of the Christian converts in Iran and Central Asia. The pastor of the Iranian Christian Fellowship and director of Elam Ministries spoke about the growing success of the Iranian Bible School, and the importance of Iranians training full time to learn to preach the Bible and spread the word of God to Persian-speaking areas of the world. He argued that because of the 'darkness of Islam' that is so evident in Iran, and the failed communism in Central Asia, these areas of the world are ready to be touched by Jesus Christ. He continued by saying that Jesus Christ is a strategist in that he had planned for a peaceful war against the Muslims. Believers and missionaries are the soldiers, the words of Jesus Christ are the ammunition, and the radio waves and technology to spread the words of Jesus Christ are their secret weapons.

There were a number of speeches throughout the day, and after each speaker the congregation would get into groups of four or five and pray. People would take turns speaking and, for example, say: 'Dear lord, please give us the strength to be soldiers and fight the darkness of Islam ... Lord we love you so much, please reach out to the missionaries and give them the strength to spread your words ... Lord, in order for our work to be carried out as you want, we need more resources ... Lord, please help us motivate those who are able to give'. As a member is praying out loud, others are humming music, or saying 'Amen', '*Isâ*'.

The Congregation

Let us now consider the different networks of Iranians who take part in the activities of the church and the Iranian Bible school. Members of the ICF consist mainly of Iranians who are from a range of socio-economic and educational backgrounds. There are a few non-Iranian members, who are either missionary workers or married to an Iranian church member. In order to discuss the social dynamics found at the ICF and the Bible school, and some of the different social forces that made them susceptible to Christianity, I have separated the congregation into three categories: first, those who converted to Pentecostal Christianity in Iran; second, those who fled from Iran (usually through Turkey) and converted to Christianity in transit to Britain; and third, those who left Iran and have converted (or are considering conversion) to Christianity in London.

Christian Conversion in Iran

Christian missionaries have for the first time been successful in converting a number of Iranians from Muslim backgrounds to Pentecostal Christianity after the revolution. The majority of the church members who converted to Christianity in Iran were neither the most nor the least affluent in Iranian society. They were mostly those with lower- to middle-class status and have some sort of social and economic independence. Many said they were searching for new channels of influence and activity.[148] They are mostly (or were in Iran) owners of small businesses and workshops, skilled workers (mechanics, plumbers, electrical technicians), musicians, workers in the bazaar, taxi drivers and construction workers.

It is important to point out that there are a number of Armenians and Assyrians who became Born-Again Christians in Iran and are now ICF members. There are also a few second-generation Iranian Pentecostalists, whose parents were born into Muslim households and were then proselytised by Anglican or Presbyterian missionary groups during the 1940s. One woman told me that her father was a student at one of the Anglican mission schools (and good friends with the now Anglican Bishop Dehqani-Tafti) and eventually converted to Christianity. Her mother, who was from a devout Muslim family, was a nurse at the Anglican missionary hospital. She too was influenced by the missionaries and eventually converted to Christianity. I asked the woman if it was difficult growing up in Iran as a Christian. She said that it was very difficult for her parents, but she was never bothered because people blamed her parents for raising her as a Christian.

I asked the first-generation Iranian Christians about their lifestyles in Iran before and after their conversion to Christianity. It was interesting how they often described the period leading up to the decision to convert through vivid accounts of dreams and visions. It important to emphasise that individuals are told by evangelising Christians that they will probably experience an insight or a sign from God that he or she should serve God and be baptised in the Holy Spirit. The content of visions and dreams are commonly interpreted by individuals as such signs from God, and are central when declaring their belief in Jesus Christ during their public testimony at their baptism. A man in his thirties, for instance, said that when he was eighteen years old he had a dream for three nights in a row that Jesus was baptising him. Prior to this he had never read the Bible and was only vaguely familiar with Christianity. He came from a practising Muslim family so he tried to ignore the dreams. One day he told his mother about his reccurring dream and she told him that it would be dangerous and sinful should he tell anyone else. A man in his early thirties reported that he was a practising Muslim and a member of a radical Islamic political group. He fell into a deep depression and decided to commit suicide by overdosing on sleeping pills. When he was about to take the pills he had an incredible vision. He stated: 'I was very far from this light which was pouring forth from the cross. I screamed for the Lord for help and the light came around me.' After that vision he went to the church in Rasht and converted to Christianity. As Martin points out: 'One must not use mechanistic terminology about these processes, or phases which imply that the transformation of the affections is just some means to a social end. People do have such ends but they are admixed with more comprehensive notions of "betterment", and wider notions of "good" as these are conveyed by "visions and revisions".'[149]

After listening to accounts of dreams and visions I would ask questions concerning their jobs, family life and religious upbringing in Iran.[150] It is important to emphasise the eagerness they had to share their testimonies. Many described the social, economic and emotional problems they were experiencing before they turned to Christianity. For example, difficulties in adjusting from rural to urban locations, loss of loved ones killed by the regime or in the Iran–Iraq war, marital or dating problems, serious illnesses, accidents, encounters of death and dealing with adolescence. Even though they all had different personal situations, many linked the root of their problems to the revolution and Islam. According to a woman in her early forties, whom I will call Zahra, the Islamic revolution created many problems for Iranians. Before the revolution, Islam was marginal in her family's life. Unless someone died or got married, the Koran sat on the shelf unused. Zahra said she didn't know what it meant to be a Muslim:

> Life was O.K. before the revolution. I never really questioned being a Muslim. After the revolution, we had to learn about Islam, whether we liked it or not. Seeing what the Islamic government did to my country has put me off Islam forever. When I started to have many problems in my life, I wanted to turn to God but not to Islam. A girl I knew brought me to the Assemblies of God church in Tehran. They were all so friendly and happy ... they were singing instead of crying and mourning like Muslims. In Christianity there is nothing in between me and God.

The changing role of Islam, from being institutionally weak before the revolution to institutionally dominant after the revolution, has been an influential factor underlining the various trajectories that have led to conversions. Converts often described their families before the revolution as believers but not practising Muslims. Although they rejected the government's definition of Islam, the revolution brought on many tensions and insecurities in the day-to-day lives of their family members. They became frustrated by the contradictions between the way in which Islam is publicly defined (and redefined) by the government, and the ways in which Islam was defined and practised (or not practised) in the private sphere. Their comments struck a chord with Hefner's research on Christian conversion in Muslim Java. Hefner wrote:

> The basic socio-religious institutions of society and the sense of social identity they inspired, had to be placed in question before a significant number of Javanese could even begin to contemplate the Christian option. The events that brought about this loosening of tradition were quite varied, but their impact on individual evaluation was everywhere the same. People began to doubt the certainty of received ways, creating the disposition to look for new standards of self-identification.[151]

They began to lose sight of accustomed ways in post-revolutionary society and they started to question different aspects of Iranian society. Several of my informants mentioned that Islam didn't allow them space to breathe anymore and converting to Christianity was a liberating way both to create a self-identification and to channel the resentments that were built up throughout the post-revolutionary period.

I asked why they, and not millions of others experiencing difficulties in post-revolutionary Iran, became interested in Christianity. Some said they were lucky, while others said it was fate and often referred back to their dreams and visions. They usually said that it must have been Jesus' plan. The answers were usually followed by discussions recalling the individuals who first introduced them to Christianity. Although they were susceptible to change in their lives, converting to Pentecostal Christianity would not have been a remote possibility if they hadn't been individually approached by evangelising Christians. They described how they met other Christians and were eventually convinced to attend a church service. Repeated attendance, along with the evangelical socialisation at the church (including meeting Iranian Muslim converts to Christianity) was what led many towards the route to conversion.

It is also significant that most converts did not have (and still don't have) a doctrinal understanding of Christianity when they were baptised. They were impressed by the joyous disposition of the Christians, the church liturgy and music, the conservative values, the desegregation and positive treatment of women and the personal treatment that each member received. They criticised the mourning and crying for Shia religious martyrs, the dress codes, gender-specific groups for Shia religious gatherings and Islam mixed with politics. As discussed earlier, they were influenced by the Christian interpretation of a passage in the Book of Jeremiah, claiming that Islam is the darkness that has spread across Iran and that Christ will restore the fortunes of the Elamites. Although some of my informants subscribed to Christianity before having understood all its entailments, they were convinced that converting was the right thing to do and they felt secure within their new social environment.

Developing a solid sense of security and an affinity with fellow Christians was an important stage to reach before many felt prepared to tell their family and friends about their conversion experience. The social stigmatisation and the demand from friends and families to justify the radical act often prompted new converts to defend their actions, resulting in a deeper identification with their new faith and the environment provided by the church. The various families' immediate reaction to a family member converting to Christianity is quite similar. They were/are shocked, embarrassed and confused about the conversion, and were/are very concerned about their son's or daughter's safety in Iran. Many converts recalled the negative and harsh reactions from friends and family. In some cases converts have introduced Christianity to their brothers, sisters, cousins and friends, who have also converted to Christianity. It is important to add that many have chosen to hide their conversion experience in order to circumvent the problems that it could create for family members. Many feared for the safety and the well-being of their families.

The Iranians who were involved in churches in Tehran, Rasht, Isfahan, and Mashad said their activities were increasingly being monitored by government officials at the end of the 1980s and the beginning of the 1990s. The Iranian Christian converts, who fall into the category of 'unprotected infidels' were threatened either to be sentenced to prison or killed if they were caught evangelising. Many churches were then closed by the government. As outlined above, the situation worsened in the beginning of the 1990s when Pentecostal church leaders were threatened, imprisoned and executed for their beliefs. Although members of the congregations were not targeted by the government, there have been reports of harassment and discrimination against Iranian converts. I have come across numerous accounts of Iranian converts being temporarily detained, threatened and discriminated against at their workplace and academic institutions, without actually being charged with apostasy or faced with violent persecution. For example, a man reported that once it became known that he was a Born-Again Christian he was expelled from reading law at the University of Tehran. He added that during his military service he spent time in prison because of his Christian faith. Other converts said that although they did not experience any persecution or harassment in Iran they always felt vulnerable and at risk. Many are afraid to openly practise Christianity due to the unpredictable and unevenly applied forms of persecution which could be carried out not only on themselves but on family members as well. While some reported that they left Iran because they could no longer face the social pressure of property raids, threats and intimidation, others came for reasons not directly tied to their faith, including education, work opportunities and family reunions. Many heard about Elam Ministries and the ICF in London through Christian networks in Iran.[152]

Conversion to Christianity in Transit

Let us now turn to those who fled Iran as Muslims and arrived in Britain as Born-Again Christians. These Iranians, who have similar backgrounds to the Iranians described above, come from the lower to middle stratas of Iranian society. For a variety of reasons these Iranians claim they were forced to leave Iran in order to escape threats and harassment by revolutionary guards. Most of the Iranians in this category paid smugglers to escort them out of Iran and into Turkey, with hopes of eventually being granted asylum in a Western European country. My informants described the many pressures of their migration experience, such as devalued status, language barriers, conflicts with the Turkish officials, and problems of housing, education, health and depression. During the migration process (usually at a low point) they were approached by Pentecostal Christians (like a trainee pastor from Elam Ministries) who would take them under their wing and provide them with emotional and sometimes material support.

A man in his early thirties, whom I will call Bahram, lived in a rural village until his (nominally Muslim) family migrated to Tehran in late 1980s. He said that although he had a lot of family in Tehran it was not easy for him to adjust to the insecurities of city life. Due to the financial situation he was not able to marry the woman he loved. He said that his life became even more difficult when he became implicated in a political endeavour against the Iranian government. His parents urged him to leave Iran as soon as possible. Bahram paid smugglers $7,000 to assist him in passing through the Turkish borders, and for organising further transportation to the Netherlands.

Bahram was arrested by Turkish police when he arrived. He was able to escape, but from that point he was always running away from the police and under the threat of being arrested. By the time he reached Istanbul Bahram was in a desperate state. He had no money, food or shelter and was sleeping on the beaches. He was approached by an Iranian Christian on the beach, who took him to a Christian church and gave him food and water. Bahram said he would listen to them talk about religion and Jesus, although it meant nothing to him, because he needed their help to survive. Eventually, he was baptised. According to Bahram, the evangelical church gave him the support he needed in order to organise his exit from Turkey and passage to Britain. I asked how involved the church was in this process and I was told that they were indirectly involved because it is illegal to buy forged documents, pay smugglers, bribe immigration officers, and so on, but he would not have been able to make all the arrangements if he had not met them.

His exit from Turkey was arranged by smugglers, who bribed the immigration officers to let him pass through with fake documents. He then flew to Britain, was granted asylum and received housing and other benefits from the state. The Christian church in Turkey gave him the address of the Iranian Christian church in Chiswick and he has become a regular member. Although in the beginning Bahram did not take Christianity seriously and he used it as a means for survival, he now claims to be a true Christian. For Bahram, the Christian church in London provides the stability and supportive environment he needs to improve his socio-economic position. Through the church, by providing him with a code of ethics and networks of Iranian friends, he has been able to build a good life in London. He is a minicab driver, and is taking classes in order to become a skilled mechanic. He no longer receives full benefits from the state.

Another example is Layla. It was planned that she and her six children would leave Iran and travel to Turkey, and her Iranian husband would meet them there as soon after as he could. Layla and her children lived together in an inadequate one-room flat in Istanbul as they waited for him. It was during these two years in Istanbul that Layla met Iranians who were Born-Again Christians, who convinced her to attend the church services. Eventually she converted. She recalls that Jesus entered her life at one of her lowest points, and that her life has been getting better ever since. She was given the opportunity to leave Turkey and apply for asylum in London.[153] Layla and her children currently live in a council flat in Southall.

Finally, Amir. Before the revolution, Amir (who is currently in his early thirties) lived in a middle-class neighbourhood in Khoramshahr, a city in south Iran. His father owned an import and export company. He and his family were (are) monarchists and avid supporters of the Shah. The events surrounding the revolution led to the bankruptcy of his father's business, and they were forced to move to Tehran to find work. His mother and father were practising Muslims and his father has travelled to Mecca. He and his sister were told to pray five times a day and fast through Ramadan, but they were never forced to practise. His mother still prays, and his father is a believer but is against the idea of an Islamic country. Amir had many problems when he was a student in Tehran because he openly expressed his distaste for the government, and he was constantly being followed and harassed by the revolutionary guards. Amir said that he was not able to conform to the rules that the government imposed on him (especially the required military service), and his parents were becoming increasingly concerned about the consequences of his behaviour. It reached a point where he had no choice but to flee from Iran. His family paid $2,000 for him to be smuggled out of Iran to Turkey, and another $3,000 to be smuggled out of Turkey, with the promise of his destination, Sweden (where his sister was living). Amir had to stay in Van, Turkey for one month and then travelled to Istanbul, where he lived for about a year. The time he spent in Turkey was very difficult for him. Amir stated:

> Turkey was all corruption, bribes, being beaten up by Turkish police, seeing how they wanted to take advantage of Iranian women and teenage girls, just because of our situation, and we could not protest. On my very last day in Turkey I had my passport and ticket to Sweden (I didn't have any legal passports or legal documents, so everything was bought and forged); the police arrested me. I was on my own now, I had to take the initiative and handle these policemen by myself otherwise I could end up in a Turkish prison. I started to speak English, which was a good point because those policemen couldn't speak any English. I took out [my Swedish passport] and started to speak to them non-stop, and when one of them saw that first of all they couldn't understand me and I had my passport with a Swedish visa, which was a gamble to show it to them, they let me go. In the beginning (in Sweden) I just could not adapt myself into the big changes, not that I was in trouble or this was an extra thing to handle. BUT, all I needed was some time to forget all those hard times in Turkey, (not even in Iran I had such a hard time).

Amir was approached by Christians involved in the Philadelphia Pentecostal church and asked (along with other foreigners) to attend a summer camp. He states: 'I was just amazed when they wanted me to become a Christian, just like that with a snap of a finger, that's not the way to evangelise to somebody who is running from a religion already. [It was difficult] when they said Jesus is the Son of God without any explanation.' He continued to have faith in God but he no longer identified himself as being Muslim. He blamed the series of difficulties in his life, which started in Iran, then Turkey, then Sweden, on the corruption of Islam. He decided to attend the summer camp, which lasted for about one week. One of the nights they were swimming in a lake and one of the participants drowned. His death, according to Amir, played a significant role in his conversion to Christianity. He states: 'What is it? How is it? Today I am born and tomorrow I die? I have gone through all the trouble to save myself from Ayatollah's regime, a death such as this is lost in vain. How can I save myself is the question. And the answer is CHRIST JESUS.' Amir was also influenced by the writings of Billy Graham. He was baptised in 1990. The Pentecostal church, which required its members to adhere to a strict ethical code (for example, no alcohol, dancing, swearing, smoking; sexual relations permitted only within a traditional marriage) improved Amir's marginal social position by providing him with social base in Sweden. After Amir converted to Christianity he was no longer accepted by his Iranian friends in Sweden. He states:

> My family did also react to my decision but after a few conversations we decided not to speak about this matter at home. Because this would upset my mom and that's why we wouldn't talk about it. But now I am more accepted as a Christian in my family than I was before. And another thing is, even as a Christian, I was never thought of as an outcast or a black sheep in the family.

He and his family have not told their relatives and friends in Iran about Amir's conversion to Christianity.

Amir moved to London in 1996. He was very happy when he came across the ICF because he always thought that he was the only Iranian who had converted to Christianity. He was very excited when he learned about the Elam Ministries mission, based on Jeremiah 49:34–39. He believes that the Persian culture has stopped flourishing ever since Islam became the established religion in his country. Amir has been struggling to make a living in London. He worked as a clerk in a clothes store and was aiming to set up his own business as a translator.

The accounts discussed above have attempted to demonstrate the way in which dislocated Iranians, at times of destitution and loneliness, became exposed to evangelising Christians and their support systems. Empirical research on Iranian conversions in Turkey is needed in order to understand if or to what extent Christian missionaries assist emigration to locations outside Turkey. I was told that the ICF and Elam Ministries are not directly involved in migration matters. They see it being their duty to provide a religious service for legitimate converts who show up at their church. Iranian Christian International states in its September 2002 newsletter that it assists Iranian Christian refugees around the world by gathering evidence of support to strengthen cases. In some cases it provides lawyers for the asylum seekers as well.

Conversion to Christianity in Britain

The final group to be considered are Iranians who arrived in Britain as Muslims, and have since converted to Pentecostal Christianity. Unlike the first two categories, they come from a range of socio-economic backgrounds. Many have lived in London since the revolution, come from middle-class backgrounds, have a university education and are, for example, employed as the following: electrical engineers, computer technicians, financial consultants, solicitors, and in sales positions. These Iranians often describe themselves as the victims of the revolution and Islamic politics. Many arrived in London in 1979 and 1980; would identify as being 'Persian' and not 'Iranian'; and would draw upon glorified images of the pre-Islamic Persian heritage in constructing their identities in London. After several years of living outside Iran many said that they started feeling nostalgic about it and attended more and more Iranian cultural events in London. Some said that they also became interested in religion, and started to read about erfan and the mystical aspects of Islam. Their accounts usually led to something extraordinary or traumatic, such as a job loss, bankruptcy, a medical 'miracle', or the death of a loved one that shook their lives and forced them to change their lifestyles, that made them more susceptible to new ideas and belief systems. Many found conversion as an inroad to British society and a way to gain social capital.

For example, a man whom I'll refer to as Taghi is in his late thirties and from a middle-class family from Tehran. His father, who was a supporter of the Shah, was forced to leave Iran at the time of the revolution. He moved his family to Kensington and invested most of their money in property. Taghi spent a lot of time socialising at expensive clubs and restaurants with his Iranian and British friends. He regularly drank alcohol, and experimented with drugs. When he realised that his stay in London was not temporary he started to take part in Iranian activities in London. Although religion had not played a large role in his life he also started to think about God and religion. In 1986 some of his friends introduced him to the Shahmaghsoudi Sufi Order, which at that time was being held in a house in north London. He regularly attended the gathering with approximately thirty other wealthy Iranians. Eventually he became disillusioned with the Sufi Order because he felt that the Master was mistakenly regarded as an infallible holy figure.[154]

In 1991 his family lost their money and property in the recession and he could no longer lead the same sort of lifestyle. He was extremely hurt when people whom he considered to be his best friends, no longer called him or invited him to social events. He became very depressed and lonely. He hated both the religion and society in Iran and the Iranian society and (Sufi) religious circles in London. Taghi confided in a British man whom he knew from work and who suggested that Taghi should meet him at a church in Notting Hill Gate, named the Kensington Temple. He went to the church and was fascinated by the singing, the charismatic style of the pastor, the friendliness and openness of the multicultural congregation and the weekly healings. Every Sunday the pastor would ask, 'Who wants to be saved? Who wants Jesus Christ in their lives?' Those interested were asked to walk to the front of the church and pray together. Taghi said that one Sunday he was overwhelmed by the church service and found himself at the front of the church praying with the pastor. He was baptised soon after.

When I asked converts why they left the Sufi Orders they all commented that the Sufi master had too much power, and the hierarchical relationship between the Sufi master and the disciples was based more on obedience than on love. When I told Taghi that I was attending Sufi gatherings for my research project he became concerned, and said that I could very easily be brainwashed by the evil *zekr*. The following Sunday he gave me a video, produced by a number of evangelical Christian groups, which condemned Sufism and other esoteric religious movements.

Taghi was surprised when he heard from a church member about the ICF because he always thought that he was the only Iranian Muslim in London who had converted to Christianity. Although he found the ICF too conservative, he regularly attended the Sunday service in order to introduce his Muslim mother (who does not speak English) to Christianity. His mother, who was hurt and embarrassed by his conversion, agreed to attend the ICF's Sunday services because she wanted to understand her son's fascination with Christianity. Although she refuses to be baptised, she started to attend regularly the ICF's Sunday service, with or without her son. She has not told any

of her Muslim friends and family in London or Iran about her son's conversion to Christianity, and she has continued to follow the events on the
Shia calendar and still attends some *sofrehs* and other Shia religious events in
Iran and London. Taghi said that although he felt like a new person after his
baptism, he did not feel completely cleansed from the sins of his past. He was
told by the pastor at the Kensington Temple to find out if his ancestors, stemming back five generations, were abnormally sinful people. He found out that
his great-great-grandfather was a Mullah. Taghi, who considers Islam as a
front for the devil, decided that it was necessary for the pastors at the Kensington Temple to release him from his evil past by conducting an exorcism.
Taghi spent five nights, 8:00 pm to midnight, at the church being 'delivered'
from his ancestor's sins. According to Taghi, there are many members of the
ICF who are in need of an exorcism but the elders of the ICF are too conservative for such methods.

Baptisms and Church Members

This section focuses on individuals who have been baptised at the ICF and
are currently church members. Baptisms are held at the ICF approximately
every six months. What follows describes one of the baptisms.

The church service started with songs in Persian and in English, which
were followed by inspirational talks given by special guest lecturers. For
example, the main pastor of a Pentecostal church in north Iran spoke about
the current difficulties of practising Christianity in Iran. He no longer asked
the congregation to meet together because it was far too dangerous in light of
the Islamic government's campaign against Christian pastors. After he made
this announcement to his congregation in Iran he began to receive letters
from the church members saying they wanted to continue meeting in spite of
the threats from the government. He said the letters were often written in
blood, signifying their devotion to Jesus Christ to their death. The charismatic
pastor then talked about a woman who was arrested for converting to Christianity. He went to the prison to give her support and she said that she needed
no other support besides her faith in Christ. He was an impressive speaker
who had the ability to stir emotions, bringing many to tears. The day was full
of such inspirational stories, songs and prayers.

The lecture was followed by a presentation of each baptismal candidate's
public testimony. Each candidate stood alone at the front of the church and
described their lives as Muslims, their first encounter with Christianity, the
problems they have faced with their families and friends. They publicly
declared their love for Jesus Christ and told the congregation the reasons why
they wanted to be Christians. Similar to the Shahmaghsoudi Sufi Order, they
often describe their newly found religious practices as the purest form of
religion, unlike Islam and other organised religions which are contaminated
by politics and power. It is important to note that the testimonies are
extremely important to the members of the ICF, not only at the time of the

baptism. On numerous occasions I came across people exchanging each other's testimonies to read. It has also become popular for Iranians around the world to post their testimonies on the Internet. The testimonies are one of tools used to convince others to convert.

On this occasion three women and five men were baptised (all from Muslim backgrounds), ranging from their late twenties to early fifties. Two of the candidates were sisters and two were a married couple. In between each testimony the congregation would sing, pray and listen to special guest lecturers. After the testimonies, the baptismal candidates, who wore white gowns, took turns entering the baptismal font with the pastor (the church altar conceals a pool of water). The pastor read a passage from the Bible and then someone from the congregation, usually the person who first introduced Christianity to the candidate, would say a personalised prayer. The baptismal rights were then read out in Persian and translated into English to the baptismal candidate. The pastor placed his hand on each candidate's head in turn and proceeded by pushing each candidate into the water until fully submerged. The congregation applauded and many cried. The following three accounts are from notes taken during the baptism and from interviews with Iranians who were recently baptised.

An Iranian man in his early fifties delivered his testimony. He is an electrical engineer and a lecturer, who received his training from MIT. He is married to a Western women and they have one son. He grew up as a practising Muslim and won awards as a child for reading the Koran. When he started to study science he lost much faith in religion and he and his wife decided that religion would not play a large role in their lives. He was transferred to Kuwait and he was excited to live with his family in a Muslim country. In Kuwait, however, his wife 'was touched by Jesus Christ' and his son also became a Born-Again Christian. This was very difficult for the man to accept. Reluctantly he started to read the Bible and slowly he became interested. He did, however, have a big problem with the idea of the Holy Trinity. He said that he took all of his questions and prejudices concerning Christianity to the pastor of the ICF, who would sit with him for hours and explain the basic tenets of Christianity. With help from the pastor, several church members, his wife and his son, he slowly began to accept and understand many different aspects of Christianity. He said that he did not decide to become a Christian until he dreamt that Jesus Christ 'touched his heart' in a dream.

A woman whom I will call Sara was also baptised. She had been growing more and more depressed in Iran, after several unsuccessful pregnancies, and she was told by friends and family that it would be good for her and her husband to change their environment. They decided to move to London because they knew several Iranians who were living there. In Iran Sara regularly attended women-only Shia religious gatherings and travelled to many religious shrines. When she arrived in London she was not involved in any religious activities, other than saying her prayers. He husband worked as a mechanic where he met some Iranians who introduced him to the ICF, and he started to attend the Church services regularly. Sara was highly suspicious of the church and was worried that it was going to change her husband and their relationship. She decided to go to some of the services in order to find its faults, and then be able to convince her husband to stop attending. She said that she continued to be critical of the ICF up until the day she realised that her husband had changed into a healthier and happier man, and from that moment she started to change her attitude towards Christianity. Sara and her husband were eventually baptised together. Four or five months after their baptism Sara found out that she was pregnant. She said that at the stage of the pregnancy when she had miscarried many times in the past, she had a dream that Jesus Christ operated on her, like her doctors in Iran. According to Sara, she knew when she woke up from her dream that she was going to give birth to a healthy child. Sara and her husband have directly linked Sara's healthy pregnancy with their conversion to Christianity.

A 16-year-old girl, whom I refer to as Schirin, grew up in Shiraz. Her father was a bus driver for the army, but after the revolution he was forced to retire. He decided to move to Britain in order to find employment. Schirin, her mother and her three sisters flew to London to join their father in 1993. She said that she was very nervous going through the immigration process when she arrived in Britain. They had to prove to the immigration officer that she had a medical emergency and that her father was in the country. Her brother was not allowed to come because he was a man over eighteen years old, and thought to be able to provide for himself in Iran. He is currently living in Iran and is a practising Muslim. Her family has always been religious but they did not follow all the rules in their home, like they had to at school. Schirin stated: 'Religion was mostly in our family so that we could grow up in a right way and also to teach us who we could trust in times of need but in Islam it's wrong to ask questions about God which I never knew why.' Once they settled in London, they met several Iranians who were members of the ICF. She stated: 'I was suffering from a kidney infection since I was two years old. We had tried everything from modern medicine to Muslim shrines for healing and nothing had worked and I was on death row when I came to the U.K. We met a few Christians, they prayed for me and I was healed.' She said that doctors in London also played a part in curing her.

Schirin and her family felt that it was a miracle from God that she was cured and they all decided to learn more about Christianity. They were eventually baptised at the ICF and they have become active participants in church events. I asked her if she told her friends at school about her conversion to Christianity. She answered: 'In school my Muslim friends tell me I have sinned and some day I will pay for it but when I tell them about my medical problem they don't say anything to that but I show them respect even though they may hate me for what I did but after a while they see I'm just like any other human being.' According to Schinn many Iranians have converted to Christianity because 'in Christianity you feel more close to God and you have a more loving relationship but in Islam religion is mixed with politics and no one likes being forced into anything and they see Christianity is not like religion it's like have a close relationship with God.'

The other Iranians who have converted to Christianity in London had, in many cases, left Iran during the 1990s. They come from lower- to middle-class backgrounds. According to an elder of ICF they have had Iranians who show up at the church pretending to be interested in Christianity and wanting to be baptised in order to obtain a written document to verify their Christian status. This document would then be used to strengthen their application to the Home Office, with hopes of being granted asylum on religious grounds. According to a church elder, this puts the church in a difficult position because, on the one hand, they don't want to turn anyone away from the church but, on the other, they do not want to baptise Iranians for the wrong reasons. The church elder said that they spend a lot of time with individuals who show up at the church and are interested in Christianity. In order to be Born Again it is necessary for an individual to make an admission of sins, profess his or her belief in Jesus Christ and repent and turn away from sin. According to the elder, those who attend the church under false pretences will often become impatient with the process, which requires dedication and sincerity. He also said that there have been Iranians who have come to the church for the wrong reasons, but have eventually become committed followers of Christ.

Iranian Women as Born-Again Christians – Preserving Morals

Ladies' Fellowship Meetings

Iranian Ladies' Fellowship meetings are held once a month on a weekday, and are designed to bring the women members of the church together to pray and to discuss various church projects, such as charity events, the children's Sunday School, organising conferences, decorating the church for special holidays, producing cookbooks and so on. The first time I attended the women's fellowship, the meeting was set aside to clean and scour the church kitchen and the church hall. There were two British women present (both in their late forties), who had been Christian missionaries in Iran during the 1970s and are married to two of the five elders of the Iranian Christian Fellowship. There were two women (in their forties) from Armenian backgrounds who have been members of the ICF from the beginning. The rest of the women were from Muslim backgrounds (in their twenties, thirties, forties or fifties) and have been baptised at the ICF in the last ten years. As we were cleaning out the kitchen cupboards I asked several of the women whether or not the church allows women to be pastors or elders. The women from Muslim backgrounds said they were not sure and that they had never thought about this issue. They asked one of the British women, whom I'll refer to as Kate, who then defended the church's position. She said:

Theoretically women are not allowed to be pastors or elders. In certain situations it is O.K. One of our students who graduated from the Bible College is now a pastor at an Iranian church in Germany. There were no men who were trained as pastors in the region, so she, with our blessings, is heading the church. The Scripture gives power to men in some parts of the Bible and power to women in other parts ... overall men and women are equal in the eyes of the Lord. I do not want women to be allowed to be pastors or elders because I think men are negating many of their duties as it is. Women, in today's world, are expected to take care of everything ... if the men weren't compelled to take the leadership roles they would easily let the women take on all of the work.

The Iranian women listening to Kate tended to agree and made comments such as 'I have enough problems trying to take care of my family, can you imagine taking care of a Church', and 'Women have important jobs in this church ... jobs that are better for women'. One woman replied, 'Yes, but I think that the men should scrub the church kitchen next time.' Another replied: 'They are in charge of maintaining the building.'

The second Ladies' Fellowship meeting I attended consisted of ten to fifteen women and was held at the home of one the church members. The majority of the Iranian women were from Muslim backgrounds, and there was one woman from an Armenian background. The majority of the Iranian women from Muslim backgrounds were single women with children, and living in council flats in areas throughout London. The pastor's wife, whom I'll call Karen, began the meeting by welcoming the women and asking them to share any new testimonies (the women spoke in Persian which was followed by a translation into English).

A woman in her late twenties, whom I'll call Marjan, said that one of her relatives was very sick and was in need of an operation, so her family members, who are all Muslim, decided that they should all come together and pray. Her sick relative then went to the hospital and the doctor said that he no longer needed an operation. Although her relatives believe that Allah answered their prayers, Marjan believes that Jesus Christ listened to her prayers and healed her relative. Another woman, who was baptised in August 1998, discussed how her Muslim friends have not been able to accept her conversion to Christianity. Although they have stopped returning her phone calls and she no longer receives invitations, she decided to try one last time and invite them over for dinner. Once they accepted the invitation, she became nervous and decided to turn to the Bible for advice. She read about Paul's method of making people from different backgrounds and religions feel comfortable by taking on their customs and roles. She then, in hopes of reminding her Muslim guests that she is still Iranian even though she is now Christian, decided to go to an Iranian store and buy a popular Iranian video. She said that during the dinner, her Iranian guests felt uncomfortable and there was little conversation. However, once she took out the Iranian video this sparked conversation, and her old friends, for the first time since her conversion, seemed to feel a bit relaxed with her.

Another testimony was given by a woman in her fifties, who became a Christian in Mashad and had left Iran as an asylum seeker with her twelve-year-old son, five months previously. When she first arrived the state placed her in a hotel in Southhall which, she said, was dirty and an unbearable environment for her and her son to live in. She prayed to God that she would be moved to a better home. She said that God answered her prayers and she was placed in a nicer hotel with people who are very courteous and clean.

The women continued to discuss the ways in which Jesus Christ 'carried' them through difficult situations in their lives. Throughout the testimonies the women would mutter 'Alleluia', and 'Praise Jesus'. This was followed by a speech given by the pastor's wife, which focused on women and the importance of the home. She first spoke about how difficult it had been for her to adapt to certain aspects of Iranian culture when she first moved to Iran as a newlywed. For example, she was not accustomed to an 'open home', where unexpected visitors walk in and out of their house throughout the day. She then referred to Luke 10:38–42, and how, although it is difficult for some people to give up their privacy, it is God's wish for Christians to open their homes to friends, relatives and people in need. She argued that the home is the woman's domain and it is her responsibility for making the family members exist in harmony with each other. If the woman is not happy in the home, then the entire household will not be happy. She then read several passages in the Bible that give advice to women as to how they should manage their household and their families. The conversations resonated with the discussions I heard at the *sofreh* gatherings.

The pastor's wife stressed the point that women should be busy at home but they should not be 'busybodies'. She also discussed the importance of women being obedient and submissive to their husbands, and how it is the woman's responsibility to teach her children to be obedient so they are able to grow into the roles of 'husband' and 'wife'. She then went on to say that when women get upset they rarely forget, making women guiltier than men of not being merciful in relationships. She discussed the need for women to be able to swallow their pride and forgive their husbands and children. It is also the woman's responsibility to build up her family members through words of encouragement.

An open forum of prayer followed Karen's speech. Whereas the first part of the meeting was reserved for testimonies of positive and uplifting experiences in the women's life, the final part of the fellowship meeting consisted of the women asking Jesus Christ for help and guidance through the difficult times they are having in London, mainly as a result of poor housing conditions, visa problems, separation of family members, medical problems and language barriers. For example, the woman who hosted the meeting prayed that her family will eventually find their way in London. She, her husband and young child arrived in London from Iran two years ago and have been moved by the state into seven different hotels and council flats. She has recently received a letter from the Council saying that she and her husband must move once again, in two months' time. She was hoping that after two years she would be settled into the new environment, speaking English, and working at least part time, but instead she has been packing and unpacking from one area of London to another.

During the prayers the women would usually share their problems and describe their desperate situations and then say, for example: 'But Lord, my problems are nothing compared to other people's problems. Let's pray for the thousands of homeless in Honduras ... they know what suffering is ... I am grateful for so many things, I have my health, Lord. I need to be patient ... I shouldn't be angry that I'm the 135th on the Council-flat waiting list. I pray that the 134 people are taken care of first.' The prayers were then followed by lunch and socialising.[155] During lunch I had several women ask me about my background. I told the women about my interest in various Iranian religious associations in London, and my interest in the Iranian Christian church and its congregation. They asked several questions, such as 'Where is your family?'; 'Are you married?'; 'Do you live with friends?'; 'Is Jesus Christ in your life?'. They were happy to hear that my parents are not divorced and I have six brothers and sisters. They asked my age and whether or not I'm married. When I told them I was twenty-nine years old and not married I heard several comments about how women are getting married too late these days. When I told them that I was raised a Catholic, one of the women responded, 'as long as your heart is open to listen to the words of Jesus Christ ...' Another woman said: 'For some reason, Jesus has brought you to us and this church.'

I asked women, throughout the course of my research, to describe the roles and expectations that the church assigns to the women members (in terms of church roles, sexuality and family), and how they are similar and different from what they were accustomed to before they converted to Christianity. The majority of the women I spoke to, regardless of their diverse backgrounds, described the Iranian Church as a place where they can freely express themselves. For instance, the women who were practising Muslims before converting to Christianity often complained about wearing a hejâb in public and in front of males who were not relatives. They found the separation between sexes at prayer gatherings a waste of time. According to a 35-year-old woman named Parisa:

> It is not possible to be close to God when you're smothered in a chador and going to one women's gathering after another ... they are places to socialise, gossip and eat. Islam has so many rules for women that it brings the women further away from God than closer to God. In this Church I can stand next to a man, and pray and sing with him, without feeling shy or guilty. I can open my arms to the Lord and pray out loud.

I asked Parisa if she ever considered practising the Muslim religion in London, where in many Iranian religious circles she would not be expected to wear a chador or *rusari* and could freely socialise with men. She responded by saying that Islam is not stable. She said there may be some groups in London who practise Islam in a different way than what's happening in Iran, but that could change. In Islam one day women are forced to wear the veil, the next day they are not. She believes that the uncertainty reflects the violent conflicts that can be found in the Koran. She argued that Christianity is stable, Jesus Christ is full of love, and this can be felt during the church services.

I also interviewed a woman named Fereshteh, who is in her late forties. She was forced to leave Iran six years ago and ended up in Sweden, which is where she converted to Christianity. Although she has always believed in God she never felt comfortable practising her faith, and this intensified when worked as a nurse in a hospital in Tehran. She could no longer tolerate the religious rules imposed by the Islamic government regarding the different treatment of men and women and the overall management of the hospital. She spoke out openly against the government until her life was threatened and she was forced to leave Iran for safety. Fereshteh states:

> After I left Iran I wanted nothing to do with Islam. It is a terrible religion that talks more about war than it does about love. When I worked as a nurse in Tehran, I would see ways that I could help people who were suffering but because of some religious rules I would be stopped from doing my job. I have always believed in God ... I wanted a place to pray ... when I met Iranian Christians in Sweden and started to read the Bible I started to become interested. I was sure I wanted to be Christian when I saw the way women could take part in praying, rejoicing and singing together with the men.

Several women said it took a long time to feel comfortable singing and praying in a public gathering. A Muslim woman in her sixties (who attends the service because her oldest son has converted to Christianity) moved to Kensington after the revolution and is now a widow. She considers herself to be a good Muslim and often attends *sofrehs* and other Shi'a religious gatherings in London. In order to try to understand his conversion, she decided to attend a Sunday service and found the songs, the song leaders, and the preaching 'silly' and like 'pop music'. During the period of my research project, she became convinced that Christianity is the true religion. She said she was having terrible problems with her knee. One Sunday, when an American healer conducted the church services in Chiswick, she claims that she felt Jesus enter her life and he healed her knee. Since then she has stopped attending all Muslim religious functions and concentrates solely on Christianity.

Expectations of Women Outside of the Church

The majority of the women I spoke to find that their conversion to Christianity and their role in the Church has released them from the confines of Islam, and has given them a sense of freedom and self-worth. This is similar to several research projects discussed in Martin's work on Pentecostalism in South America, which states:

> From everything that has been suggested so far, it is clear that women are among the 'voiceless' given a new tongue in the circle of Pentecostal communication. Since this is likely to cause surprise given the emphasis of some

American evangelicals on female subordination, it is worth recollecting that
one source of female emancipation in the nineteenth century was the evangelical tradition (as well as the Unitarian and Quaker traditions).[156]

It is also interesting to point out that the Iranian women's knowledge of
Christianity in general, and their understanding of the Church's doctrinal
stance regarding the roles of women in the church, is limited. This point was
discussed in Hefner's research on Christian conversion in Muslim Java,
where he found examples of 'Christian Javanese converts, subscribing to the
faith before having understood its entailment, indicating that not all believers
need have thought through the conceptual implication of doctrines or beliefs
they endorse as their own ... Thus, an individual can be committed to a particular belief system without fully understanding its conceptual truth or social
entailments.'[157]

The women, however, are aware of the church's position regarding the
role of women outside the church and the rules that apply to the body, such
as marriage, sexuality and dietary laws. The Pentecostal church's conservative outlook towards family, marriage and sexuality provides a framework for
the women to display their commitment to 'traditional' values while maintaining their ethnic distinctiveness. For example, a woman named Mariam,
who is a housewife with two children, told me how worried she was about
raising her children in London. Mariam told me about her family in Iran and
how important it is to be raised in a close-knit and caring family, and she
stressed the importance of children being disciplined in order to know the
difference between right and wrong. Family life in London, she argued, is
very different from family life in Iran, in that the children and teenagers in
London are not properly supervised and are not taught any morals and values. She finds that smoking, drinking, swearing and sex before marriage are
considered as normal practices for teenagers in London and can be seen
uncensored on British television. Although she was never religious in Iran
and dislikes many aspects of Islam, she liked many of the morals that Islam
provided families. She (like the majority of my interviewees) feels comfortable with the moral outlook of the ICF because it is what she and her
husband are accustomed to, with the following practices being forbidden or
frowned upon: premarital and extramarital sex, alcohol, smoking, dressing
promiscuously, homosexuality, lesbianism and swearing.

Conclusions

Since the revolution, evangelical Christian missionaries have been successful
for the first time in converting a number of Iranians from Muslim backgrounds, living both inside and outside Iran, to Christianity. In order to
understand the significance of this phenomenon, it was necessary examine
several strands of Christianity in Iran, focusing particularly on the various
Protestant missionaries' projects. Central to this discussion were the varied
and changing attitudes towards Christian minority groups, depending on the

political and socio-economic processes at different historical moments. When Pentecostal churches started to appear in Iran in the late 1950s they developed as independent institutions that were mainly successful in proselytising Iranians from Armenian and Assyrian backgrounds. These factors proved to be important for the continuation of the churches during the first ten years of the Islamic government. The Anglican Church, however, was associated with foreign money and Muslim converts, and therefore faced severe persecution from the government, starting in 1979.

There has been no research that has concentrated on the growth of Iranian Muslim converts to Born-Again Christianity. In order to understand the dynamics involved in this development it was necessary to start the discussion by introducing the research undertaken by writers such as Bruce and Martin, who write about the expansion of Evangelical, Born-Again Christianity in America and around the world. They first pointed out that Pentecostalism, like Puritanism and Methodism in the past, has provided meaning and support for those coming to terms with rapid social, political and economic transitions. As a result of the growing economy in America, Bruce has argued that ascetic lifestyles have given way to more material lifestyles which have triggered the general shift from orthodox belief and practices in the supernatural to the psychologised gospel of positive thinking and the individual pursuit of personal happiness. (The therapy-based religion of the Shahmaghsoudi Sufi Order can also be placed within this trend.) In addition to providing personal therapy and self-help techniques in coming to terms with rapid social change, Martin argued that further explanations are necessary to explain the process of Muslim conversion to Born-Again Christianity. He pointed out that susceptibility to a different faith is not usually a possibility for an individual unless they have either become detached from established socio-economic and familial institutions or are a part of a mass conversion, during periods of rapid socio-cultural change.

In order to understand the complex play of forces involved in the process of conversion, I considered the Iranians in three broad categories: first, those who converted to Pentecostal Christianity in Iran and now live in London; second, those who fled from Iran (usually through Turkey) and converted to Christianity in transit to Britain; and third, those who left Iran and have converted (or are considering conversion) to Christianity in London. I argued that evangelical Christianity has operated as a liberating space for those who have experienced serious problems of coping with an ineffective or unfamiliar institutional infrastructure in Iran and Britain. The major transformations in Iranian society, which resulted in internal and external migration, unemployment, economic hardship, and political and social repression, to name a few consequences, turned people's daily existence upside down. Like Methodism in the past, Born-Again Christianity has provided an organisational base designed to help individuals who are struggling with social, economical and emotional problems. I demonstrated that conversion would not have been a possibility for Iranians who converted inside and outside of Iran if, first, they did not have some sort of social and economic independence from familial and other social and political institutions and, second, if they weren't approached by evangelising Christians.

The primary mission of the Iranian Christian Fellowship and Elam Ministries is to convert all the Muslims in the Persian-speaking world to Christianity, which is underpinned by the passage in the Old Testament in the book of Jeremiah, 49:38, 39. This goal legitimises their transformation by providing an ideal notion of a return of fortunes to Elam, which is thought to have existed in Iran during pre-Islamic times. The number of Iranian Muslims who have converted to Christianity in Iran, and especially the memory of those who have been murdered, have been also been an influential and motivating force for potential members and the members of the church in London. The theme of martyrdom, which has become central to the Iranian fellowship in strengthening their Christian identities, is heightened by the presence of the daughter of Reverend Mehdi Dibaj, and the son and niece of Bishop Haik Hosvepian-Mehr, who are students at the Bible school and members of the church. Because of their presence, Elam Ministries has become one of the important centre points for Iranian and non-Iranian Born-Again Christians around the world. Elam Ministries and its congregation are also connected to and inspired by a broader context of social dialogue through various communications and information technologies, particularly the link between the various Internet pages of a number of independent Iranian evangelical churches that have developed around the world since the revolution. I also argued that the church leaders kept the members in the dark about many of the Christian rules and doctrines.

It will be interesting to see whether the numbers of converts and church-goers decrease in relation to the political and social changes taking place in Iran. Khatami has often been described by the Iranian Christians as 'just another Mullah', or as 'one of the many faces of evil who is fooling a lot of people'. However, according to one of the elders of the church, although many 'new seeds have been planted, the number of converts at this time may have reached its peak'.

Notes

1. International Correspondence Institute (ICI) was established in 1967 by a section of the Assemblies of God church called the Division of Foreign Missions of the general council. It was first developed in Missouri and was transferred, in 1972, to Brussels. It moved, in 1991, to Irving, Texas. ICI operates in 160 countries and claims to have 1,000,000 non-degree students and 10,000 at the degree level.
2. This goal is written in several of the ICF's brochures and has been relayed to me in several interviews with the church members and organisers.
3. See in the Bible, Jeremiah 49:34, 39. The last sentence is highlighted because it is the motto of the ICF and Elam Ministries.
4. An excerpt from an Elam Ministries pamphlet.
5. *Dictionary of Religion* (1993), Missouri : InterVarsity Press pp. 834–36.
6. D. Martin (1990), p. vii.

7. B.R. Wilson (1990), p. 131.
8. See S. Bruce (1996), p. 119. He writes that in 1767 there were 23,000 Methodists; by the end of the century there were almost 100,000; by 1850 there were over 500,000 and in 1900 there were 770,000.
9. Ibid., p. 119.
10. Ibid.
11. See, for example, A. Gramsci (1971); E.P. Thompson (1963); B.S. Turner (1994), p. 113.
12. B.S. Turner, p. 113.
13. R. Niebuhr (1962).
14. S. Bruce (1996), p. 81.
15. The Holiness Movement was originally a conservative movement. By 1919 it moved away from being an ecstatic type of religion and was considered to be a more mainstream, 'respectable' middle-class religion.
16. This is based on Romans 10:9, which states: 'The word is near to you; it is in your mouth and in your heart, that is, the word of faith we are proclaiming: That if you confess with your mouth, "Jesus is Lord". And believe in your heart that God raised him from the dead, you will be saved'.
17. This step is often based on John 3:1–8 and Romans 6:4.
18. *Dictionary of Religion,* pp. 834–36.
19. Ibid.
20. Taken from Acts 2:1–3.
21. B.S. Turner (1994); also see S. Bruce (1996).
22. B.S. Turner (1994), p. 53.
23. See S. Bruce (1996).
24. Ibid.
25. Ibid., p. 138.
26. R. Wuthrow quoted in S. Bruce (1996), p. 137.
27. R.S. Lynd and H.M. Lynd quoted in ibid., p. 137.
28. A. Greeley quoted in ibid., p. 138.
29. Wuthrow, quoted in ibid., p. 137.
30. S. Bruce (1996), p. 139.
31. Ibid.
32. Ibid., p. 146.
33. These changes have been documented in a study by J. Hunter (1987).
34. See S. Bruce's example of a fundamentalist Baptist family in Virginia, (1996), pp. 141–42.
35. Ibid., p. 163.
36. Ibid.
37. Pentecostal missions tend to be more successful in societies whose religious bodies are institutionally weak but the population is religiously lore. It has been recorded that between 12% and 15% of the Latin-America population are now Born-Again Christians. See S. Bruce (1996), p. 114.
38. Ibid.
39. D. Martin (1990), p. 185.
40. Summary taken from R. Hefner (1998), p. 102.
41. Ibid., p. 102.
42. Ibid.
43. Ibid., p. 119.
44. D. Martin (1990), p. 44.
45. A term coined by D. Martin (1990), see p. 191.
46. Ibid., p. 206.
47. E. Ifeka-Moller (1974), p. 18.
48. Ibid., p. 24.
49. See B.R. Wilson (1990); S. Bruce (1996); and D. Martin (1990).
50. D. Martin (1990), p. 133.

51. Based on the following quote taken from St John Chrysostom's sixth Homily on Matthew's Gospel. 'The Incarnate Word on coming to the world gave to Persia, in the persons of the *Magi*, the first manifestations of His mercy and light … so that the Jews themselves learn from the mouths of Persians of the birth of their Messiah'. R.E. Waterfield (1973), p. 35.

52. According to the Assyrian tradition, St Thomas, one of the twelve disciples, brought Christianity to Assyrians in parts of the Persian Empire under the Sasanian rule. According to the Armenian tradition, the first Christian missionaries to introduce Christianity to Iran were Thaddeus and Bartholomew.

53. Reuters, 24 September 1999, retrieved from Human Rights Watch Report http://www.interlog.com/human.rights .

54. G. Hewitt (1971), p. 377.

55. See E. Sanasarian (2000).

56. H. Bailey (1991), p. 731.

57. E. Sanasarian (1971), p. 54.

58. R. Waterfield (1973), p. 102.

59. M. Zirinsky in S. Ansari and V. Martin (2002), p. 51.

60. E. Sanasarian (2000), p. 43.

61. G. Francis-Dehqani in S. Ansari and V. Martin (2002), p. 27

62. Ibid. Note there were several missionary groups who travelled around Iran before the 1830s. For example, two German doctors, C.F.W. Hoecher and J. Rueffer, missionaries of the United Brethren, travelled around Iran in 1774. Henry Martyn reached Persia in 1810 and translated the New Testament into Persian. Before he died, he presented the Bible to Fath Ali Shah, who would not accept it directly but through the channel of the British Ambassador. Joseph Wolff was involved in the Anglican Missionary Society and the London Society for promoting Christianity among the Jews, and visited Shiraz, Isfahan, Kashan, Tehran and Tabriz in 1824. The Edinburgh and the Basel missionaries arrived in Iran in the 1820s. These early missionaries are not known to have converted any Iranians to Protestant Christianity. See R. Waterfield (1973).

63. See, for example, Zirinsky in S. Ansari and V. Martin (2002), p. 53.

64. P. Paidar (1995), p. 44.

65. R. Waterfield (1973), pp. 87–176.

66. H. Katouzian (1998), p. 170.

67. See J. Joseph (1961).

68. Ibid.

69. H.B. Dehqani-Tafti (1981), p.16.

70. J. Joseph (1961).

71. Ibid., p. 13. According to H.P. Beach (1901), p. 124, the American Presbyterian School in Tehran in 1900 included, 'forty-one Armenians, twenty-two Moslems, two Jews and one Parsee: Of these twenty-two Moslems, two were princes of the Qajar family, being second cousins of the present Shah; two were of the family of the chief of the Bacterians; three are Sayeds, or descendants of Mohammed; one is a mullah, or priest of Islam; of the remainder all but one are of noble birth'.

72. J. Joseph (1961), p. 13.

73. R. Waterfield (1973), p.134.

74. O. Chadwick (1975), p. 489.

75. R. Waterfield (1973), p.139.

76. Ibid., p. 134.

77. Ibid.

78. Ibid.

79. J. Joseph (1961), pp. 89–90.

80. Ibid.

81. See R. Waterfield (1973), p.141.

82. M.M.J. Fischer (1980), p. 185.

83. Ibid.

84. Ibid.
85. Francis-Dehqani in S. Ansari and V. Martin (2002), pp. 33–34.
86. Laymen's Foreign Missions Inquiry Commission of Appraisal, in J. Joseph (1961).
87. Ibid.
88. M.M.J. Fischer (1980).
89. M. Hewitt (1971), p. 388.
90. Ibid.
91. R. Waterfield (1973), p. 143.
92. This ordinance was not fully enforced. See O. Chadwick (1964), p. 489.
93. Ibid.
94. R. Waterfield (1973), p. 143.
95. Ibid.
96. H.B. Dehqani-Tafti (1995), p. 20.
97. R. Waterfield (1973), p. 144.
98. H.B. Dehqani-Tafti (1981), p. 25.
99. Ibid. pp. 32–33.
100. Ibid.
101. Ibid., p. 34.
102. S. Bruce (1996), p. 114.
103. The Iranian Christian International, Inc. (ICI) was established in 1980 in California and was set up to help Iranian Christian refugees. It has developed a leadership training for Christians ministering among Muslims.
104. See http://www.farsinet.com/ici/who.html.
105. M.M.J. Fischer (1981), p. 227.
106. E. Abrahamian (1993), p. 46.
107. H.B. Dehqani-Tafti (1981), p. 10.
108. Ibid.
109. E. Sanasarian (2000), p. 123.
110. This list was written by Dehqani-Tafti, 19 September 1981, in a letter written to Khomeini, Bani-Sadr and Mohammed Ali Rajai. See H. B. Dehqani-Tafti (1981), pp. 95–96.
111. They were accused of having received $500 million from the CIA, and 300 kg of T.N.T. explosives from the British Ambassador. See H. B. Dehqani-Tafti (1981), p. 91.
112. Ibid., p. 30.
113. E. Abrahamian (1993), p. 122.
114. Abrahamian describes Khomeini's view of non-Muslims in more detail. He states: 'Even more "loathsome" were non-Muslims, including the traditionally tolerated "People of the Book" – the Jews, Christians, and Zoroastrians. Being non-Muslims, they were considered to be *kafer* [infidels] and thus, according to Shia Iranian tradition, were *najes* (unclean), they could not marry Muslims, touch the Koran, bury their dead in Muslim cemeteries, or use public places such as barbershops, town baths, and walk the streets during rainstorms'. In E. Abrahamian (1993), p. 46.
115. Ibid., p. 48.
116. Ibid.
117. Ibid., p. 51.
118. Parliamentary Human Rights Group (1996), p. 63.
119. H. Amirahmadi (1996), p. 123.
120. D. Martin (1990), p. 295.
121. Open Doors – Field Operations, retrieved in December 1995, http://ourworld.com-puserve.com.
122. Ibid.
123. Jubilee Campaign 'The Persecution of Christians in Iran', 13 November 1998. http://www.jubileecampaign.demon.co.uk/church/ira1.htm
124. Open Doors – Field Operations.
125. Jubilee Campaign.
126. Ibid.

127. *Evangelicals Now*, November 1996, p. 5; Jubilee Campaign. Open Doors – Field Operations.
128. Jubilee Campaign.
129. Ibid.
130. *Evangelicals Now.*
131. *Agence France Presse*, 31 January 1994, http://www.iran-e-azad.org.
132. *The Washington Times*, 6 July 1994, http://www.iran-e-azad.org.
133. E. Avebury and R. Wilkinson (1996).
134. UN Special Rapporteur on Religious Intolerance. M. Abdelfattah Amor's report on his visit to the Islamic Republic of Iran, in E. Avebury and R. Wilkinson (1996), pp. 68–69.
135. Anonymous, 'Soul Giver Murdered' *Evangelical Now,* November 1996.
136. More research on Pentecostalism and the Iranian Diaspora is greatly needed. This figure seems high. It can be found on http://www.farsinet.com/ici/who.html.
137. See Jeremiah 49:39.
138. See, for example, http://www. farsinet.com/elam_uk
139. The United Bible Societies is a world fellowship of national Bible societies. It is a non-denominational organisation whose goal is to translate, produce and distribute the Bible cheaply in various languages. It developed in London in 1804 and gained a reputation in the 1820s as a Protestant organisation. Catholic Popes accused the Bible Societies of being Protestant proselytisers and publishers of corrupted Bibles. An Iranian Bible Society was developed in Iran but was closed by the authorities on 28 January 1990. See http://www.biblesociety.org/index.html
140. The Great Commission in Matthew 28:16–20 says: 'Then the eleven disciples went to Galilee, to the mountain where Jesus had told them to go. When they saw him, they worshipped him; but some doubted him. Then Jesus came to them and said, "All authority in heaven and on earth has been given to me. Therefore go and make disciples of all nations baptising them in the name of the Father and of the Son and of the Holy Spirit, and teaching them to obey everything I have commanded you. And surely I will be with you always, to the very end of the age." '
141. Taken from the Constitution of the Iranian Christian Fellowship, 1 July 1986, London.
142. Ibid.
143. Ibid.
144. Quoted from the Bible, Timothy 2:13.
145. Pentecostalists believe that the spiritual gifts, which are 'speaking in tongues', the gift of healing and the gift of interpreting tongues, are essential tenets of a true Christian. Many conservative evangelical churches acknowledge the spiritual gifts but do not believe they apply now.
146. R. Hefner (1993), pp. 121–22.
147. This information has been gathered both through interviews and Elam Ministries monthly newsletters.
148. This is similar to Martin's research on Pentecostal converts in Brazil. See D. Martin (1990).
149. Ibid., p. 191.
150. I asked these questions throughout the course of my research. I spoke with Iranians individually and in groups. For example, a group of Iranians would be sitting around after church and would ask a question which would lead to a discussion about their lives in Iran, why they converted, and so on.
151. R. Hefner (1993), pp. 121–22.
152. Britain is one of the few remaining European countries that recognise religious persecution as a valid reason for obtaining asylum.
153. I am under the impression that the Iranian Christians in Turkey help Iranian refugees like Layla find their way to the U.K. The administration of the ICF said that they do not involve themselves migration and asylum issues.

154. I have met four other Iranian men who were members of Iranian Sufi Orders in London before converting to Christianity.
155. There was one Iranian rice dish served called *dolmeh*. The other dishes were pastas and a salad.
156. D. Martin (1990), p. 181.
157. R. Hefner (1990), pp. 121–22.

6

Conclusions and Findings

By tapping into the diversity and complexity of Iranian lives in London this study has demonstrated that finding a distinct Iranian place in London, and adaptation to British society, are both processes at work. The social dynamics I encountered at a big open party for *Châhârshanbeh Souri* (a celebration that marks the beginning of the Iranian New Year celebrations), can serve as a microcosm to illustrate some of the continuities and transformations of Iranian identity and practices that have been explored throughout this book. Unlike *noruz* parties in the past, where political and religio-ethnic boundaries were tightly drawn, I came across Iranians from a variety of backgrounds and orientations. During the evening I spoke to women who attend Ms. Parvizi's *sofrehs*, non-religious Iranians, members of the Shahmaghsoudi Sufi Order, Baha'is, Zoroastrians and Armenians. While some women wore headscarves, others wore revealing dresses. A few people were drinking alcohol, while others were not. The hired band, which included a musician who plays at the Iranian Christian Fellowship, performed popular Iranian music. While many danced throughout the evening, others, such as the women who wore scarves, took pleasure in watching.

Several used the celebratory occasion to introduce and share a part of their Iranian culture to non-Iranian friends. They enjoyed explaining the customs and activities surrounding the *noruz* traditions, serving *ash*, the delicious traditional soup prepared especially for the occasion, and watching their friends try to dance in an Iranian style. I was often told: 'Iranians jump over a small fire on *Châhârshanbeh Souri* to symbolise the start of a happy and healthy life in the coming New Year'; 'We eat *ash* on *Châhârshanbeh Souri* for good luck'; 'Iranians are famous for always being late' (the band arrived late); 'We love to dance'. The interaction between the different groups of Iranians demonstrated that national identity and the Persian language were the markers of identification prioritised on this occasion.

Meanwhile, I heard an array of candid remarks on the price of admission, the organisation and style of the event. Many commented on the 'types' of Iranians who were present, referring mainly to their professions, education levels, wealth and appearances. Many were making comparisons to *Châhârshanbeh*

Souri celebrations held around London and in the past. Several people noted how *noruz* celebrations are larger or done with more or less taste in Iran and Los Angeles. Such discussions and the social dynamics at the party touch on several of the themes developed in this book. Popular cultural forms, along similar lines as the religious gatherings focused on in this book, are spaces where identity and difference are contested, displayed and reworked. What Iranian culture *is,* and how it is best expressed in British society, is certainly contestable. While many of the old distinctions between Iranians exist in London, they have been shuffled and reshuffled in order to achieve coherence under the prevailing circumstances. Many new political, social and religious lines have also been drawn and have crystallised over the years. In order to throw light on the exchanges and transformations of Iranian cultural forms or, in other words, the hybridisation of Iranian cultural forms in London, this study concentrated on the foregrounded conditions that shape Iranian cultural production and identity in London. It has been argued that over the last twenty-five years the settlement experiences of the estimated 75,000 Iranians in Britain have been continually informed and structured by the situations both in Iran and Britain. The way in which the Iranian Revolution, the period around the end of the Iran–Iraq war and Khomeini's death, and Khatami's presidency, have intersected with the particular situation of the various groupings in London, has been important in moulding and remoulding their various social, economic, religious and political practices.

The Iranian Revolution

This study began by discussing the events leading up to the establishment of the Islamic Republic, and the circumstances under which the estimated one million Iranians left Iran. For the most part, the waves of Iranians who arrived in Britain, who are from a range of political, socio-economic, religious and ethnic backgrounds, did not plan on living in Britain permanently. Many described their initial years in Britain as a period of anxiety and restlessness as they were preoccupied with the transition taking place in Iran, and the ways in which families, friends, colleagues and political affiliates were dealing with the forced implementation of the new anti-secular policies. As discussed in Chapter 2, little effort was made to maintain an Iranian cultural identity in London during the years following the revolution. For example, many Iranians reported that that they did not feel comfortable organising or attending *noruz* events, such as the *Châhârshanbeh Souri* party, because they did not want to mix with other political and social groupings of Iranians and/or they did not feel that it was appropriate to attend a celebration when Iranian society was experiencing social, economic and political turmoil. The family unit and subgroupings, based on politics and religio-ethnic identities, were reported as principal bases furnishing a sense of belonging, thus facilitating the initial stages of the adjustment process.

The Settlement Process

A number of factors, including the end of the Iran–Iraq war, Iran's dire economy, Khomeini's death in 1989 and their continued absence from their
homeland, combined to ensure the realisation that Iranians' displacement
from their homes was not temporary. Although, generally speaking, the
diverse groupings of Iranians continued to socialise with the various social,
religio-ethnic and political circles they were associated with in Iran, many
said that their topics of conversation, which used to be centred on Iran and
their social, economic and political positions, shifted to discussions concerning the settlement process and their particular situations in London. While it
has been important for Iranians to adapt successfully to aspects of British
society, many feared losing their sense of being Iranian and have resisted
complete cultural assimilation. As discussed in Chapter 2, a growing number
of Iranian cultural, media, religious and business centres and activities have
emerged in London. I described the increasing number of Iranian New Year
events, which provided a glimpse into the internal divisions (based on socio-
economic backgrounds, religion, political affiliation and ethnicity) which
were drawn during that period among Iranians living in London. Much
research is needed to understand the ways in which Iranian identity is
expressed through these different cultural and media forms. These are
complex and multifaceted, and must be examined in relation to interrelated
factors, including gender, politics, wealth, religion, ethnicity and 'cultural
capital'.

This book concentrated on an aspect of the process of emigration by focusing on different forms of Iranian religious practices and representation that
developed or redeveloped around this period in London. I became particularly interested in religious practices when I repeatedly heard Iranians from
Muslim backgrounds criticise the brands of Islam propounded by the Islamic
Republic and other Islamist groupings around the world (particularly in
Britain). I was told time and time again that 'real' Shia Islam can not be judged
by politicised notions of Islam, nor the negative stereotypes and media images
that portray Muslim women as 'oppressed' and men as 'terrorists'. I found that
concentrating on Iranians who wished actively to practise a religion, in light
of the sentiments towards the many and different interpretations and misin-
terpretations of Islam, to be an important area of research.

A study of this kind is particularly significant at a time when the social and
political implications of Islam are centre stage for politicians, journalists and
academics in the West, as well as in Muslim-majority societies. As argued in
the introduction, there has been a growing trend for commentators to treat
followers of Islam as a single community, possessing an all-encompassing
world view that is not compatible with 'Western' ideas. The claims of a shared
Muslim identity are not only based on the geographical areas where the
majority of Muslims live, but are also projected by and to Muslim people living in Western European states. The steady influx of Muslims to Britain has
raised numerous questions on the social and political ramifications of their

presence in Britain. The place for Muslims in British secular society was heightened by a number of developments, including the Iranian Revolution, the Salman Rushdie affair and the concerns about the future of British national identity within a broader European framework. These discussions have been given added impetus since the horror of September 11.

The case studies that I concentrated on have questioned the essentialist notion that religion, ethnicity and other forms of identity, have a constant and authentic set of characteristics that bind individuals and determine their experiences. In order to make sense of the continuity, discontinuity and transformation of different Iranian religious practices, I analysed the formation of various Iranian religious networks in relation to the socio-political processes at different historical periods in Iran. I introduced several research projects which focused on Iranian women's religious gatherings, and Sufi Orders, at different points during the twentieth century. These illustrated the manifold and changing meanings and roles of the gatherings, and the various ways they have been used as channels to express religious, socio-economic and political identities. The exposition of Protestant missionary activity in Iran, across various historical periods, revealed the rarity of Muslim conversion before the revolution. By focusing on these different forms of Iranian practices and representation, which developed or redeveloped during the 1980s and the beginning of the 1990s, several of the key aspects involved in constructing identities during the process of migration were identified.

In line with the findings of many research projects on migrant groups, a number of Iranians turned to a religious framework, and/or base, to help come to terms with their lives outside Iran. Many reported that they wished to disassociate themselves from the religious perspective of the Iranian government and the ensuing debates on the position of Muslims in Britain at the time. There was also a need for facilities and figures of authority to accommodate Iranian customs and religious traditions. The Nimatullahi and the Shahmaghsoudi Sufi Orders, for example, provide their members with a social and religious base for belonging and differentiation. The combination of a number of factors, including their sacred heritage and the Masters' lineages, which are thought to trace back to the prophet; practising what is thought to be the purest form of religion; being involved in one of their many active Iranian *Khâneqâhs*; and linking themselves with like-minded Iranians around the globe, are all forces which created a powerful sense of being a part of both a real and 'imagined' community, and were thought to bypass clearly the contaminated religion of the Islamic regime and other politicised notions of Islam. The *sofreh* gatherings provided a centrally located domain for women to meet together and 'push God' in their favour by directly asking him to help them with personal and family problems. It is a place where women discussed and debated whether or not the discourses and practices endorsed at many of the other new and unfamiliar religious centres were authentic and truly Islamic.

The emergence of communities, both real and 'imaginary' and reclaiming a pure and authentic past is also a pattern I revealed in Chapter 5, which focused on Iranian Muslims who converted to Born-Again Christianity.

Many became convinced that the root of their social, economic and/or emotional problems are inextricably linked to Islam and the emergence of the Islamic Republic. Several felt that the pervasiveness of Islam in Iran has had a deleterious effect on the glorious Persian culture found in pre-Islamic Iran. Converting to Christianity served as a way to channel their resentment, which was building up, for many different reasons, throughout the post-revolutionary period. I described the charismatic and convivial style of Evangelical Christianity, and the ways in which it attracted Iranians who were in need of a supportive base and of hope for the future.

This study has also revealed the number of interpretations found in a range of Iranian religious practices and traditions. Contested notions are particularly evident during the process of migration, when it is unclear how one should live as an Iranian outside Iran. I came across, for example, many, and often conflicting, definitions of what it means to be an Iranian Shia Muslim in London. Although the vocabulary of key terms and many of the components of the various gatherings – such as the food items, the stories and their primary purpose of the *nazr* at *sofreh* gatherings and the similar terminology conceptualising the spiritual path, or *tariqat*, used at both Sufi Orders – were maintained or reproduced in London with little change, the implementation and observance of the content was often varied and negotiated. I showed how themes such as family, dress codes, codes of pollution, rules of purification and what is proper and improper Islamic conduct were discussed and debated by Iranians in relation to different religious interpretations and views generated in the different social and religious associations, their households, and the workplace. I also found how the various perspectives relate to Iranians in terms of demographics, education, political standing and socio-economic distinctions.

The analysis revealed how adherence to 'popular' forms of Islam can not always be clearly distinguishable from 'orthodox' forms of Islam, making it necessary to look at a wide range of practices and institutions in order to comprehend the complexity of Islam. The Shahmaghsoudi Sufi Order, for instance, has incorporated the five pillars of Islam and the Islamic Calendar into a new design, which is similar to many other California-styled, therapy-based religious movements. I argued that by strategically locating itself at the heart of Islam it has constructed itself as a neutral and apolitical space, and has therefore not been dismissed by or isolated from some of the other Shia circles, including the embassy, as being heretical. My discussions with the Sufis outside of the meetings, described in the loose categories 'the devout', 'the dilettantes' and 'the shoppers', revealed many different levels of commitment to the Pir and his teachings.

By examining a number of religious institutions and practices and the variegated allegiance of the practitioners at many different levels of investigation, one of the central aims of this study has been to demonstrate that 'religion' cannot be treated as an isolated cultural phenomenon, divorced from political and socio-economic relations of power. Whether the Iranian religious practices and traditions were considered to be Muslim or Christian, heterodox or orthodox, traditional or modern, for women or for men, and so on, they are in fact contested notions, which must be examined in light of historically situated processes. The study has demonstrated that religion can not be understood as a homogeneous entity. Instead of assuming that religious texts and symbols determine the way religions are experienced, I have focused on the ways in which religions are practised and constructed by individuals in local situations. In order to understand the complexities involved in the local situations it was necessary to examine forces across and between national boundaries, within a broader context of social dialogue through various communications and information technologies and/or articulated by my informants who have multiple affiliations and associations between London, the Iranian diaspora at large and Iran.

Khatami and the Programme of Reforms?

During the years which followed the revolution there was a clear distinction between those who supported and those who opposed the brand of Islam implemented by the regime. This became blurred when Mohammad Khatami became president of Iran in 1997. The newly formed policies, and the office in the government attending to the cultural affairs of Iranians abroad, as discussed in Chapter 2, have made it easier for Iranians to travel back and forth between Britain and Iran. Although there are many Iranians who have not warmed to any element of the Iranian government, President Khatami and his programme of reforms have certainly stimulated among Iranians in London a renewed interest in the political, economic and social situation in Iran. The several and varied shifts in opinions and attitudes towards elements of the Iranian government since Khatami's victory, were made evident in the case studies featured in this book. They demonstrated how religious and cultural gatherings in London are a few of the many spaces used to discuss the changes in Iran and become familiar with and/or aligned or realigned to the various strands of religious and political thought currently debated in Iran and in the wider diaspora.

It remains to be seen how Iranian social spaces continue to develop in Britain, and to what extent they serve as platforms for greater participation and representation in the public domain. The increase of Iranians and non-Iranians travelling to Iran, on the one hand, and the increase in Iranians seeking asylum for political and religious persecution in Britain, on the other, are indicators of the complicated power struggles in Iran and the pathways that continue to be forged between Britain and Iran. Nevertheless, Khatami's reformist camps' landslide victory in the February 2000 parliamentary elections, the upgrade in diplomatic relations between Britain and Iran along with social factors, including Iran's victory over the United States in the 1998 football World Cup, Shirin Ebadi winning the Nobel Peace Prize in 2003, as well as the success of Iranian filmmakers, have all contributed to a new conjuncture for Iranians to negotiate their identities in Britain.

Bibliography

Abrahamian, E. 1993. *Khomeinism: Essays on the Islamic Republic.* London and New York: I.B. Tauris.
—— 1989. *Radical Islam: The Iranian Mojahedin.* London and New York: I.B. Tauris.
—— 1982. *Iran: Between Two Revolutions.* Princeton: Princeton University Press.
Abu-Lughod, L., ed. 1998. *Remaking Women: Feminism and Modernity in the Middle East.* Princeton: Princeton University Press.
Adelkhah, F. 2001. 'Les Iraniens de Californie: si la République islamique n'existait pas ...', *Les Études du CERI* no. 75.
—— 1999. *Being Modern In Iran.* London: Hurst & Company.
Afkhami, M. 1994. 'Women in Post-Revolutionary Iran: A Feminist Perspective'. In M. Afkhami and E. Friedl, eds. *In the Eye of the Storm: Women in Post-Revolutionary Iran.* London: I.B. Tauris.
Afshar, H. ed. 1993. *Women and the Middle East: Perceptions, Realities, and Struggles for Liberation.* London: Macmillan Press.
Afshar, H. 1998. *Iran: A Revolution in Turmoil.* London: Macmillan Press.
Ahmadi, A., Ahmadi, F. and Campling, J. 2000. *Iranian Islam: The Concept of the Individual.* Hampshire and London: Macmillan Press.
Ahmed, A., and Donnan, H. 1994. *Islam, Globalisation and Postmodernity.* London and New York: Routledge.
Ahmed, L. 1992. *Women and Gender in Islam: Historical Roots of a Modern Debate.* New Haven and London: Yale University Press.
Al-Azmeh, A. 1996. *Islams and Modernities.* London: Verso Publishers.
Alexander, J. and Seidman, S. 1994. *Culture and Society.* Cambridge: Cambridge University Press.
Al-e-Ahmad, J. 1982. *Gharbzadegi.* Trans. J. Green and A. Alizadeh. Lexington, KY: Mazda.
Algar, H. 1997. *Encyclopaedia of Islam.* In C.E. Bozworth, V. Dozel, W.P. Heinrichs and G. Lecomte, eds. New ed., vol. 8. Leiden: Brill.
—— 1991. 'From Nadir Shah to the Islamic Republic'. In P. Avery, G. Hambly and C. Melville, eds., *The Cambridge History of Iran.* Vol. 7. Cambridge: Cambridge University Press.
—— 1991. 'Religious forces in twentieth century Iran'. In P. Avery, G. Hambly and C. Melville, eds, *The Cambridge History of Iran.* Vol 7. Cambridge: Cambridge University Press.
—— 1990. 'Caliphs', *Encyclopaedia Iranica* vol. 4. New York: Colombia University Press.

Amanat, M. 1993. 'Nationalism and Social Change in Contemporary Iran'. In R. Kelley and J. Friedlander, eds., *Irangeles: Iranians in Los Angeles.* Berkeley: University of California Press.

Amirahmadi, H. 1996. 'Iran's development: evaluation and challenges'. *Third World Quarterly* vol. 17, no. 1: 123.

Anderson, B. 1983. *Imagined Communities: Reflections on the Origin and Spread of Nationalism.* London: Verso Publishers.

Angha, M. 1996. *The Fragrance of Sufism.* London: University Press of America.

—— 1992. *The Mystery of Humanity Tranquillity and Survival.* London: University Press of America.

—— 1988. *Dawn.* California: Maktab Tarighat Oveyssi Shahmaghsoudi Publishers.

Angha, N. 1991. *Principles of Sufism.* California: Association of Sufi's publications.

Ansari, A. 2000. *Iran, Islam and Democracy: The Politics of Managing Change.* London: Royal Institute of International Affairs.

Ansari, M. 1988. *Iranian Immigrants in the United States: A Case of Dual Marginality.* New York: Associated Faculty Press.

Ansari, S. and Martin, V., eds., 2002. *Women, Religion and Culture in Iran.* Surrey: Curzon Press.

Antoun, R. 1968 'On the Modesty of Women in Arab Muslim Villages: A Study in the Accommodation of Tradition', *American Anthropologist* vol. 70, 671–97.

Anwar, M. 1998. *Between Cultures: Continuity and Change in the Lives of Young Asians.* London and New York: Routledge.

Arberry, A.J. 1979. *Sufism: An Account of the Mystics of Islam.* London: George Allen and Unwin Press.

Arjomand, A. 1984. *The Shadow of God and the Hidden Imam: Religion, Political Order and Societal Change in Shi'ite Iran from the beginning to1890.* Chicago: University of Chicago Press.

Asad, T. 1997. 'Islam against Europe: Islam in Europe', *The Muslim World* vol. 37: 183–95.

—— 1993 *The Genealogies of Religion.* Baltimore and London: The Johns Hopkins University Press.

Asayesh, G. 1999. *Saffron Sky.* Boston: Beacon Press.

Avebury, E. and Wilkinson, R. 1996. *Iran: State of Terror – An Account of Terrorist Assassinations by Iranian Agents,* Parliamentary Human Rights Group London.

Ayubi, N. 1991. *Political Islam – Religion and Politics in the Arab World.* London and New York: Routledge.

Bafekr, S. and Leman, J. 1999. 'Highly-qualified Iranian immigrants in Germany: the role of ethnicity and culture', *Journal of Ethnic and Migration Studies* vol. 25, no. 1: 95–112.

Bahrampour, T. 2000. *To See and See Again: A Life in Iran and America.* California: University of California Press.

Bainbridge, W. 1997. *The Sociology of Religious Movements.* London and New York: Routledge.

Bailey, H. 1991. *The Cambridge History of Iran.* Cambridge: Cambridge University Press.

Baldick, J. 1993. *Imaginary Muslims: The Uwaysi Sufis of Central Asia.* London: I.B. Tauris.

—— 1989. *Mystical Islam: An Introduction to Sufism.* London and New York: I.B. Tauris.

Balmer, R. 1993. *Mine Eyes Have Seen the Glory: A Journey into the Evangelical Subculture in America.* Oxford: Oxford University Press.

Bamdad, B. 1977. *From Darkness into Light: Women's Emancipation in Iran,* trans. F. Bagley. New York: Exposition Press.

Bani-Sadr, A. 1991. *My Turn to Speak,* trans. W. Ford. Washington, WA: Brassey's.

Banton, M. 1983. *Racial and Ethnic Competition.* Cambridge: Cambridge University Press.

Barker, M. 1983. *The New Racism.* London: Junction Books.

Barth, F. 1969. *Ethnic Groups and Boundaries.* London: George Allen and Unwin.

Bashiriyeh, S. 1984. *The State and Revolution in Iran.* New York: St. Martin's Press.

Bauer, J. 1991. 'A Long Way Home: Islam in the Adaptation of Iranian Women Refugees in Turkey and West Germany'. In A. Fathi, ed., *Iranian Refugees and Exiles since Khomeini.* Costa Mesa, CA: Mazda Publisher.

—— 1985a. 'Demographic Change, Women and Family in a Migrant Neighbourhood of Tehran'. In A. Fathi, ed., *Women and Revolution in Iran.* Leiden: Brill.

—— 1985b. 'Sexuality and the Moral "Construction" of Women in an Islamic Society', *Anthropology Quarterly* vol. 58, no. 3: 120–29.

Baumann, G. 1996. *Contesting Culture.* Cambridge: Cambridge University Press.

Bayat, M. 1982a. *Mysticism and Religious Traditions.* Oxford: Oxford University Press.

—— 1982b. *Mysticism and Dissent: Socio-religious Thought in Qajar Iran.* Syracuse: Syracuse University Press.

Beach, H.P. 1901. *A Geography and Atlas of Protestant Missions: their environment, forces, distribution methods, problems, results and prospects at the opening of the twentieth century.* New York: Student Volunteer Movement for Foreign Missions.

Beck, L. and Keddie, N.R., eds., 1978. *Women in the Muslim World.* Cambridge, MA: Harvard University Press.

Behrooz, M. 2000. *Rebels with a Cause: The Failure of the Left in Iran.* London and New York: I.B. Tauris.

Berger, P. 1974. 'Substantive Definitions of Religion', *Journal for the Scientific Study of Religion* vol. 13: 125–33.

Betteridge, A. 1993. 'Women and Shrines in Shiraz'. In D.L. Bowen and E.A. Early, eds., *Everyday Life in the Muslim Middle-East.* Indiana: Indiana University Press.

—— 1985. 'Gift Exchange in Iran: The Locus of Self-Identity in Social Interaction', *Anthropology Quarterly* vol. 58, no. 4: 190–202.

—— 1980. 'The Controversial Vows of Urban Muslim Women in Iran'. In N. Falk and R. Cross, eds., *Unspoken Worlds: Women's Religious Lives in Non-Western Cultures.* Belmont: Wadsworth Press.

Bhabha, H. 1995. 'The Commitment to Theory'. In E. Carter, J. Donald and J. Squires, eds., *Cultural Remix: Theories of Politics and the Popular.* London: Lawrence and Wishart.

Bhachu, P. 1985. *Twice Migrants: East African Settlers in Britain.* London: Tavistock.

Bibby, R. and Brinkerhoff, M. 1973. 'The Circulation of the Saints: A Study of People who Join Conservatives Churches', *Journal for the Scientific Study of Religion* vol. 112: 273–85.

BiParva, E. 1994. 'Ethnic Organisations: Integration and Assimilation vs. Segregation and Cultural Preservation with Specific Reference to the Iranians in theWashington D.C. Metropolitan area', *Journal of Third World Studies* vol. 11: 369–404.

Bill, J. 1988. *The Eagle and the Lion: The Tragedy of American-Iranian Relations.* New Haven: Yale University Press.

Blackstone, T., Parekh, B. and Sanders, P., eds., 1998. *Race Relations in Britain.* London and New York: Routledge.

Blair, B. 1991. 'Personal Name Change among Iranian Immigrants in the U.S.A'. In A. Fathi, ed., *Iranian Refugees and Exiles since Khomeini*. Costa Mesa, CA: Mazda Publisher.

Bloom, W. 1991. *The New Age: An Anthology of Essential Writings*. London: Rider/Channel 4 Publications.

Bonine, M. and Keddie, N.R., eds., 1981. *Modern Iran: The Dialectic of Continuity and Change in Modern Iran*. Albany: State University of New York Press.

Borot, R., ed., 1993. *Religion and Ethnicity: Minorities and Social Change in the Metropolis*. The Netherlands: Kok Pharos.

Bottomley, G. 1998. 'Anthropologists and the Rhizomatic Study of Migration', *Australian Journal of Anthropology*, Sydney Special Issue 9:1.

—— 1992 *From Another Place*. Cambridge: Cambridge University Press.

Bourdieu, P. and Wacquant, L.J.O. 1992. 'Toward a social Praxeology: The structure of logic of Bourdieu's sociology'. In *An invitation to Reflexive Sociology*. Chicago: University of Chicago Press.

Bowen, K. 1996. *Evangelism and Apostasy*. Montreal and Kingston: McGill/Queen's University Press.

Bowker, H. ed., *Women in Religion*. London and New York: Pinter Publishers.

Boyce, M. 2001. *Zoroastrians: Their Religious Beliefs and Practices*. London and New York: Routledge.

—— 1995. *A History of Zoroastrianism,* 2 vols. Leiden.

—— 1977. *A Persian Stronghold of Zoroastrianism*. Oxford: Clarendon Press.

Bozorgmehr, M. 1998. 'From Iranian Studies to Studies of Iranians in the United States, *Iranian Studies* vol. 31, no. 1: 5–31.

—— 1997. 'Internal Ethnicity: Iranians in Los Angeles', *Sociological Perspectives* vol. 40 : 387–408.

Bozorgmehr, M., Sabagh, G. and Der-Martirosian, C. 1993. 'Beyond Nationality: Religio-Ethnic Diversity'. In R. Kelley and J. Friedlander, eds., *Irangeles: Iranians in Los Angeles*. Berkeley: University of California Press.

Bozorgmehr, M. and Sabagh, G. 1991. 'Iranian Exiles and Immigrants in Los Angeles'. In A. Fathi, ed., 1991. *Iranian Refugees and Exiles since Khomeini*. Costa Mesa, CA: Mazda.

Bozorgmehr, M. and Sabagh, G. 1988. 'High Status Immigrants: A Statistical Profile of Iranians in the United States', *Iranian Studies* vol. 21: 5–36.

Brah, A. 1996. *Cartographies of Diaspora: Contesting Identities*. London and New York: Routledge.

Bruce, S. 1996. *Religion in the Modern World: From Cathedrals to Cults*. Oxford: Oxford University Press.

—— 1992a. *Religion and Modernisation*. Oxford and New York: Clarendon Press.

—— ed., 1992b. *Religion and Modernisation: Sociologists and Historians Debate the Secularisation Thesis*. Oxford: Oxford University Press.

—— 1990. *A House Divided: Protestantism, Schism and Secularisation*. London and New York: Routledge.

Bruce, S. and Wallis, R. 1989. 'Religion: the British contribution', *British Journal of Sociology* vol. 40, no. 3: 493.

Bynum, C.W., Harrell, S. and Richman, P., eds., *Gender and Religion: On the Complexity of Symbols*. Boston: Beacon Press.

Çalgar, Q. 1997. 'Hyphenated Identities and the Limits of "Culture" '. In T. Modood and P. Werbner, *The Politics of Multiculturalism the New Europe: Racism, Identity and Community*. London: Macmillan.

Campo, J.E. 1991. *The Other Side of Paradise: Explorations into the Religious Meanings of Domestice Space in Islam*. California: University of Southern California Press.

Carter, E., Donald, J. and Squires, J., eds., 1995. *Cultural Remix: Theories of Politics and the Popular*. London: Lawrence and Wishart.

Carter, L. 1987. 'The "New Renunciates" of the Bhagwan Shree Rajneesh: Observations and Identification of Problems of Interpreting New Religious Movements', *Journal of the Scientific Study of Religion* vol. 26: 148–72.

Cashmore, E. 1994. *Dictionary of Race and Ethnic Relations*. London and New York: Routledge.

Chadwick, O., ed., 1975. *The Pelican History of the Church*. London: Hodder and Stoughton.

Chaichian, M. 1997. 'First Generation Iranian Immigrants and the Question of Cultural Identity: The Case of Iowa', *International Migration Review* vol. 31: 612–27.

Clifford, J. and Marcus, G. 1986. *Writing Culture: The Poetics and Politics of Ethnography*. Berkeley: University of California Press.

Cook, G., ed., 1994. *New Face of the Church in Latin America*. New York: Orbis Books.

Cornell S. 1996. 'The variable ties that bind: content and circumstances in ethnic processes', *Ethnic and Racial Studies* vol. 19: 265–89.

Cowen, J. 'Displaced Persons: A Study of the Acculturation and Reestablishment of Social Networks of Iranian Women Immigrants to Western Canada', Ph.D. diss. Vancouver, 1993.

Crapanzano, V. 1973. *The Hamadsha: A Study in Moroccan Ethno Psychiatry*. Berkeley: University of California Press.

Cross, R. and Falk, N., eds., 1989. *Unspoken Worlds: Women's Religious Lives in Non-Western Cultures*. Belmont: Wadsworth Press.

Dawood, N.J. trans. 1998. *The Koran*. London: Penguin Books.

De Groot, J. 1996. 'Gender, discourse and ideology in Iranian Studies: Towards a new scholarship'. In Kandiyoti, D., ed., *Gendering the Middle East: Emerging Perspectives*. London: I.B. Tauris.

Delvecchio-Good, M. and Good, B. 1988. 'Ritual, the State and the Transformation of Emotional Discourse in Iranian Society', *Culture, Medicine and Psychiatry* vol. 12: 43–63.

Delvecchio-Good, M. 1978. 'A Comparative Perspective on Women in Provincial Iran and Turkey', *Women in the Muslim World*. Cambridge, MA and London: Harvard University Press.

Deqani-Tafti, H.B. 1981. *The Hard Awakening*. New York: Seabury Press.

—— *Dictionary of Religion* 1993. San Francisco: Harper Collins.

Der-Martirosian, C., Bozorgmehr, M. and Sabagh, G. 1993. 'Beyond Nationality: Religio-Ethnic Diversity'. In R. Kelley and J. Friedlander, eds., *Irangeles: Iranians in Los Angeles*. Berkeley: University of California Press.

Donaldson, B.A. 1938 *The Wild Rue: A Study of Mohammadan Magic and Folklore in Iran*. London: Luzac and Company.

Drury, C. 1994. 'Christianity'. In Bowker, H., ed., *Women in Religion*. London and New York: Pinter Publishers.

Eade, J. 1994a. 'Educated Young Bangladeshi Muslims in London's "East End",' *International Sociology* vol. 9, no. 3: 377–94.

—— 1994b. 'The Impact of Globalisation on Sociological Concept: Community, Culture and Milieu', *Innovation* vol. 7, no. 4: 371–89.

—— 1991. 'The Political Construction of Class and Community: Bangladeshi Political Leadership in Tower Hamlets'. In Pnina Werbner and Muhammad Anwar, eds., *Black and Ethnic Leadership in Britain*. London: Routledge.

—— 1989. *The Politics of Community: The Bangladeshi Community in East London.* Aldershot: Avebury.

Eickelman, D. and Piscatori, J., eds., 1990. *Muslim Travellers: Pilgrimage, Migration and Religious Imagination.* New York and London: Routledge.

Ellis, J. 1991. 'Local Government and Community Needs: A Case Study of Muslims in Britain', *New Community,* April: 365.

Elwell-Sutton, L.P. 1970. 'Mystic making', *New York Review of Books,* 1 July: 35–37.

Esfandiari, H. 1997. *Reconstructed Lives: Women and Iran's Islamic Revolution.* Baltimore and London: The Johns Hopkins University Press.

Eskandari-Qajar, M. 2002. 'Consider the Facts: Prognosis For a Return of Kings'. Iranian.com, December 28; 11.

Esposito, K. and Haddad, Y., eds., 1998. *Islam, Gender and Social Change.* Oxford: Oxford University Press.

Falk, N. and Cross, R., eds., 1989. *Unspoken Worlds: Women's Religious Lives in Non-Western Cultures.* Belmont: Wadsworth Press.

Fanon, F. 1963. *The Wretched of the Earth,* trans. Farrington, C. New York: Grove.

Fathi, A. 2002. 'Communities in Place and Communities in Space: Globalization and Feminism in Iran'. In S. Ansari and V. Martin, eds, *Women, Religion and Culture in Iran.* Richmond: Curzon Press.

—— ed., 1991. *Iranian Refugees and Exiles since Khomeini.* Costa Mesa, CA: Mazda.

Fernea, E. and Bezirgan, B., eds., 1977. *Middle Eastern Muslim Women Speak.* Austin, Texas: University of Texas Press.

Fernea, R. and Fernea, E. 1972. 'Variation of Religious Observances among Islamic Women'. In N.R. Keddie, ed., *Scholars, Saints and Sufis.* Berkeley: University of California Press.

Fischer, M.M.J. 1980. *Iran: From Religious Dispute to Revolution.* Cambridge, MA: Harvard University Press.

—— 1978. 'Persian Women'. In L. Beck and N.R. Keddie, eds., *Women in the Muslim World.* Cambridge, MA: Harvard University Press.

—— 1977. 'Review of Boyce M., "A Persian Stronghold of Zoroastrianism"', *Iranian Studies,* Autumn: 294–99.

Fischer, M.M.J. and Abedi, M. 1990. *Debating Muslims: Cultural Dialogues in Postmodernity and Tradition.* Madison, WI: University of Wisconsin Press.

Friedl, E. 1994. 'Religion is Power'. In M. Afkhami and E. Friedl, eds., *In the Eye of the Storm: Women in Post Revolutionary Iran.* New York: I.B. Tauris.

Friedl, E. 1989. 'Islam and Tribal Women in a Village in Iran'. In N. Falk and R. Gross, eds., *Unspoken Worlds: Women's Religious Lives in Non-Western Cultures.* Belmont: Wadsworth.

Galin, M. 1997. *Between East and West: Sufism in the Novels of Doris Lessing.* New York: State University of New York Press.

Gellner, E. 1992. *Postmodernism, Reason and Religion.* London and New York: Routledge.

—— 1983. *Muslim Society.* Cambridge: Cambridge University Press.

Gerholm, T. and Yngve, L., eds., 1988. *The New Islamic Presence in Western Europe.* London: Mansell.

Ghods, M.R. 1989. *Iran in the twentieth Century: A Political History.* London: Adamantine Press.

Gilanshah, F. 1990. 'The Formation of Iranian Community in the Twin Cities from 1983–89', *Wisconsin Sociologist* vol. 27, 4: 11–17.

Gilroy, P. 1990. 'It ain't where you're from, it's where you're at… The Dialectics of Diasporic Identification', *Third Text* vol. 13.
—— 1987. *There Ain't No Black in the Union Jack*. London: Hutchingson.
Gilsenan, M. 1992. *Recognising Islam*. London: I.B. Tauris.
—— 1973. *Saint and Sufi in Modern Egypt – Sociology of Religion*. Oxford: Clarendon Press.
Giorgi, L. 1992. 'Religious Involvement in a Secularised Society: An Empirical Confirmation of Martin's General Theory of Secularisation', *British Journal of Sociology* vol. 43: 639–56.
Gordon, H. 1971. *The Problem of Success – A History of the Church Missionary Society 1910–1942*. London: SCM Press.
Gramlich, R. 1981. *Die schiitischen Derwischorden Persiens: Brauchtum und Riten* vol. 3. Wiesbaden: Steiner.
Gramsci, A. 1971. *Selections from the Prison Notebooks*, ed. and trans. Q. Hoare and G. Nowel Smith. London: Lawrence and Wishart.
Greeley, A. 1989. *Religious Change in America*. Cambridge, MA: Harvard University Press.
Grillo, R. 1999. *Pluralism and the Politics of Difference: State, Culture, and Ethnicity in Comparative Perspective*. New York: Oxford University Press.
Hall, J. 1985. *Powers and Liberties: the Causes and Consequences of the Rise of the West*. Oxford: Blackwell.
Hall, S. 1995. 'Fantasy, Identity and Politics'. In E. Carter, J. Donald and J. Squires, eds., *Cultural Remix: Theories of Politics and the Popular*. London: Lawrence and Wishart.
—— 1992. 'New Ethnicities'. In J. Donald and A. Rattansi, eds., ' *"Race", Culture and Difference'*. London: Sage.
—— 1990. 'Cultural Identity and Diaspora'. In J. Rutherford, ed., *Identity: Community, Culture and Difference*. London: Lawrence and Wishart.
Halliday, F. 1996. *Islam and the Myth of Confrontation: Religion and Politics in the Middle East*. London: I.B. Tauris.
—— 1992. *Arabs in Exile: Yemeni Migrants in Urban Britain*. London and New York: I.B. Taruris.
Hamilton, M. 1994. *The Sociology of Religion*. London and New York: Routledge.
Hammond, P. 1993. 'Religion and Ethnicity in Late Twentieth-Century America', *Annals of The American Academy of Political and Social Science* vol. 527: 55–66.
Hamzeh, N. and Dekmejian, R. 1996. 'A Sufi Response to Political Islamism', *Middle East Studies* vol. 28: 217–29.
Hannassab, S. 1998. 'Sexuality, Dating, and Double Standards: Young Iranian Immigrants in Los Angeles', *Iranian Studies* vol. 31, no. 1.
Harbottle, L. 2000. *Food For Health, Food For Wealth: Ethnic and Gender Identities in British Iranian Communities*. Oxford: Berghahn Books.
—— 1995. ' "Palship", Parties and Pilgrimmage: Kinship CommunityFormation and Self-Transformation of Iranian Migrants to Britain'. In *Representation of Places and Identities*. Keele: Keele University Press.
Harding, S. 1987. 'Convicted by the Holy Spirit: the rhetoric of fundamental Baptist conversion', *American Ethnologist* vol. 14, no. 1: 167–81.
Heelas, P. ed., 1998., *Religion, Modernity and Postmodernity*. Oxford: Blackwell.
Hefner, R. 1998. 'Secularisation and Citizenship in Muslim Indonesia'. In P. Heelas, ed., *Religion, Modernity and Postmodernity*. Oxford: Blackwell.

Hefner, R. 1993. 'Of Faith and Commitment: Christian Conversion in Muslim Java'. In *Conversion to Christianity - Historical and Anthropological Perspectives on a Great Transformation*. Berkeley and London: University of California Press.

Hegland, M. 1983. 'Two images of Hussein: Accommodation and Revolution in an Iranian Village'. In N.R. Keddie, ed., *Religion and Politics in Iran: Shi'ism from Quietism to Revolution*. New Haven: Yale University Press.

Hermansen, M. 2000. 'Hybrid Identity Formations In Muslim America: The Case of American Sufi Movements', *Muslim World* vol. 90, 1/2.

Hesse-Lehmann, K. and Spellman, K. 2003. 'Iranische transnationale religiöse institutionen in London und Hamburg'. In Roth, K., ed. *Zuwanderung und* Integration. München: Münchner Beiträge zur Volkskunde.

Hesse-Lehmann, K. 1993. *Iraner in Hamburg: Verhaltensmuster im Kulturkontakt*. Berlin and Hamburg: Dietrich Reimer Verlag.

Hewitt, G. 1971. *The Problem of Success, A History of the Church Missionary Society 1910–1942*. London: SCM Press.

Higgins, P. 1985. 'Women in the Islamic Republic of Iran: legal, social and ideological changes', *Journal of Women in Culture and Society* vol. 10, no. 31.

Hinnells, J.R. 1984. *The Penguin Dictionary of Religions*. Harmondsworth: Penguin.

Hobsbawm, E. 1991. *Nations and Nationalism Since 1790*. Cambridge: Cambridge University Press.

Hobsbawm, E. and Ranger, T., eds., 1983. *The Invention of Tradition*. Cambridge: Cambridge University Press.

Höfert, A. and Salvatore, A., eds., 2000. *Between Europe and Islam: Shaping Modernity in a Transcultural Space*. Brussels: P.I.E. – Peter Lang.

Humphrey, M. 1999. *Islam, Multiculturalism and Transnationalism: From the Lebanese Diaspora*. London: I.B. Tauris.

Hunter, J. 1987. *Evangelicalism: The Coming Generation*. Chicago: University of Chicago Press.

Huntington, S. 1993. 'The Clash of Civilisations?', *Foreign Affairs,* New York: Council of Foreign Relations. Summer: 22–49.

Ifeka-Moller, C. 1974. 'White Power, social-structural factors in conversion to Christianity: East Nigeria 1921–1966', *Canadian Journal of African Studies* vol. 8, no. 1: 17.

Jacobson, J. 1998. *Religion and Identity Among British Pakistani Youth*. London: LSE and Routledge.

Jamzadeh, L. and Mills, M. 1986. 'Iranian *Sofreh*: from collective to female ritual'. In C.W. Bynum, S. Harrel and P. Richman eds., *Gender and Religion: On the Complexity of Symbols*. Boston: Beacon.

Joseph, J. 1961. *The Nestorians and Their Muslim Neighbours*. New Jersey: Princeton University Press.

Kamalkhani, Z. 1998. *Women's Islam: Religious Practice Among Women in Today's Iran*. London: Kegan Paul International.

—— 1993. 'Women's Everyday Religious Discourse'. In H. Afshar, ed., *Women in the Middle East: perceptions, realities and struggles for liberation*. London: Macmillan Press.

—— 1983. *Iranian Immigrants and Refugees in Norway*. Bergen: University of Bergen Press.

Kandiyoti, D., ed., 1996. *Gendering the Middle East: emerging perspectives*. London: I.B. Tauris.

—— ed., 1991. *Women, Islam and the State*. London: Macmillan Press.

Kaplan, S., ed., 1995. *Indigenous Responses to Western Christianity*. New York and London: New York University Press.

Katouzian, H. 1998. 'Liberty and License in the Constitutional Revolution in Iran', *Journal of the Royal Asiatic Society* series 3, vol. 8, no. 2: 159–80.

Katz, S. 1983. *Mysticism and Religious Traditions*. Oxford: Oxford University Press.

Keddie, N.R. 2000. 'Women in Iran Since 1979', *Social Research* vol. 67, no. 2.

—— ed., 1983. *Religion and Politics in Iran: Shi'ism from Quietism to Revolution*. New Haven: Yale University Press.

—— 1981. *Roots of Revolution: An Interpretative History of Modern Iran*. New Haven: Yale University Press.

Keddie N.R. and Bonine, M., eds., 1981. *Modern Iran: The Dialectic of Continuity and Change in Modern Iran*. Albany: State University of New York Press.

—— 1972. *Scholars, Saints, and Sufis: Muslim Religious Institutions in the Middle East Since 1500*. Berkeley: University of California Press.

Kelley, R. 1993. 'Wealth and Illusions of Wealth in the Los Angeles Community'. In Kelley, R. and Friedlander, J. *Irangeles. Iranians in Los Angeles*.

Kelley, R. and Friedlander, J., eds., 1993. *Irangeles: Iranians in Los Angeles*. Berkeley, Los Angeles, Oxford: University of California Press.

Kennedy, J. and Fahim, H. 1974. 'Nubian Dhikr Rituals and Cultural Change', *Muslim World* vol. 64, no. 3: 205–19.

Kepel, G. 1997. *Allah in the West: Islamic Movements in America and Europe*. California: Stanford University Press.

Kepel, G. 1994. *The Revenge of God. The Resurgences of Islam, Christianity, and Judaism in the Modern World*. Cambridge: Polity Press.

Khan, V.S. 1979. 'Pakistanis in Britain: Perceptions of a Population', *New Community* vol. 5: 222–29.

Khomeini, Ruh Allah Ibn Mustafa 1981. *Islam and Revolution: Writings and Declarations of Imam Khomeini*, trans. H. Algar. Berkeley: Mizan Press.

Leman, J. and Bafekr, S. 1999. 'Highly-qualified Iranian Immigrants in Germany: the Role of Ethnicity and Culture', *Journal of Ethnic and Migration Studies* vol. 25, no. 1: 95–112.

Levitas, R. 1986. *The Ideology of the New Right*. Cambridge and Oxford: Polity Press.

Lewis, B. 1985. 'The Shi'a', *New York Review of Books* vol. 32.

Lewis, P. 1994. *Islamic Britain: Religion, Politics and Identity among British Muslims*. London: I.B. Tauris.

Lings, M. 1975. *What is Sufism?* Berkeley: University of California Press.

Lynd, R.S. and Lynd, H.M. 1929. *Middletown, a Study in Contemporary American*. New York: Harcourt, Brace.

Malamud, M. 1994. 'Sufi Organisations and Structures of Authority in Medieval Nishapur', *Middle East Studies* vol. 26: 427–42.

Mandel, R. 1990. 'Shifting Centres and Emergent Identities'. In D. Eickelman and J. Piscatori, eds., *Muslim Travellers: Pilgrimage, Migration and Religious Imagination*. New York and London: Routledge.

Mann, M. 1986. *The Sources of Social Power* vol. 1. Cambridge: Cambridge University Press.

Mansur, F. 1972. *Bodrum: A Town in the Aegean*. Leiden: Brill.

Martin, D. 1990. *Tongues of Fire: The Explosion of Protestantism in Latin America*. Oxford: Basil Blackwell.

Martin, V. and Ansari, S., eds., 2002. *Women, Religion and Culture in Iran*. Richmond: Curzon Press.

Martyn, H. 1892. *Saint and Scholar: The First Modern Missionary to the Mohammedians 1781–1812*. London: Religious Tract Society.

Masse, H. 1954. *Persian Beliefs and Customs*. New Haven: Human Relations Area Files.

Miles, R. 1993. *Racism after 'Race Relations'*. London and New York: Routledge.

Mills, M. 1982. 'Iranian "sofreh": from collective to female ritual'. In C.W. Bynum, S. Harrell and P. Richman, eds., *Gender and Religion: On the Complexity of Symbols*. Boston: Beacon.

—— 1982. 'A Cinderella Variant in the Context of a Muslim Women's Ritual'. In C. Dundes, *Cinderella: a Folklore Casebook*. New York: Garland Publishing.

Mir-Hosseini, Z. 1999. *Islam and Gender: The Religious Debate in Contemporary Iran*. Princeton: Princeton University Press.

Moaveni, A. and Zagorin, A. 2002. 'Just Don't Call Him 'King of Kings'', *Time Magazine* 15/4. vol. 159, 15: p. 8.

Modarres, A. 1998. 'Settlement Patterns of Iranians in the United States', *Iranian Studies* vol. 31, no. 1. 1998: 31–49.

Modood, T. and Werbner, P., eds., 1997. *Debating Cultural Hybridity*. London: Zen Books.

Moghissi, H. 1994. *Populism and Feminism in Iran*. New York: St. Martin's Press.

Moin, Baqer. 1999. *Khomeini: Life of the Ayotollah*. London: I.B.Tauris.

Momen, M. 1997. *A Short Introduction to Bahai'i Faith*. Oxford: Oneworld.

Momen, M. 1985. *Introduction to Shi'I Islam*. New Haven: Yale University Press.

Moslem, M. 2002. *Factional Politics in Post-Khomeini Iran*. Syracuse: Syracuse University Press.

Mottahedeh, R. 1986. *The Mantle of the Prophet*. New York: Chatto and Windus.

Muir, J. 2002. 'Straw Heads for Iran Talks', BBC News: 9 October.

Murray, C. 1994. 'Race, Genes and I.Q: an Apologia: The Case for Conservative Multiculturalism', *The New Republic*. 31 October.

Murray, N. 1986. 'Race and the Press in Thatcher's Britain', *Race and Class*. London: Institute of Race Relations and the Transnational Institute.

Naficy, H. 1998. 'Identity Politics and Iranian Exile Music Videos', *Iranian Studies* vol. 31, no. 1: 51–64.

—— 1993. *The Making of Exile Cultures: Iranian Television in Los Angeles*. Minneapolis: University of Minnesota Press.

—— 1991. 'From Liminality to Incorporation: Iranian Exile, Television in the USA'. In A. Fathi, ed., *Iranian Refugees and Exiles since Khomeini*. Costa Mesa, CA: Mazda.

—— 1990. 'Exile Discourse and Television: A Study of Syncretic Culture: Iranian Television in Los Angeles'. Ph.D. diss. California.

Najmabadi, A. 1998. 'Crafting an Educated Housewife in Iran'. In L. Abu-Lughod, ed., *Remaking Women: Feminism and Modernity in the Middle East*. Princeton, New Jersey: Princeton University Press.

—— 1998. 'Feminism in an Islamic Republic: Years of Hardship, Years of Growth'. In K. Esposito and Y. Haddad, eds., *Islam, Gender and Social Change*. Oxford: Oxford University Press.

Namazi, S. 1998. 'Some Observations on Iran's Policies Towards Iranians Abroad', *CIRA Bulletin*. March.

Nasr, H. 1991. *Islamic Spirituality II*. New York: Crossroad Publishing.

—— 1988. *Shi'ism Doctrines, Thought and Spirituality*. New York: State University of New York Press.

—— 1980. *Living Sufism*. London: George Allen and Unwin Press.

Nassehi-Behnam, V. 2000. 'Diaspora Iranienne En France Changement Et Continuité', *Cahiers d'études sur la Méditerranée Orientale et le Monde Turco-Iranien* no. 30.
—— 1991. 'Iranian Immigrants in France'. In Fathi, A., ed., *Iranian Refugees and Exiles since Khomeini*. Costa Mesa, CA: Mazda.
—— 1990. 'L'exil occidental'. In N. Firouzeh, ed., *Regards sur l'Iran, Civilisations* vol. 35, no. 2: 209–47.
Nazeri, H. 1996. 'Imagined Cyber Communities, Iranians and the Internet', *MESA Bulletin* vol. 30: 158–64.
Niebuhr, R. 1962. *The Social Sources of Denominationalism*. New York: Meridian.
Nielson, J. 1992. *Muslims in Western Europe*. Edinburgh: Edinburgh University Press.
Nurbakhsh, J. 1997. 'Pilgrimmage', *Sufi* no. 33: 40.
—— 1996. *Discourses on the Sufi Path*. London: Khaniqani Nimatullahi Publications.
—— 1989. *In the Paradise of the Sufis*. London: Khaniqani Nimatullahi Publications.
—— 1984. *Spiritual Poverty in Sufism*. London: Khaniqani Nimatullahi Publications.
—— 1981. *Sufism, Meaning, Knowledge, and Unity*. London: Khaniqani Nimatullahi Publications.
—— 1978. *In the Tavern of Ruin: Seven Essays on Sufism*. London: Khaniqani Nimatullahi Publications.
Nyang, S. 1995. 'Introduction'. In S. Angha, *The Fragrance of Sufism*. University Press America.
OPCS/GROS 1992. *1991 Census Ethnic Group and Country of Birth Report, Great Britain*.
Owen, D. 1992. '1991 Census Statistical Paper no. 1', *Ethnic Minorities in Great Britain: Settlement Patterns*. Centre of Research in Ethnic Relations, University of Warwick.
Paidar, P. 1996. 'Feminism and Islam in Iran'. In D. Kandiyoti, ed., *Gendering the Middle East: Emerging Perspectives*. London: I.B. Tauris.
—— 1995. *Women and the Political Process in Twentieth-Century Iran.* Cambridge: Cambridge University Press.
Papastergiadis, N. 1997. 'Tracing Hybridity in Theory'. In T. Modood and P. Werbner, eds., *Debating Cultural Hybridity*. London: Zen Books.
Peach, C. 1992. 'Ethnicity in the 1991 Census', vol. 2, *The Ethnic Minority Populations of Great Britain*, Office For National Statistics.
—— 1990. 'The Muslim Population of Great Britain', *Ethnic and Racial Studies* vol. 13, no. 3: 414–19.
Peach, C. and Vertovec, S., eds., 1997. *Islam in Europe: The Politics of Religion and Community*. New York: St. Martin's Press.
Peach, C. and Glebe, G. 1995. 'Muslim Minorities in Western Europe', *Ethnic and Racial Studies* vol. 18, no. 1: 26–45.
Pinault, D. 1992. *The Shiites: Ritual and Popular Piety in a Muslim Community*. London: I.B. Tauris.
Pinto P., 2002. *Mystical Bodies: Ritual, Experience and the Embodiment of Sufism in Syria*. Ph.D. diss., Boston University.
Piscatori, J. and Eickelman, D., eds., 1990. *Muslim Travellers: Pilgrimage, Migration and Religious Imagination*. New York and London: Routledge.
Pliskin, K. 1987. *Silent Boundaries: Cultural Constraints on Sickness and Diagnosis of Iranians in Israel*. New Haven and London: Yale University Press.
Poole, E. 2002. *Reporting Islam: Media Representations of British Muslims*. London, New York: I.B. Tauris.

Rahnema, A. 2000. *An Islamic Utopian: The Political Biography of Ali Shari'ti*. London, New York: I.B.Tauris.

Reina, R. and Schwartz, N. 1974. 'The structural context of religious conversion in El Peten, Guatemala: status, community and multicommunity, *American Ethnologist* vol. 9, no. 1: 157–91.

Rex, J. 1996. *Ethnic Minorities in the Modern Nation State*. New York: St. Martin's Press.

Rex, J. and Tomlison, S. 1979. *Colonial Immigrants in a British City*. London and New York: Routledge and Kegan Paul.

Rice, C. 1923. *Persian Women and Their Ways*. Seeley: Service and Company.

Richard, Y. 1995. *Shi'ite Islam* Oxford. Blackwell.

Riesbrodt, M. 1993. *The Pious Passions: The Emergence of Modern Fundamentalism in the United States and Iran*. Berkeley: University of California Press.

—— 1916. *Mary Bird in Persia*. London: Church Missionary Society.

Roy, O. 1998. 'Tensions in Iran: The Future of the Islamic Revolution', *Middle East Report*, Summer: 38–41.

Rubin, M. 2001. 'A Return of Kings? Alternative Outcomes for the Middle East', October 11, *Telegraph*.

Runnymeade Trust. '1997. Commission on British Muslims and Islamophobia'. In *Islamophobia: a Challenge for us all*. London: Runnymede Trust.

Sabagh, G., Der-Martirosian C. and Bozorgmehr, M. 1993. 'Beyond Nationality: Religio-Ethnic Diversity'. In Kelley, R. and Friedlander, J., eds., *Irangeles: Iranians in Los Angeles*. Berkeley: University of California Press.

Sabagh G. and Bozorgmehr M. 1991. 'Iranian Exiles and Immigrants in Los Angeles'. In A. Fathi, ed., *Iranian Refugees and Exiles since Khomeini*. Costa Mesa, CA: Mazda.

Sabagh, G. and Bozorgmehr, M. 1988. 'High Status Immigrants: A Statistical Profile of Iranians in the United States', *Iranian Studies* vol. 2: 5–36.

Said, E. 1993. *Culture and Imperialism*. New York: Alfred A. Knopf.

Said, E. 1978. *Orientalism*, New York: Pantheon.

Saleh, S. 1972a. 'Women in Islam: Their Role in Religious and Traditional Culture', *International Journal of Sociology of the Family* vol. 2: 35–42.

—— 1972b. 'Women in Islam: Their Status in Religious and Traditional Culture', *International Journal of Sociology of the Family* vol. 2, no. 2: 193–201.

Salvatore, A. and Höfert, A., eds., 2000. *Between Europe and Islam: Shaping Modernity in a Transcultural Space*. New York: P.I.E. – Peter Lang.

Sanadjian, M. 1995. 'Temporality of "Home" and Spatiality of Market in Exile: Iranians in Germany', *New German Critique. Germany: East, West, and Other* no. 64, Winter: 3–36.

Sanasarian, E. 2000. *Religious Minorities in Iran*. Cambridge: Cambridge University Press.

Schimmel, A. 1997. *Nightingales Under the Snow*. London: Khaniqani Nimatullahi Publications.

Seidel, G. 1986. 'Culture, Nature and "Race" in the British and French New Right'. In R. Levitas, ed., *The Ideology of the New Right*. London: Polity Press.

Shaida, M. 1992. *The Legendary Cuisine of Persia*. London: Penguin.

Shariati, A. 1990. 'Fatima is Fatima', *Zan* 21: 97.

Shashaani, A. 1993. *Promised Paradise: Agha Jan-Sufism's Secret Divulged*. New York: University Press of America.

Smithies, B. and Fiddick P., 1969. *Enoch Powell on Immigration*. London: Sphere.

Shashanah, F. 1998. 'From the Rivers of Babylon to the Valleys of Los Angeles: The Exodus and Adaptation of Iranian Jews'. In Warner, R.S. and Wittner, J.D. eds., *Gatherings in Diaspora.*

Sheil, Lady 1856. *The Life and Manners in Persia.* London: John Murray.

Spooner, B. 1963. 'The Function of Religion in Persian Society', *Iran*, vol. 1: 83–95.

Sreberney, A. 1998. 'Media and Diasporic Consciousness: An Exploration among Iranians in London'. Paper. International Association for Media and Communication Research Conference. Glasgow.

Sreberney-Mohammadi, A. 1987. 'Post-Revolutionary Iranian exiles: a study of impotence', *Third World Quarterly* vol. 9, no. 1: 108–21.

Sreberney-Mohammadi, A. and Mohammadi, A. 1991. 'Iranian exiles as opposition: some thesis on the dilemmas of political communication inside and outside Iran'. In A. Fathi, *Iranian Refugees and Exiles since Khomeini.* Costa Mesa, CA: Mazda

Sullivan, Z. 2001. *Exiled Minorities – Stories of Iranian Diaspora.* Philadelphia: Temple University Press.

Sullivan, Z. 1998. *Eluding the Feminist.* In L. Abu-Lughod ed., *Remaking Women: Feminism and Modernity in the Middle East.* Princeton: Princeton University Press.

Tapper, N. and Tapper, R. 1987. 'The Birth of the Prophet: Ritual and Gender in Turkish Islam', *Man* vol. 22, no. 1: 69–92.

Tarack, A. 1996. 'U.S.–Iran relations: heading for Confrontation?' *Third World Quarterly:* 159.

Taylor, C., ed., 1994. *Multiculturalism.* Princeton NJ: Princeton University Press.

Thaiss, G. 1972. 'Religious Symbolism and Social Changes, the Drama of Husain'. In N.R. Keddie and M. Bonine, *Scholars, Saints and Sufis.* Berkeley: University of California Press.

Thomas, T., ed., 1986. *The British: Their Religious Beliefs and Practices 1800–1986.* London and New York: Routledge.

Thompson, E.P. 1963. *The Making of the English Working Class.* London: Random House.

Torab, A. 2002. 'The Politicization of Women's Religious Circles in Post-Revolutionary Iran'. In S. Ansari and V. Martin, eds., *Women, Religion and Culture in Iran.* Surrey: Curzon Press.

—— 1998. 'Neighbourhoods of Piety: Gender and Ritual in South Tehran', unpublished Ph.D. diss., School of Oriental and African Studies.

—— 1996. 'Piety as Gendered Agency: A Study of Jaleseh Ritual Discourse in an Urban Neighbourhood in Iran', *Man* vol. 2, June: 235–52.

Trimmingham, J. 1971. *The Sufi Orders in Islam.* Oxford: Oxford University Press.

Turner, B.S. 1994a. *Orientalism, Postmodernism and Globalism.* London and New York: Routledge.

—— 1994b. *Religion and Social Theory.* London: Sage.

Van den Bos, M. 2002. 'Sufi Authority in Khatami's Iran, Some Fieldwork Notes', *Oriental Moderne* XXX (LXXXII), n.s. 2: 351–378.

—— 2000. *Mystic Regimes.* Leiden, Boston: Brill.

Van der Veer, P. 1994. *Religious Nationalism: Hindus and Muslims in India.* Berkeley: University of California Press.

Vertovec, S. and Peach C., eds., 1997. *Islam in Europe: The Politics of Religion and Community.* New York: St. Martin's Press.

Vidler, G. 2001. Research Paper, House of Commons Library, 9 March.

Wallman, S., ed., 1979. *Ethnicity at Work.* London: Macmillan.

Waterfield, R. 1973. *Christians in Persia: Assyrians, Armenians, Roman Catholics and Protestants.*

Watson, J.L., ed., 1977. *Between Two Cultures*. Oxford: Blackwell.

Weber, M. 1991. Reprint, 1930. *The Protestant Ethic and the Spirit of Capitalism*. London: HarperCollins.

—— 1978. *Economy and Society*, vol. 1. Berkeley: University of California Press.

Werbner, P. 2001. 'The Limits of Cultural Hybridity: On Ritual Monsters, Poetic Licence and Contested Postcolonial Purifications', *Journal of Royal Anthropological Institute*, NS vol. 7: 133–52.

—— 2000. 'Divided Loyalties, Empowered Citizenship? Muslims in Britain', *Citizenship Studies* vol. 4, no. 3.

Werbner, P. and Basu, H., eds., 1998. *Embodying Charisma: Modernity, Locality and the Performance of Emotion in Sufi Cults*. London, New York: Routledge.

Werbner, P. and Modood, T., eds., 1997. *Debating Cultural Hybridity*. London: Zen Books.

Werbner, P. and Anwar, M., eds., 1991. *Black and Ethnic Leadership in Britain*. London: Routledge.

Westermarck, E. 1933. *Pagan Survivals in Mohammedan Civilisation*. London: Macmillan.

Wilcox, L. 1995. *Sufism and Psychology*. Chicago: Abjad Books.

Wilford, R. and Miller, R. 1998. *Women, Ethnicity and Nationalism*. London, New York: Routledge.

Willis, C.J. 1883. *In the Land of the Lion and Sun*. London: Macmillan.

Wilson, B.R. 1990. *The Social Dimensions of Sectarianism – Sects and New Religious Movements in Contemporary Society*. Oxford: Clarendon Press.

Woodward, K., ed., 1999. *Identity and Difference*. London: Sage.

Wright, D. 1988. 'Introduction' Cloake, Margaret Morris, *A Persian at the Court of King George 1809–10*. London: Berrie & Junkers.

Wuthrow, R. 1976. 'Recent Patterns of Secularisation: A Problem of Generation', *American Sociological Review* vol. 41: 856–67.

Yuval-Davis, N. 1997. 'Ethnicity, Gender Relations and Multiculturalism'. In Werbner, P. and Modood, T., eds., 1997. *Debating Cultural Hybridity*.

Zubaida, S. 1995. 'Is there a Muslim Society?', *Economy and Society* vol. 24, no. 2: 151–88.

—— 1993. Reprint, 1989. *Islam, the People and the State*. London: I.B. Tauris.

Newspaper Articles

Agence France Press, 'Iranian opposition accuses Tehran of "murdering", Mehdi Dibaj', 6 July 1994.

—— 'Murder and Disappearance', 4 July 1994.

—— 'Relatives say Iranian pastor murdered in connection with his religious activities', 31 January 1994.

Amnesty International, 'Assassination of Community Leaders by State Security Agents', 12 January 1994.

CNN Interactive, 'Transcript of Interview with Iranian President Mohammad Khatami', 7 January 1998.

Comite Iranien Contre La Repression et Le Terrorisme D'eta, vol. 3, March 1993.

Daily Telegraph, 'Prince Charles is wrong: Islam does menace the West', 19 December 1996: 26.

The Economist (Anonymous), 'Come Home, almost all is forgiven', 2 May 1992: 52.
Evangelical Now, "Soul-Giver' Murdered", vol. 11, no. 11, November 1996.
Guardian, Wilson. J. 'Culture of Charity', 21 June 2002.
Human Rights Watch Report, http://www.interlog.com/human.rights.
Independent, Cornwall, R, 'Britain names Ambassador to Tehran', 5 May 1999, p. 5.
Independent, anonymous, 'Exiles press West towards Tehran Spring', June 21, 1996, p. 8.
Iranian Christian International, Inc., http://wwwfarsinet.com/ici/index/html.
Jubilee Campaign (1998) 'The persecution of Christians in Iran', 13 November in
  http://www.jubileecampaign. demon.uk/church/ira1.htm.
The New York Times, 'Iran wages fierce campaign against Christian minority, 1 August
  1994.
Open Doors- Field Operations- December 1995 in: http://ourworld.
St. Louis Dispatch, Nejat, K., 'Where is Mohammed Khatami's moderation?' 2 June
  1999.
The Sunday Times, Grimston, J. 'Iran Gift Sparks University Row' 24 October 1999.
Time, 'Islam, Should the World be Afraid', 15 June 1992, p. 4.
Today, 'In the Name of Islam', 20 April 1995, p. 4.
Time, 'Just Don't Call Him 'King of Kings'15 April 2002, Vol. 159 Issue 15, p8, 1p, 1c.
Telegraph, (2001), Rubin, M. 'A Return of Kings? Alternative Outcomes for the Middle
  East' October 11.
Washington Post, Mufson, S. and Lippman, T. Saturday 1 May, 1999 A10.

Background Papers

'Background Paper on Refugees and Asylum Seekers from Iran', United Nations High
  Commissioner for Refugees, Geneva, 1995 and 1998
The Baha'is (1995), the Bahai Publishing Trust of the United Kingdom.
The Iranians Community centre annual report for March 1988, printed at 266–268
  Holloway Road, London N7.
Iranian Association Newsletter, printed in London.

Index

www.ingramcontent.com/pod-product-compliance
Lightning Source LLC
Chambersburg PA
CBHW072105040426
42334CB00042B/2329